BETWEEN HOPE AND DESPAIR

Advance Praise for *Between Hope and Despair*

'Rajeev Bhargava, a scholar of eminence, has over the years written a good deal on the principles of political ethics with specific reference to contemporary Indian society. The present work sums up the challenge in its opening lines: "India's collective ethical identity is under duress. We don't seem to agree currently on what our collective good is." This makes for unsettling reading, more so in the light of his detailed commentary on the basic principles of our Constitution. But it also gives us hope because it reminds us of what as a nation we should and can achieve. Mandatory reading for those who wish to make India a better, more humane society.'

Hamid Ansari, former vice president of India and chairman, Rajya Sabha (2007–2017)

'Rajeev Bhargava writes because he cannot but write. Even as Ustad Rashid Khan cannot but sing, Malavika Sarukkai cannot but dance, Jatin Das's brush cannot be still and I cannot but read him for I want to see current affairs subjected to ethical analysis, valuational norms and the litmus test of "What is the intention?" And there, Bhargava's writing never fails me.'

Gopalkrishna Gandhi, former governor of West Bengal

'Rajeev has been writing, objectively and analytically, on various issues now emerging as challenges to our constitutional ethos. This collection of essays is but a small sample of his thoughts written with uncanny foresight. He raises many provocative questions in his essays and tells us where we are in fulfilling the dream of a just, fair and equal society and where our constitutional democracy is taking us, slowly but surely.'

Madan Lokur, former justice of Supreme Court of India

'Rajeev Bhargava's *Between Hope and Despair* is a thoughtful look at the social and moral turmoil that faces us in modern India. Examining the nation's past and present while looking towards its future, Bhargava's writing covers a wide range of issues, producing an elegant reflection on India's crisis of ethics.'

Shashi Tharoor, MP, author and public intellectual

'Rajeev, the optimist, through his latest book, *Between Hope and Despair*, wishes to heal the growing divisions in India over its identity. He lucidly, insightfully states his own views and hopes a proper response from others will start a meaningful dialogue. Indeed, each of us can dip into this collection, choose an essay on one of the many relevant issues, reflect on it and contribute to this conversation.'

Anu Aga, former chair of Thermax and Teach for India

'The nuance and complexity that Rajeev brings into every question is invaluable. He nudges us towards the possibility of a more equal and just society.'

T.M. Krishna, musician and writer

'This is a deep and probing analysis of India's democracy as it is today. It was born out of a dream of inclusivity. But the fact is, it stands over an area marked by age-old fault lines of caste, class, religion and gender. These essays are a profound analysis of how the unavoidable seismic jolts have shaped and reshaped India in the last 75 years.'

Mrinal Pande, writer and former chief editor of Hindustan Dainik

BETWEEN HOPE AND DESPAIR

100 Ethical Reflections on Contemporary India

Rajeev Bhargava

BLOOMSBURY
NEW DELHI • LONDON • OXFORD • NEW YORK • SYDNEY

BLOOMSBURY INDIA
Bloomsbury Publishing India Pvt. Ltd
Second Floor, LSC Building No. 4, DDA Complex, Pocket C – 6 & 7,
Vasant Kunj, New Delhi, 110070

BLOOMSBURY, BLOOMSBURY INDIA and the Diana logo
are trademarks of Bloomsbury Publishing Plc

First published in India 2023
This edition published 2023

ISBN: PB: 978-93-94701-37-3; eBook: 978-93-94701-50-2
2 4 6 8 10 9 7 5 3

Typeset in Bembo Std by Manipal Technologies Limited
Printed and bound in India Gopsons Papers Pvt. Ltd.

To find out more about our authors and books visit www.bloomsbury.com and sign up for our newsletters

For my grandson, Miran,
and the future of all the children of his generation

Contents

PART III: OUR RIGHTS, OUR VALUES

PART IV: OUR RELIGIOUS AND SECULAR IDEALS

PART V: DEEP ISSUES THAT MATTER

Acknowledgements

In more than forty years of my academic life, I had written all of five newspaper articles. Yet for some reason, I was approached, in the past decade, by several national and international dailies and weeklies to write for them. I declined out of diffidence, reticence and a feeling that I didn't have the competence to write for the larger, non-academic audience. So when Mini Kapoor of *The Hindu* asked me to write a column, I balked at the very idea of a weekly deadline. I felt the sheer pressure of producing a regular column would interfere with academic writing.

But my daughters, Vanya and Aranyani, and my sons-in-law, Shiva and Ganesh, unfailingly persuaded me to move beyond the classroom and commit myself to public writing. Vanya and Shiva, in particular, insisted that their friends and acquaintances desperately needed exposure to political theory. Tani, my wife, pushed me to take the plunge as enthusiastically as she always has. I must thank them all for helping me turn from an academic to a more public-spirited writer.

I must also thank the editorial team of *The Hindu*, particularly Mini Kapoor and V.R. Srinivasan, for not giving up on me when I first prevaricated. Eventually, I relented on three conditions. First, that I would write every fortnight not every week. Second, that I would be free to choose the topic of every column. And third, that the content need not be tied to current affairs but have general social, political or philosophical significance. Vanya insisted that each piece focus on conceptual clarification for a primarily young readership. Both Tani and Vanya helped with the choice of themes and went over the writings to ensure that they were accessible. So did the copy editors at *The Hindu*: Murali Krishnaswamy, Radhika Santhanam and G.L. Narayanan.

Initially, the column was called 'The Public Eye' and appeared in the *Sunday Review*. Later when the Sunday supplement was discontinued, I got a little more space as it moved to the op-ed page. After fifty-odd articles, I began to lose steam and wanted to cry off. At that stage, Srinivasan egged me on. Several friends read me regularly and carefully, and offered critical comments. Foremost among them were Alok Rai, Shalini Advani and Charles Taylor. Other consistently supportive readers include Patrick Olivelle, Hamid Ansari, Pamela Philipose, Ranjini Obeyesekhere, Neeladri Bhattacharya, Dr Ambrish Mittal, Laura Weisberg, Sanjeev Bhargava, Daniel Bell, Raghavendra Gadagkar, Ritu Menon, Anu Chenoy, Hilal Ahmad, Nikolas Kompridis, Shabana Azmi, Javed Akhtar, Joe Carens, T.M. Krishna and Jack Hawley. Pratap Bhanu Mehta, Mukul Manglik and Yogendra Yadav assured me that they were circulating these pieces among their students. That motivated me to keep going. The value of instant feedback was also brought home to me by Chitra Joshi, Nilufer Gole, Asaf Savat, Dr Navin Dang, Anup Jhalani, Sudipta Mandal, Rakesh Pande, Ananya Vajpeyi, Pogy Menon, Dr Amit Sen, Kamalini Dutta, Tanika Sarkar, Mini and Abhi Chatterjee, Nilanjana Kaviraj, Madan Lokur, Romila Thapar, Deepak Nayyar, Deepankar Gupta, Ajay Shankar, Seema Chishti, K.T. Ravindran, Sanjaya Baru, David Wong, Anthony Barnett, Pamela DeLargy, Andrew and Peggotty Graham, Aube Taylor, Nissim, Mannathukkaren, Ramesh Dixit, Rajendra Prasad, Aryama, Sudha Mohan, Parthiv Shah, Anant Shah and Anvesh Sathpathy. I am sure there are many others who I ought to thank but have missed out. I am equally unable to mention the names of innumerable young men and women, probably students, who messaged me; I can't thank them enough for their stimulating comments. By their online comments, several readers of *The Hindu* spurred me to keep writing. Others took the trouble of locating my email address. Perhaps the most pleasant and satisfying remark came from one of them, Vivek, CEO of a startup. 'I am not a bad person,' he said, 'but out of ignorance and lack of mentorship, I moved into pursuit of external goods and not internal goods. Now that I know the difference, I ask myself the core question of what kind of a good I want and why. You articulated the differences between external and internal goods really well.'

I am very pleased to have sustained the column for over three years from 2017 to 2020 and then briefly in 2022. Newspaper articles have an ephemeral shelf life. But short articles give the opportunity to those with less time on hand to read on important, complex issues. They can reach a much larger audience. So, when it was suggested that I put them together in a book, I seized the opportunity. The benefit of such a collection is that readers can pick one or two articles on a theme of immediate interest, as if it were a newspaper piece, and be spurred into further thinking of their own. I am grateful to Hilal Ahmed for putting Chandra Sekhar of Bloomsbury India in touch with me. I hope that the readers of this collection will find this collaborative effort valuable and read it with pleasure and profit.

Introduction

India's collective ethical identity is under duress. Currently, we don't seem to agree on what our collective good is. Some groups have entirely lost faith in the story that we are a pluralist, constitutional democracy. For them, India, now changing for the better, is finally rediscovering its Hindu identity and becoming a great nation-state. For others, who retain faith in the vision formulated during the anti-colonial struggle, this deeply troublesome change has brought us on the verge of losing our civilisational character. They despair. We seem today to be divided into at least these two camps. Is it possible to bring these groups with divergent views to discuss each other's points of view—and do so with an open mind, reasonably? I think it is. Through reflections on contemporary events, I, who retain faith in the inclusive vision, take the first step towards beginning a dialogue with the other side. By taking you back to the big founding narrative of the republic, I hope to clarify the constituents of our ethical ideals. I believe that the legitimate concerns of all those disenchanted with this inclusive, pluralist idea of India can actually be addressed *within* the basic framework of India's constitutional democracy. If we get our fundamentals right and properly understand the ethical language of the original vision, we might still be able to save our country from further polarisation and may even heal some of its divisions. I hope that by reading this short book, those who have recently become sceptical of this vision will be less so, and those who have rejected it altogether will reconsider their views. At any rate, I hope that they will be motivated enough to better articulate their deep disagreements with me and others like me. It is important for all of us to begin or continue a conversation if our nation is to flourish or, perhaps, even survive.

All of us dream. We dream about better futures and how to realise them. This gives our lives direction, a purpose, a sense of movement from where we currently are to where we aim to reach. It makes life meaningful and worthwhile. None of us merely exist or survive; we undertake life's journey during which we experience the full force of the drama of hope and despair.

Each of us dreams individually but we also come together to dream collectively. We dream as family, community, a country and, even, as humanity. Collective dreams need communication—a conversation. We need to listen to and learn about each other and exchange our views on the ideal collective life. How else can the I's become we? After all, collective dreams require or presuppose a common mind, and this common mind has to be forged first. In the late nineteenth and early twentieth centuries, we began to form such a collective mind—to think of ourselves as 'Indians'. Together, we realised that the country as a whole was subject to the rule of an alien power. Alien not because they were of a different colour or religion and had come from afar but because most of them were clueless about our culture, the way we understood ourselves or how we wished to lead our lives. In the mid-nineteenth century, these power wielders stopped intermingling with us and began to view us as inferior beings. Most of them viewed us instrumentally and used us to fulfil their own dreams in which there was no place for us.

Our first big dream was to rid ourselves of them and establish self-government. People from all walks of life and different parts of the country came together to fight this colonial rule and, in the process, realised that they were one people. Swaraj (self-rule) was an important part of the dream. But what was to be done after attaining it? What kind of society or nation were we going to build after we had gained collective power?

It is always easier to come together against something, especially an oppressor, but when we begin to think more positively or more concretely about the kind of society we envision, differences emerge—big differences. This is especially the case with a people whose history goes back thousands of years and who have had a series of rich encounters with new peoples and ideas. Diversity and its associated tensions make collective dreaming a trifle difficult, yet we dreamed of creating solidarity. Rather than allow these differences to destroy us, we sought to revel in them, be enriched by them and created a vision that gave us direction and purpose for a better collective life.

We dreamed of building a society of free and equal people. We dreamed of dismantling crippling hierarchies that beset our society. We dreamed of giving each person the opportunity and the ability to dream about the life he or she wanted to live. Having lived under an empire, we dreamed of finding our rightful place in the post-colonial global order and helping people in other parts of the world realise freedom and equality. These short essays are written in the hope that this dream is still alive.

I have spoken of having a collective vision of pursuing our dreams. Implicit in these phrases is the idea of the 'good'. I could easily replace 'dreams' with the technical, philosophical term 'conceptions of the good life'. When Martin Luther King said he had a dream, he did not mean that he had a psychic event in his sleep but that he visualised a good life for all Americans, Black and White. The good is something more than what we simply happen to desire. It is a desire that we evaluate to be worthwhile and significant. This is why we often strive to achieve it, and to secure it we are even prepared to sacrifice some of what we consider less significant. During Covid-related lockdowns, it was good to desire to stay home rather than go out to meet others. Keeping oneself safe and healthy is a good that overrode the desire to socialise. To excel at music or cricket, to lead a self-reflective life, to live a life in pursuit of God, to be recognised as a great weaver, to help create an oppression-free, egalitarian society are all different conceptions of the good, not unevaluated desires.

Because a strong connection exists between the good (what we evaluate to be significantly more worthwhile than mere desire) and ethics, I have used the term 'ethical' throughout the book and 'ethical reflections' in the book's title. The term 'ethics' covers two extremely important dimensions of human life. The first involves evaluation of something as good or bad, praiseworthy or repugnant. It is a fact that we became independent on 15 August 1947. But if we say that it was *good* to have achieved independence on 15 August, it turns into an *ethical* statement. It is because we evaluate national freedom positively as something worth desiring and achieving—that it is a 'good'. This is why we celebrate the day we gained independence.

But ethics is not just about the good and the bad. A second component of ethics is the evaluation of something as right or wrong. If I say that Jai took money from Veeru, then nothing ethical has been stated. But if I say that Jai borrowed some money from Veeru that he does not intend to return, then Jai has done something wrong. Right and wrong are attributes of individual acts in relation to others. Some traditions and societies use the special term 'morality' to talk about right and wrong actions. If we accept this then ethics in the broad sense includes morality, which is a distinct part of ethics but not the whole of it. To go back to our example, we will then use the term 'immoral' for what Jai did. In the ordinary life of many cultures, these terms are used interchangeably, but it is helpful to treat them as partially distinct. The crucial point behind this distinction is to highlight that in realising our own good, we may harm or do some wrong to others. It is wrong to trip my competitor in order to win the race. A football player can't push his opponent when he is speedily heading towards the goalpost. Winning is the good here, but you should not achieve it by wrong actions. Clearly, while it is important to realise our own vision of the good life, it must not be done at the expense of the good of others, immorally. This is what made, for example, colonialism wrong and immoral. Colonialism helped colonisers to realise their dreams, bringing at least some good to them, but it harmed the colonised, oppressed and exploited them. This was plainly wrong. Upper-caste men are entitled to realise their idea of a good life, but they can't do it by oppressing other castes or women. It is wrong to have created an entire institution that systematically and routinely oppressed and humiliated a vulnerable group. This makes the hierarchical caste system immoral.

The reflections in the essays are ethical because they speak consistently about the good and the bad and the right and the wrong. Many of them relate to the Constitution of India because it too is an ethical document. India's Constituent Assembly (1946–1949) came together to discuss not only the organisation of power or the structure of government but also to formulate a common constitutional ethic that *should* be followed by all individuals and groups living in India. The Constitution tries to specify which among the many desires we have are qualitatively better, worthwhile or good. And it attempts to provide a moral framework of right actions within which to realise our good. It asks us to shape our own pursuit of the good life in the light of moral standards, for instance, without infringing on the freedom of others to pursue their good life and without oppressing or subordinating them. It must be clear by now that terms like 'freedom', 'equality' and 'justice' are not mere words, because crystallised around them is a comprehensive vision of the common good life for all Indians and a common ethic that includes a common public morality. If we follow this morality, another part of what we collectively imagine as our common good will likely emerge and flourish: solidarity or fraternity.

A major part of the book deals then with our constitutional ethic. In many essays, I take up a troubling contemporary event and by reflecting on it try to clarify the meaning of ethical and moral concepts, the significance of our constitutional values and the adverse consequences of undermining them. The core features of this ethic can be further elaborated. First, it includes a commitment to pluralism. Our Constitution acknowledges that all of us do not and need not strive to realise a uniform idea of the good life. It recognises that India is a diverse country and, therefore, has multiple conceptions of the good life and many ways of finding ultimate self-fulfilment. This plurality of conceptions about how to lead a good life was always part of our landscape, and it is neither possible nor desirable to disturb it. People sought fulfilment with the help of world views that were either dependent on one God (as in the case of Sikhs, Muslims, Christians and some Hindus) or many gods and goddesses (as in the case of many Hindus) or entirely independent of any god (as in the case of Jains, Buddhists, some Hindus and modern atheists). These conceptions of the good life were believed to be objective in the sense that there was widespread agreement that they were higher in status than subjective desires or needs. No one believed there was one single answer to the question 'What is the good life and how to lead it?' Christians, Muslims, Parsis, Jews, Jains, Buddhists and the wide variety of Hindu groups—the Shaivites, Vaishnavites, Shaktas, Tantriks and yogis—all had their own distinctive ideas of how best to lead one's life. It was always accepted that there were multiple higher goods or multiple truths or, at the very least, that there was one God or Truth but multiple ways of getting to Him or of reaching there.

The Constitution is designed to protect each of these different, community-specific collective visions and their distinctive interpretations by individuals. Freedom is assumed to be a primary good because the pursuit of a worthwhile life is inconceivable without it. This gives a richer meaning to the constitutional guarantee of freedom of religion, which includes freedom from organised religion. No one may thwart the pursuit of these valuable conceptions of the good life. Yet, this religion-related freedom is not the only freedom granted to us by our Constitution. Other significant freedoms include freedom of movement, freedom of expression, personal freedom and liberty (to eat or wear what we choose to) and political freedom such as the freedom to question the government and to peacefully assemble, mobilise or protest. To legally guarantee and make their infringement punishable, these freedoms were incorporated within a framework of rights. A small number of these rights, such as the right of a religious or linguistic community to set up and maintain its educational institutions, were related to groups or communities.

Apart from freedom, the other key good or value endorsed by the Indian Constitution is 'equality'. In the Indian context, this was nothing short of a social and political revolution, a radical break from much of the past. By the late nineteenth century, India had become a land of major and minor hierarchies. Two of these were pivotal and related to caste and gender. Enshrining equality in the Constitution was a major step to begin to dismantle caste- and gender-based hierarchies. By the nineteenth century, partly because of the colonial logic of governance, the caste system had become extremely rigid. The exclusion of the Atishudras and Shudras from important public domains and the repugnant practice of untouchability were rampant. Therefore, when equality was made a central value of the Indian Constitution, it was seen as a radical break from pernicious hierarchies. Equality also challenged gender inequality and the doctrines that justify it, which are present in virtually every single religious and non-religious world view of the past.

The other important ideal encouraged by our Constitution and given a pre-eminent position in its preamble is justice. The idea is that everyone must be given what is due to him or her on fair and equal terms. And the sole manner in which justice was to be brought to society was peacefully by discussion and deliberation. In short, justice was to be brought democratically.

While democracy is often equated by many people simply with elections, it is in fact not reducible to elections but is concerned with the realisation of political freedom and equality. In our Constitution, many features of democracy are spread over the entire section on fundamental rights. What did these guarantee? First, inclusive citizenship. No one is excluded on grounds of religion, colour, etc. Yet, inclusion does not automatically entail equality. One may be included in a group but given a secondary status within it, subordinated to those higher up. Therefore, equality of citizenship needed to be guaranteed. There are no first- and second-class citizens. Third, a modicum of material well-being. This was important for an individual to effectively act as a citizen. The assumption, rightly, was that a connection exists between material well-being of ordinary people and democracy. This was mentioned not in the fundamental rights section but in the directive principles of state policy. All three ideas were new. Before the birth of democracy, we were subjects of this or that empire, some of which certainly had the idea of inclusive subjecthood. Inclusive subjecthood may even have meant that in the eyes of the emperor all of us were equal regardless of language or religion. Or that we were to be equal beneficiaries of the emperor's generosity. Both inclusiveness and pluralism were present in our imperial political traditions. But in 1950, with one stroke we made citizenship available on equal terms to all persons living in a well-defined territory regardless not only of their language or religion but also their class, race, caste or gender. All became equal members of a new political community.

Making citizenship inclusive and equal linked democracy not only to pluralism but also to the principle of non-exclusion and non-discrimination. This maximum inclusiveness and equality also entailed that the Indian state would not have a strong alliance with any one religious or ethnic group that permits exclusion of and discrimination against others. This feature of political secularism ensures that the Indian state maintains a principled distance from all religions for the sake of freedom, equality and fraternity. Without this important feature, one religious group could easily dominate and oppress others. Additionally, the ideal practice of democracy presupposes the maximum possible 'pacification of politics'. This means the following three things. One, that political power has to be transferred from one person or group to another peacefully, not violently as it used to in the past in many kingdoms. Two, there should be an open public sphere where common issues are freely discussed, debated and contested. Because it enables this free exchange of views, dissent is not suppressed but tolerated. And those with different viewpoints are viewed only as temporary adversaries not permanent enemies. Three, that there is a willingness to negotiate and compromise in the interest of building fraternity among citizens with radically different conceptions of the good life.

We built this idea of democracy on the basis of several such elements within our traditions. This included polytheism, a pluralist social practice that has been a continuing feature in India since the Vedic period; the tradition of government-by-discussion associated with ancient clan republics; and mutual respect between communities and rejection of war as a way to resolve conflicts, both associated with Emperor Ashoka. Democracy was also built by breaking away from some anti-democratic elements in our traditions. The new ethic rejected the hyper-masculine ethic of the early Vedic period, the realpolitik of the *Arthashastra*, the hierarchical varna order found in the *Dharmshastras*, the autocratic elements in virtually all kingships and imperium all the way down to the exploitative rule of the British Empire. Both continuities and discontinuities with our traditions are to be found in our constitutional ethic.

The continuing presence within India of some anti-egalitarian, anti-democratic, anti-freedom traditions explains why the threat to this freedom-loving, egalitarian constitutional ethic of a just social and political order may come not only from outside but equally from within. The essays in this book continuously draw attention to these internal threats and factors that undermine the ethical vision of the Indian Constitution. This is to make citizens aware of the adverse consequences on their collective life by the ill-conceived actions of certain social and political actors.

The need to have this awareness is felt acutely by many Indians. Seventy-five years of a collective journey is bound to yield much that causes misgivings and sorrow. Many of the essays here express judgements that things in India are going badly. They capture the sense of despair about where we went astray, the mistakes we made. They forewarn the reader about the moral dangers that beset our society and try to identify the sites where we might find the resources to somehow combat them. Quite like the terrible pollution of our environment, which happens insidiously behind our back and is noticed only when we fall sick, our social and cultural environment starts to get contaminated long before it affects our personal life. Very often, we realise the full significance of something only after we have lost it. But we cannot afford to wait for the loss of our constitutional values in order to understand their importance. We must not be indifferent to its fate or negligent of the myriad ways in which all of us are undermining it in varying degrees.

These essays are also written in the belief that the Constitution directs each one of us to fearlessly raise questions such as 'Have plural and secular spaces expanded or contracted in our country? Are we becoming more or less inclusive? What is the state of our democracy? Are we free to criticise our government? Is a policy of the government violating any of our freedoms? Is one group free to criticise another and is that freedom being misused to demean each other? As we answer them, the Constitution encourages us to make value judgements: it is despicable that Dalits are mistreated; the government's policy on personal laws is imposing more restrictions on women, there is excessive concentration of power in one office holder, which is bad for our democracy. The judiciary may be the final judge and the ultimate arbiter on these constitutional matters but citizens must make judgements too. Adopting this freedom-loving egalitarian ethic, born during the national independence movement and crafted over many years with painstaking labour, makes it almost mandatory to make value judgements in the light of these constitutional values and principles.

But making value judgements in the light of constitutional values is exceedingly difficult in our times. The difficulty comes in two forms from two opposite directions. The lesser difficulty is due to a habit among the educated to refuse, at least until recently, to make value judgements altogether—or at least they were trained not to make their judgements public. Whatever the reason for this refusal, this ended up shaping a public sphere virtually emptied of value judgements, creating a huge moral vacuum. There was very little to be viewed in the light of constitutional values because judgements were simply not forthcoming.

One pernicious reason behind this suspension of value judgements and the reluctance to use moral and ethical terms is the belief that nothing objectively right or good exists. The general thinking is that anything good for one person may be bad for another. The corollary being, what is right for one may be wrong for another. Such thinking assumes that what we call 'good' is an entirely subjective matter, a simple issue of mere preferences, of likes and dislikes, of private feelings, a matter of taste. This has another consequence. Can a good reason ever be given for why you like the colour red and I blue?

How can reason decide which is objectively better? It cannot. If this indeed is so and all issues relating to the good (i.e., all ethical matters) are merely subjective preferences, then they are inherently beyond reasonable arbitration too. We can never arrive at an ethical consensus by dialogue and deliberation. Any agreement must then be a result of force imposed by power. The implication for our constitutional ethic is also clear. This would mean that there is no objective good or right to be found in the Constitution, and it only articulates the subjective good of those who happened to be in power. If ethics and morality were really that elastic and power-laden, then neither the Constitution nor these short essays would have any relation to truth. They would simply be subjective opinions masquerading as truth. The tone of truth-seeking in these essays would only be a devious, rhetorical ploy. Mere propaganda. I must confess that if I thought I was trying only to manipulate the mind of the reader to agree with me, I would simply not write at all. I don't see myself as a salesman of dreams or an advertiser of ideas.

Another reason for scepticism about ethical judgements is understandable. Many ordinary people feel that they are being constantly judged by those in positions of power: parents, teachers, bosses, religious leaders and other self-appointed gatekeepers of moral boundaries. A lot of people find themselves in situations where they are constantly being judged for doing 'something wrong'. You are bad because you are wearing the wrong kind of dress or meeting the wrong person. You are not putting in enough effort because you are lazy. For people who face them, the term 'judgement' is laden in our discourse with oppressive misrecognition. Now, it is true that judgements of good or bad and right or wrong are easily corrupted by wealth, fame and, most of all, power. This is why a judgement pronounced from the pulpit or the throne should be taken with a pinch of salt. Most likely, it is not truth that we receive from others but a lie or self-interest in the guise of morality. It expresses power and status not truth. But the lesson to be learnt from this is not that we should not judge at all but that we should not allow power, wealth or fame to contaminate our judgements.

To be sure, there does exist a pretty good reason to refrain from making value judgements. This brings me straight to the second, bigger difficulty in making such judgements in the light of constitutional values. The deeper problem today is not the refusal to judge but an excess of value judgements. Our public sphere is dominated by fierce negative value judgements about others and self-congratulatory positive value judgements about ourselves. Most are pronounced instantly without proper understanding or without looking at an issue from the perspective of the other. Typically, these judgements are prejudicial. None seem to be made in the light of constitutional values. On the contrary, most are made in defiance of those values. The consequences of such judgements can be disastrous because they generate distrust and disharmony and harvest conditions of hatred and violence. If being judgmental means making hasty, ill-informed judgements of these sorts, then it is a terrible mistake to be judgmental. It is simply wrong to reach instant, half-baked conclusions about a community, the ethical and moral quality of an individual and social or political acts. I believe that these instant judgements have contributed massively to our current social and political crisis.

If judgement without understanding is hollow and causes harm, understanding alone is not enough. On the other hand, understanding without judgement may do little good to the judged, and without practical import, might be pointless. For a start, it is impossible to ask people not to make value judgements. Refraining from value judgements does not come naturally to humans. On the contrary, it is natural for humans to be moved by some good/value or other. Since we are inescapably ethical creatures, we cannot but help being oriented to the good or the bad or to the right or the wrong. It is pointless to deny or suppress this fact about us. If so, it is more realistic and desirable to ask people to make informed, considered judgements. Besides, value judgements play an important role in society. Good objective judgements alone detect our real shortcomings and can help transform us to become better and enable us to grow as a person. If we as individuals, communities or society are keen to evolve, we must seek an honest appraisal, a suitably objective judgement, one that follows rather than precedes a proper understanding of our motives, intentions, goals, desires and values. Judgements with empathy are crucial for self-improvement of individuals, communities and nations. No society becomes 'great' without ethical self-reflection and critical assessment. The essays in the book do not shy away from making ethical judgements—to condemn or praise, as the case may be. But they seek to do so with empathy and understanding. They make these value judgements in the light of the values enshrined in the Indian Constitution. My hope is to encourage my readers to also make judgements self-reflectively with empathy and understanding and in line with our constitutional tradition.

These essays assume that if we reason with proper understanding of one another with an open mind and shed our deep-rooted prejudices and narrowness of spirit, we can reach agreement on what is good and right. By taking it beyond *subjective* opinions, this agreement establishes the objectivity of good and right. Overall, I reject the idea that ethics and morality are mere opinions, that all morality, ethics and truth are relative to the subjectivity of individual persons. There are a wide range of good that are *objective* in the sense that they are considered worth pursuing not just by me or you but an entire community (e.g., going around a ritual fire in order to be married). Some are considered worth pursuing by an entire nation and not just a community. This is what our Constitution-makers tried to articulate, and the consensus they reached was and remains an objective common good. And to continue with this line of reasoning, some goods are worth realising not by one group or nation alone but by entire humanity (e.g., prosperity, peace, openness, etc.) and some are worth not only for humans but the entire planet (e.g., preventing pollution or global warming, promoting inter-species universalism, etc.). In short, objective goods exist even if they have varying degrees of objectivity. Likewise, it is patently wrong to deliberately injure any human being, indeed even animals, punish an innocent, snatch food from the hungry, demean or humiliate others, etc. These are more or less objective wrongs. It follows that there are objective rights too. It is objectively right not to harm others.

But how can we be sure that our understandings have overcome prejudice? How am I certain that my own understanding is not tainted by prejudice? As a matter of fact, I am not. Why then make them public? Because I believe my own prejudicial judgements can be altered only by conversation and dialogue over time. All our judgements then are provisional. They make a claim to truth, which is itself neither final nor immutable. Truth, in my view, is not equivalent to the aggregate of subjective opinions whose content happens to be the same. Only subjective opinions that pass through legitimate public scrutiny and withstand it have a strong chance of being true. This is why we must make our opinions public.

Constitutional ethic is not the only topic of these essays. A second set of issues is concerned with other aspects of public and private ethics and morality. What is the good in universities? What precisely is their importance? What is the value of intellectuals and what specific standards of excellence must they strive to fulfil? Why should we develop a scientific temper? When is it right to forgive? What is the reparative power of an apology? Is love compatible with criticism?

Other essays are about a deeper understanding of the human condition and experience. Why language matters. What is the role of myths and rituals in our society? How is statelessness experienced? What are the full ramifications of humiliation? What psychological devastation is caused by sexual assault? Some essays lament the present state of our country—its lack of minimal decency, its coarse public culture, the perilous state of intellectual life, its toxic masculinity, the deadly role played by rumour and fake news in public life. A whole section of the book is devoted to our collective experience of the pandemic, particularly the enormous social suffering of migrant workers. Yet others express hope in the power of the ordinary people, the depth of folk wisdom, the healing touch of a prayer, the moral power of the Mahatma's example.

I was trained as a theorist—as a social and political philosopher. Like in other professional disciplines, I was inducted into its special vocabulary, which from the outside appears to be unnecessary jargon. I have tried my best to stay away from it. If I have failed to make my point in a simple language, it is only because intellectual habits, like other habits, are difficult to shed.

As an academic, I wrote for several decades only for other academics in dense, argumentative prose found in long articles and books. Initially, I felt ill-equipped and reluctant to write a column in newspapers for the general reader. But some former students and members of my family persuaded me to take the plunge. They had a motive, which they did not hide. They were horrified by the public cacophony generated by many social and political terms and were dismayed by the astonishing confusion and misunderstandings surrounding them. They were disheartened by the widespread failure to understand the significance of our constitutional ethic and, more generally, moral ideas. They appealed to the teacher in me and nudged me to go beyond my echo chamber and widen my pedagogic reach. Meanwhile, I was troubled by the indifference of my own acquaintances to the semantic structure of moral and ethical concepts. They did not know the precise meaning of terms such as democracy or secularism that dominated our public discourse. Many did not know what the term 'minority' refers to, that 'scheduled castes and scheduled tribes' are not listed as minorities in the Constitution or that there is no constitutionally guaranteed reservation for religious minorities. Nor had they ever thought about the usefulness of the fundamental rights or the value of institutions. They had rarely asked, 'What harm does the collapse of institutions bring? Why is the right to free speech crucial to a democracy? How does the persistent failure of democracy affect our private life?' I felt I must garner my training and teaching experience for a wider public purpose and try to answer some of these questions.

I have been a teacher for most of my adult working life. Though not associated with any university currently, I continue to lecture. Teachers often develop a pedagogic mode of communicating ideas even outside the classroom. Though I have always tried to view my students as interlocuters or equal partners in an ongoing conversation, I hope I have not ended up addressing my readers as pupils.

PART I

Our Nation, Our Constitution

1

Why Have Faith in the Great Indian Experiment?

India's independence from colonial rule launched an unprecedented experiment of introducing democratic equality in a deeply diverse society. Scholars and political observers the world over predicted its failure. Successful nation-states and democracy require one language, one culture and, perhaps, one religion—how could democracy thrive in a poor, illiterate society with mind-boggling religious, cultural and linguistic diversity? Today, when brazen attempts are afoot to suppress such differences, it appears that the sceptics and pessimists were correct. But I remain unmoved. Even in these hopeless times, I have faith in the success of the experiment.

There are many reasons why I remain hopeful, but I focus here on two: one general and the other India-specific. The general reason is that humankind benefits more from diversity than brute uniformity. No one person or group can develop the entire range of thoughts, practices and the good necessary for survival and flourishing. To fulfil constantly evolving human needs, different skills honed by sustained collective, inter-generational effort are required. When a group spends time on one set of skills, it necessarily neglects the others. This means that any cultural group's capacity to fulfil multifarious human needs is limited. Fulfilling all needs demands a pooling together of different skills and a high degree of mutual dependence and learning. The realisation of a better, richer life makes diversity necessary. Those who understand and endorse this are pluralists. Anti-pluralists, who deny and fight diversity, are doomed to lead a fractured, truncated life and may not even survive in the long run. Just as biodiversity is necessary for the larger ecosystem, so is cultural diversity for the much smaller human world.

My second reason is to do with the character of India's historically evolved collective unconscious—our deepest habits and temperament of respect and mutual acceptance. A particular variant of high-strung, deeply insecure modernists masquerading as preservers of Indian tradition but imitating the worst European mode of nation-making pose a challenge to this. But my guess is that

India's age-old moral habits will prevail over this seemingly unifying but utterly claustrophobic and corrosive force.

Critics will immediately dismiss my statement in favour of India as crazily utopian. Am I not making this claim by turning a few happy episodes into a character trait of a whole people? I do not think so. The extent and depth of religio-philosophical diversity in India or an enviable degree of peaceful religious coexistence in its past has been noted globally. Yet, contemporary scholars adopt two contrasting perspectives on this religio-philosophical coexistence. Some explain it by the unique quality of tolerance in Hindu culture that a surfeit of invaders took advantage of until some Indians said enough is enough. Others argue that Indian culture is no different from others—that it always contained a propensity for religious conflict, violence and persecution, and, therefore, the coexistence of different groups occurred because of an accidental balance of power as no group was ever strong enough to rid society of other groups. The clear implication is that the moment any group acquires disproportionate power, it will eliminate other groups or consign them to a life of slavery. It is also argued that this balance of power in society was made possible by political expediency; rulers abhor social and political instability. So peaceful coexistence in India was a result of balance of power between communities underpinned by political necessity.

I disagree with both views. That India's past was also not always harmonious—rocked as it was by religious conflict, violence and persecution—cannot be denied. Hindus and Jains, Hindus and Buddhists, Shaivites and Vaishnavites and even Hindu ascetic orders fought and smashed each other's temples. Occasionally, political rulers, such as the Senas in the eleventh–twelfth century Bengal, were extremely partial to their own Hindu sect. Those who came to India in search of wealth and territory, such as the Greeks, Sakas, Kushans and Huns, indulged in violence too. So did Turks, Afghans and Uzbegs. But an average Hindu selectively remembers only the violence of Muslims. Worse, he forgets that not one but many Islams came to India from cultural regions as far apart as Arabia and Mongolia at different times and with different motives. Only some came with religious zeal against idol worshippers. Some of them plundered and returned while others, such as Mohammad Ghori and Mahmud of Ghazni, fanatically destroyed temples and stayed back to rule. If Persian sources are right, they forcibly converted too.

What an average Hindu also fails to remember is that most Muslim political adventurers fought other Muslim rulers, not Hindu. After all, the much-maligned Babar defeated the Lodhis not some Hindu king! Indeed, many new settlers, attracted to India's pluralist imagination, adapted their beliefs and practices to be in tune with it. For many Hindus and Muslims, Allah became one of the many gods; others thought of Prophet Mohammad as an avatar sent down from heaven to restore righteousness, and for still some such as the Ismailis, Ali, a cousin of Mohammad, was the long-awaited tenth incarnation of Vishnu. Depicting Rama and Krishna as prophets, many made them an integral part of the Islamicate world. Rulers in this pluralist world frequently acted impartially towards everyone. In quarrels between Hindus and Muslims, Hindu rulers, such as the one in the fifteenth century Mangalore, were quick to punish fellow Hindus when found guilty. In 1713, the highest Muslim government official in Ahmedabad had to bear the wrath of some of his own coreligionists when justice prompted him to rule in favour of Hindus. The same spirit of impartiality made Muslim royalty mediate in sectarian disputes to bring together warring sects of Jain, Sikh or Hindu. Royal patronage was extended to non-Muslims, modelled on a pattern set by previous Hindu, Jain and Buddhist rulers. For example, the Gorakhnath math in Jakhbar (in Jammu) received grants from virtually every Mughal ruler. So did the math in Gorakhpur.

I hope these few examples suffice to demonstrate that India's pluralism successfully inhibited religious adversaries from turning into permanent enemies and encouraged peaceful cohabitation. It restrained the recurrence of religious violence. Hatred and demonisation of others are found in medieval Hindu and Muslim literature, but in practice, it disappeared as quickly as it materialised. Pluralism may not have always been formulated as a religious or philosophical doctrine but has become an integral component of our social imagination, being present as a tacit common understanding and default setting in our background. It is this moral imaginary—not timeless philosophical doctrines, time-bound balance of social power or political convenience—that explains peaceful religious coexistence in India.

This unstated confidence in the value of cultural diversity and peaceful religious coexistence shaped Gandhi's thought as well as the thoughts of several other leaders of the anti-colonial movement and the makers of the Constitution of India. Our social imaginary made religious violence, persecution and partiality of political rulers an aberration rather than a norm in India. This unspoken common mentality is too deep-rooted to vanish overnight. Sooner or later, the Indian people will act upon it. This is why I continue to repose faith in the great Indian experiment that was launched on 15 August 1947.

2

A Nation Is a People in Conversation

What is a nation? Above all, it is a people self-consciously bound together by common or overlapping concerns about their past, present and future. This self-conscious awareness of commonality is not genetically encoded. Nor does it drop from the sky. It grows when people talk and listen to one another and through oral and written communication understand each other. This is easy among families and in villages concentrated in a small territory where people meet face to face, but how do common concerns develop among an entire people, virtual strangers to one another, and spread over a large territory?

The short answer is that without a public culture forged first by print and then an electronic media, there would be no conversation among the people, no development of common concerns and, therefore, no nation. So it is entirely apt to say that a nation exists only as long as there is a continuous conversation among its members about what it was, is, will and should be. A disruption of this conversation is the undoing of a nation.

Matters of Common Concern

This conversation is also about what the nation should do. This is an unprecedented achievement of our age, for conversations now are not just passive, contemplative and mere post-facto reflections but yield decisions on which the people may act.

A modern nation is a collective agent; its members can together strive to realise goals they have set for themselves. For example, India must together discuss and find ways to reduce unemployment, resolve the conflict in Kashmir and alleviate the distress of its farmers. This was impossible in earlier societies where decisions about the future of society were taken by a small band of elites, notably chieftains and kings, primarily to protect their own interests rather than the interests of the people, which were always secondary.

To be sure, such conversations and interconnected actions existed in the past. Some elites, dispersed across large territories, may well have had a conversation about things in common. How else does one explain the spread of Bhakti or Vedantic ideas across large swathes of India? Yet, what is new in our time is that, in principle, any Indian can begin a conversation on any matter and turn it into an issue of common and pervasive concern. An issue of a particular community—say triple talaq adversely affects only Muslim women and is primarily a matter between Muslim men and women—can be viewed, at least secondarily, as a matter of common concern. Likewise, the exclusion of Hindu women from some temples may not affect non-Hindus but can be raised by them as a matter of general concern.

The philosopher Jean-Paul Sartre says somewhere that the distinguishing mark of intellectuals is that they stick their nose into every other person's business. However, in modern nations with democracy, this trait is widespread. Provided they empathetically understand it in all its complexity and nuance, virtually anyone can make another person's interest a matter of common concern.

If this is so, an important implication ensues for the ethics of nationhood: No one should be prevented from turning a particular matter into an issue of common concern or be excluded from this conversation, not even those with whom one profoundly disagrees. For having a conversation is not the same as reaching an agreement.

When a large group begins a conversation, different voices, interests, ideas about the common good participate in it. Some of these differences go deep and surface for the first time only during a conversation and cause dissonance. For example, currently, issues pertaining to Kashmir are so fraught with controversy that even an academic argument by a professor causes intense heat.

Not surprisingly, public arenas where such conversations take place are a frequent site of conflict. Both the expression of conflict and its artful management (ensuring that it does not blow up) are crucial for a productive conversation.

If a nation is a people in conversation, then anyone stopping this conversation is damaging it. Such 'conversation stoppers' act in two ways. First, under the illusion that they are managing or resolving conflict, they forcibly remove some groups from the public arena, depriving them of the means to express their concerns and arguments. Some violent extremists do so for other reasons; for instance, it is the avowed aim of terrorists to terminate this conversation. Such suppression of disagreement or conflict undoes a nation.

Second, after allowing different voices to enter the arena, they adopt disruptive tactics—shout down, abuse and troll them—making participation so unpleasant and fearful that interlocutors are compelled to give it up. This too contributes to the unravelling of a nation.

For the Sake of the Nation

One final point: A nation—a people in conversation on common issues—is not the same thing as a state, which is public power concentrated in specific institutions such as the parliament, government, judiciary, army, police and bureaucracy.

Nations may exist without states and states without nations. Moreover, the nation is ethically prior to the state; the state exists for the sake of the nation. At no point must the state hijack the conversation, dictate its agenda or control it. It is a part of the conversation not its permanent leader. Indeed, it is the duty of the state to rein in those who disrupt or block the conversation. The nation expects it.

3

Why Do We Celebrate Republic Day?

The preamble to the Constitution declares that India is a republic. This self-description must be taken seriously; being a republic is integral to India's political identity. Moreover, this is not just a descriptive but a strong ethical, normative claim. Being republican is an ideal to which we are meant to consistently aspire; and when we go astray, we should know that we have done something wrong; we must be remorseful and then make amends. If our political identity loses its republican character, we must quickly act to restore it. It is because we cherish being a republic that we annually celebrate its founding moment on 26 January 1950. The parade and the ritual surrounding it are meaningless unless we get the spirit behind the event.

Against Monarchy

What is meant by a republic and what is its significance? For a start, the primary collective intent behind a republic is anti-monarchical. The Greeks defined monarchy as the 'rule of one (mono)', a form of government where one person rules and all others obey; one is sovereign, all others his subjects. We usually associate it with the hereditary rule of maharajas and maharanis, but the Greek definition of the term also covers rule by modern dictators (autocracy). But what's wrong with the rule of one person? Why fear rule by one person? Perhaps the most pernicious quality about monarchy is that it subjects people to the whims and fancies of one person and his arbitrary will. One day he likes us and gives us, say, a land grant, and the next day, he withdraws the grant and puts us in jail. All powers are vested in him. God-like, he becomes the judge and the jury, makes and executes laws, decides when they are violated and rewards and punishes as he pleases. All these decisions affecting us are taken mysteriously and privately without discussion and expressed as revealed truth. The entire decision-making process remains close to his chest. Hidden from everyone, it brooks neither transparency nor accountability. It is this tyrannical potential of the rule of one person, the absolute and arbitrary use of power, that we dread.

Government by Discussion

What alternative does a republic offer? The English word 'republic' is derived from Latin—'res publica', the public thing. This translates in the political domain into decision-making in the open in full view of all. A republic then is associated with what we today call the public sphere, an open space where people put forward claims about what is good for the community (its collective interest). After discussing, debating and deliberating upon them, they reach decisions about which laws to have and what course of action to take. A republic is 'government by free and open discussion'.

The contrast between monarchical and republican forms of government couldn't be sharper. Monarchy entails surrender to the arbitrary power of another person, allowing whimsical intrusion in our choices and living at the mercy of the master. It breeds slavery. Those who live for long periods under subjection of others tend to develop slavishness, a mental torpor difficult to dispel. Silenced for long, they lose a vibrant sense of their own agency and are rendered without the capacity to think for themselves or take decisions about their own lives. For this reason, Gandhi used the idea of Swaraj to challenge not only political colonisation by the British but also the colonisation of our minds. It is because rule by one enslaves people and makes them unfree, that the republic, its alternative, is strongly associated with freedom. To have a republic is to have a free people. This is why Gandhi's Swaraj is an important republican idea and the reason why the republican tradition emphasises the importance of citizenship. After all, to be a citizen is to belong to a political community where one can express and act freely. Citizens alone have political liberty. Without it, we are mere subjects.

For republic lovers, political liberty means not unbridled freedom to do whatever one pleases (negative liberty) but to live by laws made by citizens themselves, laws that are a product of their own will not the arbitrary will of another person. This explains why republics have a constitution generated by a deliberative body of citizens that provides the basic law of the land, the fundamental framework of governance. The phrase 'we the people' in our Constitution is not a mere literary embellishment but central to a republican constitution. The willingness to live by self-made regulations but enforced by public power or the state also means that those who value a republic are not against states per se but against those that take away our political freedom.

Democratic Republic, Republican Democracy

It appears from what is said above that the word 'republic' covers all that is meant by the term 'democratic'. Our own Constituent Assembly initially took the view that since the word 'republic' contains the word 'democratic', it may be unnecessary to use both. This may have been in keeping with the French republican tradition, where the two terms are used interchangeably. Yet, after announcing its commitment to sever its links with an external, imperial monarch and all existing and future claims of local rajas and make India a republic, Ambedkar and Nehru conceded that since an undemocratic republic is conceivable, a separate commitment to democratic institutions is necessary.

This decision was correct. It was wise to keep both terms in the preamble. The idea of the republic conveys that decisions shall be made not by a single individual but by citizens after due deliberation in an open forum. But this is consistent with a narrow criterion of who counts as a citizen. The ancient Roman Republic was not inclusive. Ancient India probably had aristocratic clan republics that were far from democratic. In ancient Greece, slaves, women and foreigners were not considered citizens and excluded from decision-making. Indeed, for many Greek thinkers, democracy had a negative connotation precisely because it was believed to involve everyone, including plebians, who we contemptuously call 'the mob'.

What the term 'democratic' brings to our Constitution is that citizenship be made available to *everyone*, regardless of their wealth, education, gender, perceived social ranking, religion, race or ideological belief. Democracy makes the republic *inclusive*. No one is excluded from citizenship; *all* of us have the right to vote. At the same time, if voting is restricted, for practical reasons, only to choosing representatives who make laws and policies in the name of the people, then citizens must at least have the right to be properly informed and seek transparency and accountability from their government. A republic must, at the very least, have perpetually vigilant citizens who act as watchdogs, monitor their representatives and retain the right to contest any law or policy made on their behalf. By going beyond mere counting of heads, the term 'republic' brings free public discussion to our democratic Constitution. It gives depth to our democracy. It is mandatory that decisions taken by the representatives of the people be properly deliberated, remain open to scrutiny and be publicly and legally contestable even after they have been made.

When the farmers came out on the streets to peacefully challenge the three farm laws made by the current government, they exercised not only their democratic rights but exhibited the highest of republican virtues. It is to celebrate such political acts of citizens that we have a designated republic day.

4

Why We Need a Constitution

The judgement by the Supreme Court clarifying the jurisdictions of Delhi's lieutenant governor and its elected representatives and specifying the limits of their powers once again underscored how fortunate we are to have the Constitution. Why should gratitude be expressed for living under a constitutional democracy? Why do we need a constitution?

Since an individual's own personal power is severely limited, nothing valuable can be attained without the collective effort of individuals. A boulder cannot move even by an inch when pushed by an individual but with help from others, it can go places. Most human good—health, education, infrastructure, peace and harmony, economic growth, leisure and enjoyment, art and literature, narratives of self-understanding and collective heritage—are realised by assembling power. However, once constituted, this indispensable collective power to do or achieve things can be used not to realise the collective good but for one's own exclusive advantage—to secure things only for oneself. This can be done by forcing others to do what they would not otherwise do—to get them to act against their will—for one's own benefit.

Checking Tyranny

A typical feature of all, particularly modern, societies is that this public or collective power is largely vested in the state relatively separate from society. It follows that state power meant for everyone's good can be used by some over other members of society to benefit just a few of its functionaries and their friends. Since the formation of states, humans have felt the need to not only garner collective power but also limit it so that it is not exercised whimsically and arbitrarily for self-aggrandisement and against the basic interests of the people. This is the key reason why we have the Constitution, which is not just any odd assortment of law and institutions but a framework of ground rules that acts as a bulwark against the tyrannical use of state power to dominate and oppress others.

In short, constitutions strive for a delicate balance to ensure that the collective power of society invested in the state is neither dissipated or fragmented to become ineffective (for this results in lawlessness and anarchy detrimental to the realisation of the good life) nor so tightly organised and untrammelled that it takes away our freedom and becomes oppressive. The potential to abuse public power, an ever-present possibility in all states, is inherent in the very exercise of it. Thus, the earliest constitutions of the world developed to check the tyranny of our rulers.

This idea of the Constitution presupposes an unbridgeable distance between the people and the state—a powerless people who need the help of constitutional law to control state power. But what if people themselves wield state power? What if the power of the state comes from the power that resides in the demos (the people)? State power may be limited not by some higher law but by the power of the people. Democracy, it could be argued, can function as an alternative to a constitution. Why, then, have a constitution?

This is an attractive but flawed idea. In practice, democratic power never really resides in the people but in a temporarily constituted majority. Sometimes, this majority can become permanent. Here, the tyranny of a ruler is replaced by the tyranny of the majority group. Thus, we need a constitution to check the tyranny of a majoritarian democratic state. This entails that very important issues pertaining to minority groups be freed from the contingencies of majority will and taken out of the decision-making arena of electoral democracies and made more or less non-negotiable. This is the point behind rights—rights of individuals and minorities must not be trumped by majority preferences. This is the second reason why we need a constitution or constitutional democracy.

Prevent Self-harm

But a constitution is required for a third reason: to protect everyone against human vulnerability in general. It is important not to forget that human beings are fallible, that they sometimes forget what is really good for them; they yield to temptations that bring them pleasure now but pain later. It is not unknown for people to act in the heat of the moment (out of anger, fear or intense hatred)—electing a person with strong authoritarian traits, for example—only to rue the consequences of the decision later. By providing a framework of law culled from years of collective experience and wisdom, a constitution prevents people from succumbing to fashionable whims and fancies, anticipating and redressing the excessively mercurial character of everyday politics. The guardians of India's Constitution have ensured that the destabilising swings of legislative moods generated by ephemeral passion or myopia do not alter its basic structure.

Enable Power to Do Good

India provides a particularly instructive case of another valuable function of a constitution: to provide a moral framework for profound, non-violent social transformations. This is Ambedkar's great contribution. But Nehru was equally eloquent: 'The Constituent Assembly is a nation on the move, throwing away the shell of its past political and possibly social structure, and fashioning for itself a new garment of its own making.' The Indian Constitution was designed to break the shackles of traditional social hierarchies and usher in a new era of freedom, equality and justice. Thus, by disenabling the state from doing certain things, a constitution enables it to do other important things more effectively. Once restrained, public power can be deployed to achieve the good life. Thus, a constitution is needed not only to limit wielders of existing power but to empower those traditionally deprived of it—to give vulnerable people the power to help realise an inclusive collective good.

5

No Other Book Can Trump the Indian Constitution

A minister of the West Bengal government, Siddiqullah Chowdhury, reportedly remarked that for Muslims 'our holy scripture, the Quran Sharif, is supreme and if any constitutional provision ... contradicts the Quran, then our scripture will prevail and not the Constitution'.[1] This statement is deeply condemnable in a constitutional democracy and nothing justifies it. He might have been better off paying heed to his own chief minister who, a few years ago, categorically said that while 'we respect all holy books ... the Constitution is *the* holy book in a democracy'.

There is a great deal of truth in this assertion. On 26 January 1950, for the first time in Indian history, we—believers and practitioners of diverse philosophies and religions—decided to also become the people of a single book. This was the only way to knit ourselves together into one modern nation, not only because, taken collectively, we find the ultimate worth in many books but

[1] *The Statesman*, 'Bengal Minister Siddiqullah Chowdhury Says Quran Will Prevail over Constitution,' 22 September 2018.

also because we live with traditions where books are religiously irrelevant—devotional singing, ritual performance, meditation, truthful self-examination are enough. Each of us had to find a fit between our distinctive way of reaching the ultimate—one god, many gods and goddesses or indeed no god at all—and a common, basic framework for living together. No matter how inadequate our Constitution is, an enduring consensus exists that it provides a strong, secure foundation for an inclusive, dignity-protecting and freedom-sensitive society. Devised by men and women of diverse faiths and castes speaking different languages, the basic structure of the Constitution is sound and needs no altering.

Religion and the State

Implicit in the Constitution is a subtle yet deeply interesting view of religion: first, it is a path to the ultimate; second, it constitutes a historically sedimented tradition; and third, it specifies a set of norms for social interaction. Wisely, the Constitution commits the state to a complex stance towards this 'religion', a point the minister fails to understand. First, the state should not interfere in the choice of individuals or groups in their quest for ultimate self-fulfilment. This is precisely what religious freedom means. Second, the Constitution acknowledges the value of distinct traditions but also simultaneously recognises that aspects of any tradition putrefy over time, and unless reinterpreted, reinvigorated and refashioned, they fall off like dead skin or destroy healthy tissues of the social body. This is also true of religion. The attitude of the state to religious traditions can therefore be neither wholehearted acceptance nor outright rejection. On the third issue, the overall position of the Constitution, despite a few ambiguities and temporary retreats, is unequivocal. It demands nothing short of a profound social revolution. It signifies a break from unjustifiable hierarchical norms of the past to build a defensible egalitarian ethos in the present, where everyone can live with dignity and respect. Thus, the state must have critical respect; respect because some aspects of religion need nurturing and preservation, and critique, because some unworthy ones need modification and still others destruction.

To realise critical respect, the state does not need strict separation but principled distance from all religions. Principled distance requires the state to eschew a formal alliance with religion but not to build an insurmountable wall between the two. The state disengages from religion or engages with it—engages positively (actively promoting religion) or negatively (intervening to inhibit it)—and in order to treat all as equals, does not accord the same treatment but helps or hinders one religion more than others, as the occasion demands. Thus, without abandoning respect for Hinduism, the state must engage to abolish the degrading practice of untouchability justified by certain Hindu texts and commentators, which some declare as part of Hinduism itself. This constitutional intervention was required to do justice to those Dalits who did not disown Hinduism. In fact, if, despite formal doctrinal commitment to equality, this degrading practice persists in other religions such as Indian Islam and Christianity, the state must intervene in them too. Not doing so is tantamount to treating Muslim and Christian Dalits unfairly.

Hindus who complain that state intervention has been unfair to their religion have got it completely wrong. This is like a situation where a patient who has benefited from surgery is resentful of those who also need it but are not fortunate enough to receive the treatment. Nothing can be more absurd. In short, the state acted in a pro-Hindu manner and with indifference to the injustices within other religions. Much the same is true when in 1956, thanks to the efforts of Ambedkar, Nehru and several progressive Hindus, the Parliament partially reformed Hindu personal law by passing the Hindu code bills. They saved Hinduism from decay by giving Hindu women a stake in their received religion. For the first time, they could remain Hindus and yet move towards greater equality and freedom. The majority of Hindus benefited from it even if a section of the orthodox Hindu was displeased. Alas, Muslim women could not benefit from this reform and continue to be victimised by their patriarchs.

Stop Abominable Practices

No matter how suspicious the minister was of the motives of the central government to reform Muslim personal laws and how illegitimate the ordinance route to 'reform' is, the fact is that instant triple talaq is an abominable practice rejected by many Muslim countries. It gives enormous power to Muslim men and is deeply degrading to Muslim women. Perpetuating it when other forms of civil contractual practices compatible with both the Constitution and a more meaningfully interpreted Quran are available is akin to festering the injustice against Muslim women and disrespecting the 'holy book' of democracy.

6

The Importance of a Nation's Self-image

In 2017, the remark by the outgoing Indian vice president, Ḥamid Ansari, that there is growing unease among Dalits and minorities caused rancour among some of our fellow citizens. It is a bit puzzling why, for this was not an unusual observation. Many Indians, including former president Pranab Mukherjee, had raised concerns about growing intolerance in our country and the threat to our pluralist ethos. But Ansari's remark was seen by some as particularly disturbing because of the apparent damage it inflicted on the country's image. Some went as far as to say that it was an insult to the country.

Concern for the country's image is not to be scoffed at or dismissed as inconsequential. A country's image is important. Since a country is made up of its people, its image is the collective self-image of the people. Each one of us wants to be viewed by others favourably because how one is treated is frequently determined by how one is seen. We don't wish to be misrecognised by others. We all wish to be recognised for what we truly are and not be seen through a distorting lens. Besides, a positive self-image is crucially linked to our self-esteem. If our self-image is damaged, our self-esteem will necessarily be lowered and we are bound to feel humiliated and insulted. This is equally true of our collective self-image. If our country is portrayed negatively, we feel ashamed, angry or even outraged. There is no denying the importance of a country's image.

Self-Image: A Double-Edged Sword

Yet, a self-image should not be confused with a person's real self. There is always a gap between how one is seen (by others or by oneself) and what one really is. Moreover, there are two kinds of self-images. The first kind is constructed self-reflectively, which constantly realigns between how one appears and what one really is. Conscious of the pitfalls of self-deception, it relentlessly unmasks defects and vulnerabilities. Building a real self and constructing a self-image are here part of the same ethical process.

The other thrives on deliberate distortion. Though carefully crafted, such a self-image is far removed from reality. Disconnected from the real self, the image overtakes it and becomes all that matters. Indeed, it even masks the real self and its flaws. An obsession with this self-image undermines the growth of the real self; wasteful energy is spent on polishing the self-image even as the real self is tarnished by neglect. This as is true for a nation as it is for an individual.

Publicly acknowledging and attending to one's flaws rather than ignoring them is pivotal to nurturing a healthy and positive self-image. Cosmetically engaging with them or being indifferent to the creeping malaise damages the self and its real image. What or who then is damaging a country's self-image? And who among us is nurturing it positively? Consider a teenager who habitually cheats in exams but is caught one day by an observant and scrupulous teacher. Though his act reflects badly on his own moral character, it probably tells us even more about the poor quality of moral life in his family. The appropriate thing to do here is for the parents to own up their mistake and find ways of rectifying the moral ambience at home so that this does not occur again. But what happens instead is bizarre. The parents begin to blame the teacher for publicly ruining the reputation or image of the family. How twisted can a mind be!

Some years ago, the country was hit by a series of corruption scandals. Imagine if those who exposed the scandals were blamed for damaging the country's image and the scamsters came through unscathed? Today, it is clearly the lynch mobs who are damaging the image of the country not those who express concern over the lynchings and want the government to put a stop to them. Surely, there is some perverse logic operating here.

Internal and External Image

A second feature of the obsessive preoccupation with image is this: those persistently anxious about the country's image do not clarify that their embarrassment is due solely to the tarnished image of the country in the external world. But equally, if not more importantly, is the image of the country within, amongst its own people. Do we not need to ask what the image of the country is in the eyes of Dalits, minorities, ravaged farmers and others who feel alienated and excluded? Can we please start getting concerned about the country's internal image and the imprint this intolerance leaves on our alienated citizens?

Quite like an individual, no country is perfect. We all make mistakes, stray from the path, get misdirected, temporarily lose our way and even reach the wrong destination. But the intelligent and wiser lot among us are self-correcting. They can tell when and where we have gone wrong and take steps for course correction. The ability to tell right from wrong, the courage to acknowledge that a wrong has been committed and the collective resolve to fix it—these are all crucial for the health of a nation.

The image of a country is greatly enhanced when its citizens speak out against any wrong committed in their name or their land. It is even more reassuring to hear people in the highest positions of authority acknowledging public wrong with responsibility and purpose. It shows that we are a vibrant, self-examining and introspective people. It also shows that we are an assured democracy. That, indeed, is the image that we should wish to have of ourselves within the country and abroad.

7

Taking Pride in Our National Culture

Who must have legitimate cultural pride and why? Should humans take pride in their respective cultures? Yes! Why not? All Indians must be proud of the absence of major religious wars in India, no significant instance of religious persecution and, at least until the nineteenth century, no large-scale communal violence.

Should we all have pride in each and every aspect of our past and present culture? Of course, not! How can Hindus take pride in socially sanctioned untouchability or the continuing control of their women, who are still mostly unable to lead a free public life? So, there must be a distinction between legitimate and illegitimate cultural pride.

And how assertive must we be about cultural pride? Should we shout from the rooftops that 'we are the greatest', always wear our pride on our sleeve or instead allow it to shine through, with humility and calm self-confidence, in our actions and achievements?

Vociferous Assertion?

Assertive cultural pride is understandable, even justified, only when a group is breaking away from prolonged cultural subjugation and humiliation, as was the case in mid-nineteenth century India, when profound distortions were introduced in our self-understandings by cultural imperialism. But already by the early twentieth century, we see an articulation of legitimate cultural pride in the expressions of Vivekananda, Tagore and Gandhi that behoves a confident cultural community. What then is the need for such vociferous assertion now?

And why invent originality or greatness in the face of all evidence to the contrary when there is much else to be legitimately proud of? Why have false pride in *pushpak vimaan* or 'plastic surgery' when there are real things, ideas and values in our own culture to give us profound self-satisfaction? The great Indian epics, Buddha's and Upanishadic teachings, Panini's grammar, Aryabhatta, the magnificent Kalidasa, Kabir's poetry, etc., are just a few examples.

Finally, what precise form must cultural pride assume, particularly in a religiously and culturally plural world? I would put it like this: we are all proud participants in a historically connected, worldwide flow of cultural resources; we too contribute in our own distinctive way to the rich, large, complex and variegated cultures of humanity. Cultural communities must mutually recognise their historically grounded and validated contributions. This collective achievement is not an illusion or exaggeration but very real.

Allow me to illustrate. We know that Leo Tolstoy had a profound impact on Mahatma Gandhi. Now, Tolstoy—a Russian aristocrat by birth, an army officer in his youth and, later, a great writer and thinker—underwent a radical spiritual conversion, culminating in a dramatic renunciation of worldly success to lead an ascetic life of non-violence and social service.

Apparently, the catalyst for this change was his reading of a Georgian fable that captures a poignant human predicament: a man running away manically from a diabolical beast falls into a well but escapes instant death by somehow clinging to a creeper. But alas, the creeper is being persistently nibbled at by white (day) and black (night) mice. It is only a matter of time before he drowns in the well. The man's death is overdetermined.

This story made Tolstoy realise that in the end, despite wealth, fame and power, life in itself is meaningless because death is imminent. His response was to turn away from the material world of pomp and power. The fable was part of Christian hagiography on the lives of Saints Barlaam and Josaphat. It spread from Damascus to Baghdad to Greece and Rome to western Europe and became a part of medieval Christian consciousness. Its dominant motif was the renunciation of worldly power and wealth by a young prince, Josaphat, who, coming under the influence of a hermit named Barlaam from the Sinai desert, abdicated his throne in order to seek moral and spiritual truth.

The Narrative Loop

But here is the interesting twist in this Christian story. The prince in the tale woven by Georgian monks from Greek, Latin and Arabic sources was Indian! The prince in the story is none other than Prince Siddhartha Gautama, the Bodhisattva, the future Buddha! Georgian Christians learnt about him from Arab Muslims, who had taken it from the Manichees in Central Asia, who in turn obtained it from Buddhist sources.

In Manichean versions, Bodhisattva became Bodisaf in Arabic, Yudasaf in Georgian, Iosaph in Greek and Josaphat in Latin. But the origin story does not stop here. Wilfred Cantwell Smith, a great admirer of India's religious diversity and founder of the department of world religions at Harvard University, from whom I got this account, goes on to say that the Buddhist story itself may have Jain and ancient Hindu roots.

So a story that originated in India returned to it via Greece, Rome, Baghdad, Georgia and Kiev through the vehicle of Buddha, Tolstoy and Gandhi. Millions of such stories originated from West Asia, China, Europe or Africa, finding their way to different parts of the world.

If this is how things, ideas and values circulate, virtually nothing belongs wholly to any one group. This is why the only right way of expressing cultural pride must not be by claiming greatness for oneself but rather for each cultural community, by showing that it too contributes to historically connected worldwide cultures of humanity. Deep down, the real subject of cultural pride is invariably a host of interconnected cultural communities.

PART II

Our Democracy: People, Politics and Leadership

8

Why We Treasure Democracy

Politics anywhere and anytime is messy, and democratic politics is messier, if only because its dirt is in full public view. It has the appearance of perpetual chaos and continual disorder. Why do all of us put up with it then? Why do so many prefer it to other political orders?

For Peace, Freedom and Well-being

The attractiveness of democracy lies in its ability to give us a peaceful transfer of power. To be sure, it is not for those in search of equanimity and inner peace or for those easily unnerved by disagreements and conflicts. It is for the street-smart with a flair for some adventure in public life. It draws on our agonistic energies, bringing conflict upfront. But it frees us from the bloody battles and gory coups d'etat through which wealthy and powerful super-elites conventionally settled their conflicts. It is a non-violent substitute for the marauding warrior ethic.

Second, it eliminates the most basic fears and anxieties to which social and political life is prone—the fear of being killed, beaten or humiliated for doing or saying what we want or for challenging the powerful. It promotes the maximum possible openness in how we think, speak and behave. None of us can survive without some limits to our speech and action, but democracy allows us to test and stretch them tantalisingly close to breakdown before deftly pulling back. An extricable link exists between democracy and public freedom.

Third, no other political system takes people's own view of their needs, wants and goals more seriously than democracy, giving the people the best possible shot at satisfying them.

The Difficulties of Democracy

Alas, democracy does not come easy. And Indian democracy has been built in the most difficult circumstances. Many expected it to fail even after the introduction of universal adult franchise and constitutionally mandated institutions. A culture of equality is believed to be crucial to democracy but India inherited a social structure replete with hardened gender and caste inequalities. A democracy's success depends on fairly high levels of growth, but India's rate of growth in 1947 was virtually zero, with 65–70 per cent of its population trapped in extreme poverty. To be successful, democracies supposedly need a fair degree of cultural, linguistic and religious homogeneity, but India has deep cultural, religious and linguistic diversity. Most Western democracies have high levels of literacy and education, but a substantial section of the Indian population was illiterate, with virtually no formal education.

Yet Indian democracy has survived. Indeed, democratic mechanisms have been deployed to attack gender and caste inequalities, to bring millions out of poverty and to nurture its famed diversity. Besides, lack of education has not lessened popular enthusiasm in its favour. And this brings us to the most admirable feature of Indian democracy: born amid various forms of social illness and new diseases that had been exacerbated by colonialism, it has had to fight these and incessantly reproduce its own conditions of survival. In the absence of social conditions crucial to its durability, it has had to continually give birth to its own nurturing conditions and heal itself after falling sick. Indian democracy is largely self-sustaining. This feature of a polity is praise-worthy in the same way as respect is due to self-made, autonomous individuals.

Helping Democracy Grow

Largely but not entirely, like other claims of self-creation, this one too is a trifle exaggerated. Two external conditions help democracy to grow. First, a stateless society can't be democratic because the conditions of democracy are not automatically reproduced but need an effective state. But just any state won't do. Though Indian democracy was preceded by a relatively modern state, the very same state hindered it too. The colonial state apparatus inherited by us was insensitive to the needs of the people, working almost entirely for the British Empire. A number of colonial laws were repressive and excessively regulatory. Their primary objective was the creation of a 'nuisance-free' public order, controlling a defiant population and exploiting them for the benefit of the empire. The colonial state was built to resist democracy, not facilitate it. This repressive apparatus, a permanent threat to our democracy, always comes in handy for authoritarian officials/leaders, as it did during the Emergency. So democracy needs a competent state, but one that is tamed to work for it.

Second, to be democratic, the state must be relatively independent of classes and ethnic groups in society. No class or ethnic group (religious or linguistic community) must completely control state power, or use it to push its own agenda in its entirety. Therefore, each class and ethnic group must learn to live with this fact—that all its objectives cannot be met. This realisation occurs either when each class or ethnic group has enough power to prevent intergroup domination or when, for the sake of a more inclusive moral vision, every group forsakes part of its interests and achieves a principled compromise. By curbing the inclination to impose our agenda on others, and instead arriving at negotiated settlements, we produce stable democracies. This precisely is achieved in the Indian Constitution.

Any attempt to subordinate the state to the whims of a powerful individual or to use it disproportionately in favour of one group disturbs this delicate consensus, destabilises Indian democracy and wrecks the collective future of its citizens. The nasty experience of our own Emergency and the unsavoury condition of societies plagued with attempts at domination (by the Sinhalese in Sri Lanka or Sunnis in Pakistan) teach us to treasure democracy. Forgetting this lesson is disastrous.

9

Bicycle Ride as a Metaphor for Democracy

What is democracy? Abraham Lincoln's phrase that it is political rule of the people, by the people and for the people is now a cliche. For some it is more a frivolous shorthand than a serious elucidation. But I reckon it remains an apt description of democracy, carrying more weight than what we have come to suppose.

The Cycle as a Metaphor

Let's take a simple example. A village has a bicycle to fetch goods of daily use. So far, the bicycle is used exclusively by the pradhan (village headman) to procure goods only for himself and his family;

but now, following a change of heart or popular pressure, the pradhan also uses the bicycle to ferry goods he thinks would meet the basic needs of other village folks. The bicycle is now used, at least sometimes, also *for* the people. On receiving some articles of subsistence, they begin hoping that a day will come when they would be able to ride the bicycle; see, touch and smell the goods themselves; and choose what they really want. Instead of being content with things handed out to them, they can now go to the market, see the entire range of goods on display and decide what, by their own reckoning, best satisfies them. So, they somehow manage to persuade the pradhan to let them ride the bicycle and visit the market. They now realise that there were many things that they had not even conceived they needed. They also begin to enjoy the ride to the market and back. Indeed, the bicycle takes them to entirely new worlds, beyond the market and the immediate world of things they need. It fires up their imagination, helps them forge new relations and conjure up new worlds. Riding the bicycle has its own rewards—its own thrill. The bicycle now doesn't merely work for them but is also worked *by* them, and for that reason, it works even better.

At this stage, however, the pradhan changes his mind and takes this bicycle away from them. The village is back to square one; the people return to their deprived state. In a fix, the poor villagers realise that the mere opportunity to use the bicycle was never enough. It should always have belonged to them. They should have claimed it as theirs—have had a greater stake in it. They, not the pradhan, should have collectively owned it because its use, in the last instance, depended on their having a permanent, inalienable right to it. So now they strive to make the bicycle theirs and to prevent it from remaining an exclusive possession of the pradhan. They realise that they should not even view the bicycle as a thing of instrumental value. Rather, it should always have been something of intrinsic value—indeed, an integral part of who they are. Losing it would not just be a temporary deprivation from which they can recover easily and quickly by getting a replacement, but an alienation of the basic capacity to determine the course of their life, a shattering blow to their self-confidence, self-esteem and their very sense of self. Once they reclaim it, they can legitimately say that the bicycle not only functions for and is run by them but also belongs to them. It is theirs—for them, by them and, even more importantly perhaps, *of* them.

Decision-making and Identity

I hope the reader has understood that what is true of a simple bicycle is also true for the far more complex practice of democracy. Democracy is an institutional mechanism that helps us obtain resources that potentially satisfy and enable us to lead the life we wish and choose. But it works for us only if we all take part in running it. If we allow some elites (pradhans) to take charge and rely exclusively on them to get us the resources we need, chances are that we may never get the resources or receive them sporadically, depending on the elites' whims and fancies. Besides, we would be deprived of the sheer pleasure of decision-making, of taking an active part in choosing and allocating resources and of determining the course of our collective and individual lives. And, finally, if we don't have a stake in democracy—if we feel we don't own it and don't see it as belonging to us as a constitutive part of our identity—then one day it might even be taken away from us by someone. So we must ensure that democracy is not just for the people and run by the people but also is *of* the people. It belongs to us; that is to say, it is *ours*. A lot of thought, it appears, was invested by Lincoln in this short, by now cliched, phrase.

10

What the Ruler and the Ruled Owe One Another

The *Arthashastra* is not the only source of political thinking in India. Another tradition exists from which we can learn much, which is as relevant in our own very different context of popular rule (democracy) as it was in ancient times.

I am thinking here of a tradition in which the idea of the chakravartin, the wheel turner, is of great significance. The wheel that these great rulers turn is the wheel of dhamma (law inspired by morality). Just as the Buddha turned the wheel of dhamma in the religio-philosophical sphere, just so, the chakravartin turns it in the political sphere. The turning of the wheel is a metaphor for a radical restructuring of the world in accordance with a politico-moral vision. The king launches an entirely new set of political and administrative measures inspired by public morality and becomes a normative ruler—the just ruler who brings peace and prosperity to his subjects. If he conquers other kingdoms, he does so not by physical force but by moral appeal. People submit to his rule not from coercion but voluntarily, out of respect for his adherence to the principles of dhamma.

The Ashoka Template

The king who first embodied the idea of a moral ruler—the 'normative king'—is none other than Ashoka. Before him, or before he turned his back on the tradition of physical conquest and violence to become the chakravartin, the rightness or wrongness of actions was determined solely by the king. The law was not applied consistently or uniformly but in an extremely partial and arbitrary manner. Thus, rajas often rewarded or punished their subjects to serve their own idiosyncratic moral sense or personal interests. However, by fashioning the idea of dhamma, Ashoka detached his personal views from what is morally right. By submitting to what is morally right, he sought to save himself from acts that he might come to regret later and to tame the institution of kingship itself, which would limit his own absolute power.

If dhamma is a higher moral principle not just above the ruled but also the ruler, we have within our midst not just what the ruled owe their rulers but also what the ruler owes the ruled. The politico-moral order stands above the king, at least partially. The head of the family is as much part of it as his wife and children are. Likewise, the king is part of the political order just as much as his subjects are. And just as all members of the family owe something, though not the same thing, to each other, the king also owes something to his subjects, though qualitatively different from what the subjects owe him.

What the subjects owe to the king and his officials is obedience to his commands. But these commands are not his whims but flow from dhamma itself. Furthermore, the Ashokan Pillar Edict VII clarifies that compliance to dhamma must arise largely from *nijjhattiya* (persuasion) not solely from *niyama* (legislation). And we can be persuaded only when something makes sense to us—when what is commanded accords with what one understands dhamma to require. Everyone must follow dhamma out of an inner disposition to comply with one's conscience, as it were. In short, rule by dhamma may also be viewed as an attempt to transform brute power into moral authority; commands are followed because they are seen to be good, not merely because the ruler so commands.

This does not exhaust the political dimension of dhamma, however. For it must also include what the king owes his subjects. Pillar Edict VI elaborates what this is: *lokassa hitasukhaye* (welfare and happiness of all living beings in this world) and hereafter in swarga (heaven). According to Pillar Edict IV, the king's officials also owe something to the subjects: *samata* (impartiality), *viyohala* or *vyavahar samata* (impartiality in the social domain) and *damda samata* (impartiality in the domain of retributive punishment).

In the reign of dhamma, the king is not just a ruler but a leader, one who leads his subjects by example. Apart from being a father to all (important in that context), Ashoka tried to be someone who saw further and clearer than others, sometimes even teachers and healers; he was always a moral exemplar.

Lessons for Today

What is the takeaway from this ancient conception of dhamma-inspired chakravartin? Not the idea of kingship or the rule of one man, which is of no value in a democratic republic. Nor the idea of the ruler as our father—our maibaap. In a democracy, we rule collectively; at least as equal citizens, we rule and are ruled in turn. But even our own rule can become arbitrary, where power is exercised by popular whims rather than predictable, stable norms emanating from collective reflection. So the takeaway is that we owe it to ourselves and to each other that there are (a) impartial rule of law that checks abuse of popular power, saving us, the people, from acts that we might come to regret later, and binds even those we have temporarily chosen to govern us and (b) something like dhamma, a constitutional morality, such as justice, tolerance, freedom, equality and civic friendship, which guides us all, the ruler and the ruled. And our elected representatives owe it to us that they are not merely rulers but moral exemplars—faithful adherents of the rule of law and constitutional morality. The chakravartin tradition remains a valuable resource for our democratic republic.

11

Respecting Leaders in a Democracy

Respect for politicians is in short supply in our times. Most citizens of contemporary democracies seem to tolerate, not respect, those they elect. Are we troubled by the absence of respect in politics? Should politicians even be accorded respect? If yes, what form of respect must they get?

Directive Respect: Egalitarian

'Respect' has multiple senses, of which three are relevant here. One sense, which might be called 'directive respect', was elaborated by the late eighteenth-century German philosopher Immanuel Kant. For him, respect has the force of an authoritative moral instruction or directive. Kant understood that humans in their social interactions can never entirely eliminate using one another for personal benefit. When I approach a conductor in a bus, I do not do so out of love, affection or curiosity but with one goal in mind: to purchase a ticket to travel. And the conductor is in the bus to do a job for the bus owner: sell tickets. All of us—the passengers, the conductor, the driver and the bus owner—relate to each other as instruments to achieve our respective ends: travel home, earn a livelihood, make profit, etc. However, Kant argued, while this may well be so, each must also keep in mind that we are moral agents with distinct purposes; we have our own subjective take on the world and the capacity to endow the world with meaning, purpose and value. In short, we have inherent dignity that imposes limits on the extent to which we can use each other for personal benefit. I can't treat the bus conductor as a mere thing to be pushed around, offended or humiliated even as I buy the ticket from him. I must respect him.

To reiterate, the quality of dignity that inheres in a person is the ground for a moral directive not to treat someone only as an instrument to realise my purpose but also always as a person with distinct purposes of her own. Dignity demands respect. Put differently, to respect others is not just to have an attitude but also to act towards humans in a way that does not merely use them. This is what makes it a form of directive respect. In addition to being directive, Kant's notion is also egalitarian. This is because each of us commands this respect regardless of our differential social status, position, class, gender, race, talent or achievement.

Directive Respect: Hierarchical

This egalitarian feature alone differentiates it from another instance of directive respect where the quality that commands respect from others inheres not in the person qua person but in the social position she occupies or the role she performs. Thus, children must respect their fathers; wives, their husbands; servants, their masters; lower caste people, higher castes and so on. Indeed, this unequal status is the original site of the idea of respect, its breeding ground. The notion of respect was for long intertwined with ideas of superiority and inferiority and had deep hierarchical overtones. Virtually indistinguishable from fear and deference, it was expressed not only in words but through silences and bodily stances. Thus, persons believed to be inferior could not call a superior by his name or look him in the eye; they must always have their heads bowed or covered, could not touch any part of the superior person or could, at best, touch only his feet; they are required to always obey, do as they are told and never question or even respond.

This hierarchical notion of directive respect has not disappeared from our society (as many had hoped) and continues to permeate social relationships. But disturbingly, just when we thought that this notion of respect is fading away from politics because of our anti-colonial struggle and equality-centred reform movements led by Jyotirao Phule, Mahatma Gandhi and B.R. Ambedkar, it appears to be raising its ugly head again. Revived here is the older, deeply hierarchical idea of respect as deference, which brooks no dissent, muffles voices and demands unquestioning silence from all. It is also being used to elicit obedience to a 'supreme leader'. This appears to be happening not only in India but in many other polities of the world. I have been told that many conversations between Trump loyalists and his critics came to an abrupt halt because of complaints that the critics did not respect the president. The Hungarian Prime Minister Viktor Orbán said that any attack on his policies is a sign of disrespect for Hungary. The Turkish writer Ece Temelkuran drew attention to similar demands by Turkish President Recep Tayyip Erdogan. When charged with rigging the polls, Mr Erdogan claimed that this showed disrespect to the people of Turkey and their choice.

The hierarchical notion of respect is a one-way street and incompatible with the very idea of democracy. The egalitarian notion of respect articulated by Kant, a perfect riposte to respect as deference, is presupposed by democracies and relevant as a value in relationships among citizens but is too general to be of use in the specific context of citizen–ruler relationship. Does this mean then that respect for politicians is entirely dispensable in democracies? I don't think so.

Evaluative Respect

Another kind of respect exists. This is owed to people not because of what they are or their social position but by virtue of what they have achieved. This may manifest in some praiseworthy qualities of character, such as moral integrity or skills perfected through sheer hard work, such as by a cricketer. This respect consists in an attitude of positive appraisal of the person's moral qualities or non-moral skills. Here, respect is not presumed but earned. We can appropriately say that this attitude of respect is well-deserved when a person meets some standards of excellence integral to that practice. Precisely because it is something one achieves; it can also be a matter of degree. Rightly or wrongly, one can say that one has a greater evaluative or appraisal respect for Sunil Gavaskar than, say, Chetan Chauhan, or for Jawaharlal Nehru than, say, Govind Ballabh Pant. This quality-dependent appraisal respect is different from egalitarian, directive respect which is owed to each and every individual.

It is this notion of evaluative respect or appraisal respect that is relevant in democratic politics. Politicians occupy a contingent political position where they have a job to perform: work for the common good; ensure that everyone is treated as an equal, not suffer from negative discrimination at the hands of the government; get what the people need; ensure that there is peace and justice. Also, that they work truthfully, sincerely, transparently. When politicians achieve these goals and behave in accordance with the highest standards of political morality, they earn our respect. When they fail to do so, we begin to disrespect them.

There is no question of hierarchical respect or deference to our leaders in modern, democratic polities. It is our right to question, challenge and criticise our politicians. All power wielders must submit to these demands. All of us, the rulers and the ruled, are bound by norms of egalitarian respect more generally, and by evaluative respect specific to democratic politics in particular. To our politicians, we can only say: perform well, and earn our respect!

12

What Qualities Should We Expect from Our Leaders?

We expect individuals to be their own leaders, to take charge of their lives and to assume responsibility for their decisions. But when individuals group together, problems arise. Groups can't take charge of themselves nor can every member simultaneously take charge of the entire group. Someone from the group is invariably asked to show the way, become the primary agent and lead. This is simply a fact: groups can't do without leaders. Every sporting team has a captain, a school or college has a principal, a company has its CEO, institutions have their directors and governments their presidents, chief or prime ministers.

Yet, not everyone who occupies high office is a leader. A person who merely coordinates the actions of others or has management skills is not a leader. Moreover, not everyone who assumes the role of a leader is able to play it well. What qualities then make for a leader? Which virtues are required to provide ethical leadership? I suppose there is little new one can say on this matter. But let me still give it a shot in the hope that it serves as a good reminder. Here I can identify four.

Being Inclusive

First, if a person is chosen to lead a group, it is her responsibility to take care of the interest of each person of the entire group. This often entails putting collective interest before her own interest or that of her preferred members in the group. For this to happen, she must first be able to identify the common good, have a grasp of what is acceptable to all and formulate an inclusive vision. This requires an infinite capacity to listen to others, learn from them, have the intellectual ability to critically examine and evaluate what everyone wants and needs and then put them all together.

Second, since this intellectual formulation can only be the first step, an estimate of the real quality of a decision is not known until it is implemented; its deficiencies begin to show up only when put into practice. This requires her to keep her ear to the ground and listen patiently to criticism to judge if her policies are working. She must not be defensive when criticised or evade uncomfortable questions but face criticism head on and be able to sift the wheat from the chaff. It also necessitates that a leader show flexibility and an ability for course correction by admitting mistakes. She should know that one's stature is not diminished by accepting fallibility.

Third, a leader must be a good communicator, and that is greatly helped if she has a way with words. But all the rhetorical flourish is of no avail if the speech lacks sincerity and conviction. A conviction with no relation to truth or actual outcomes is dishonest. Eloquence, though a good quality, is hollow without truth. Isn't it better to quietly do the job at hand rather than make grandiose claims or promises that can't be kept?

Finally, a good leader knows that nothing can be achieved without the collective expertise and wisdom of a support team. And when it comes to the entire country, such a team consists of a battalion of groups and institutions. How should members of such teams be picked? It is tempting to induct people who belong to one's own caste, region or religion. But such people are prejudiced in their thinking and serve their own particular group or merely themselves. They can't be good for the country as a whole. A good leader must rise above narrow, irrelevant considerations to select her team.

Unafraid of Rivals

It is equally tempting to pick those one has taken a fancy to or who are loyal. But such people often lack spine. Fearful people with poor ability can never offer good advice to their leader and could allow bad decisions to push the country down a ruinous path. Besides, they are often among the first to backstab the leader once out of power. Thus, personal likes and dislikes too must be set aside. I doubt if younger readers know that Nehru inducted into his cabinet Dr Ambedkar, his long-standing pre-eminent critic, as also the founder of the Jan Sangh, Syama Prasad Mookerjee. Abraham Lincoln, the nineteenth-century American president, was also exemplary in this matter. The man he appointed as his secretary of war was earlier his superior in legal practice and had on occasion even humiliated him. But over time, Lincoln was convinced that the interest of the nation during war would be best served by bringing this rather arrogant man into the cabinet. This led him to set aside personal resentment, forgive him and appoint him to a very crucial job in his cabinet. Great leaders don't hold grudges, are not vindictive and do not care if they have been wronged in the past by anyone so long as they are convinced that he will do no wrong in the future. Magnanimity isn't just a personal moral quality but a necessary political virtue.

Clearly then, a leader must have a knack for appointing persons best suited to his team—those who have proven ability, understand the purpose of the job, can speak their mind and are able to, without fear, disagree with the leader, if need be. Above all, they must understand the inclusive public philosophy that guides the nation. But such persons can be identified only by one who possesses these qualities and is herself devoted to this public philosophy. In India, this means that our leaders must owe supreme loyalty to nothing but our constitutional values.

13

The Importance of Listening Well

A very instructive passage on the difference in norms of debate among ancient Indian scholars, on the one hand, and kings and their subjects, on the other, is found in the ancient text *Milinda Pañha*. It records an exchange between the Indo-Greek king Milinda (Menander) and the Buddhist monk Nāgasena. When the king fails to understand a point made by Nāgasena, he asks, 'Will you discuss with me again?'

Nāgasena says, 'If Your Majesty will discuss as a scholar (paṇḍita), yes; but if you discuss as a king, no.'

'How do scholars discuss?'

'When scholars talk a matter over with each other, there is a winding up, an unravelling; distinctions are made and counter-distinctions;

one or other is convinced of error, and then acknowledges his mistake; and yet thereby, they are not angered. Thus, do scholars, O king, discuss.'

'And how do kings discuss?'

'When a king, your Majesty, discusses a matter, and he advances a point, if anyone differs from him on that point, he is apt to fine him saying: "Inflict such and such a punishment upon that fellow!" Thus, Your Majesty, do kings discuss.'

Debates in ancient India, the text seems to say, were tranquil, stress-free events in which participants did not hesitate to change their opinions where necessary, a far cry from royal (political) discussions in which disagreement with political rulers was frequently fraught with danger and winning a debate was almost, and sometimes literally, a matter of life and death.

Listening to Citizens

In fact, democracy is the only form of government where rules of scholarly and political debate are supposed to coincide, both among citizens and between governments and citizens. Debates are meant to be conducted fearlessly and in the ensuing discussion, mistakes are acknowledged and opinions changed. There is no anger or sense of humiliation if and when one is shown to be in error. Public arguments are meant to compel citizens to openly acknowledge when proven wrong and force governments to admit their mistakes and change policies. But is any of this possible without proper listening? It is said that it is the privilege of powerful people to speak and the lot of the powerless to listen. The beauty of democracy is that it obliges the powerful to listen.

To be sure, even democratic governments do not always listen to their electors. But as soon as their legitimacy dips below a certain threshold and their habit of turning a deaf ear to their people threatens their survival, they seem instinctively to know that it is absolutely crucial to start listening.

Something akin to this appears to happen frequently in India. Some time back, the present government appeared not to be listening to anyone. And although it is arguable that only a few top corporates were eventually heard, it is equally true that after months of silence on the pleadings of the 'people' to do something about the economic slowdown, the government finally listened to someone. If only this courtesy was extended to teachers, scholars, dancers, musicians, painters, town-planners, farmers and workers as well as to Tamils, Kashmiris, Dalits, adivasis and minorities! Should not good governments listen even to those who dissent against their policies?

Good governments must make a habit of listening to citizens. Indeed, in democracies, those temporarily in power need to develop the quality of being good listeners—*sushrutas*. What do I mean by this and how will this help?

Good Listening

Allowing someone to speak is, of course, the first precondition of listening. Remaining quiet while she is speaking is another. But silence can still mean not listening. One may even pretend to listen but remain disengaged or distracted. We all know that there exists what might be called 'vacant-look listening' when the interlocutor is physically present but mentally absent. Even sincere silence may just convey paternalistic assurance or be viewed as a strategy to allow the speaker to let off steam. It can betray biased judgement or a moralising readiness for instant advice. These are conversation-stoppers and roadblocks to listening. Good listening is attentive, uninterrupted and genuinely responsive.

There is more to good listening. The Indian spiritual thinker Jiddu Krishnamurti put this point across well. He said, 'There are two ways of listening: there is the mere listening to words, as you listen when you are not really interested, when you are not trying to fathom the depths of a problem; and there is the listening which catches the real significance of what is being said.' In short, good listening is empathetic and self-reflexive. It involves the capacity to step out of one's own perspective and consider things from the other's point of view: 'climb into his skin and walk around in it,' as Harper Lee put it. Good listening enables an accurate understanding of what another person is thinking, feeling, experiencing and meaning. None of this is possible if one remains self-centred or believes that truth and goodness is on one side alone. Good listening further presupposes that others have much to teach us, especially those who, in important aspects, are different from us.

Such good listening is especially needed in times of deep disagreement when we forget that there are as many views as there are people and delude ourselves into believing that the world is divided into two: us and them. We believe that only two views exist, and the one held by us is correct. This particularly crude form of binary thinking exacerbates conflicts and deepens polarisation. A polarised world contains prefect conditions for people to stop listening to each other. It is precisely at such times that we need encouragement to start listening so that we can broaden the horizon of our experience and break the horrible habit of dismissing differences. Listening helps reveal hidden commonalities that bolster cooperation. It dispels mistaken assumptions. It brings greater acceptance. In such deeply divided times, should it not be the duty of democratic governments to encourage people to de-escalate bitterness and discord and begin listening to one another?

Listening to the Many

The present government has made a good beginning by listening to a few. Since good democratic governments strive to be inclusive and win the trust of all, they must listen to the many and become *bahushruta*. Deliberative democrats often emphasise the importance of good arguments and wish the best argument to determine their decisions. But can we ever know the best argument if we haven't listened to all of them or unless we ensure that, as far as possible, all points of view have indeed been taken into account? This inclusion is impossible without listening to voices that may have been repressed before—voices of the powerless and the vulnerable.

A continuing conversation between governments and citizens and among citizens themselves is crucial in a democracy. But good conversations presuppose good habits of listening. Governments must take seriously their duty to be not only *sushruta* but also *bahushruta*. Citizens too must take more responsibility for cultivating these public virtues.

14

The Importance of Democratic Education

A persistent concern exists about democracy's failure to fulfil our expectations. While our votes are forceful 'paper stones', effective in getting rid of governments we dislike, they are powerless to give us effective, efficient, good governments. Why do we have to put up with corrupt rulers with criminal records—qualities that obstruct good governance? Why tolerate those who strive to do better for themselves than for the people and have neither vision nor wisdom? Why have mediocre politicians who shun contact with people with ability and talent?

Better, Wiser Governments

Some cynics may respond to this crisis of democracy by arguing the following: to achieve our national goals, we must assemble the best team to govern. Such a team cannot be elected by popular mandate but instead by those who have the intellectual wherewithal to select those fit for it. To such people, democracy—which is committed to the principle of one person, one vote, and which extends franchise to all regardless of ability—can never produce the best team.

They might draw an analogy from cricket where we play to compete at the highest level and win, something not possible if the best cricketers are not selected. But this is not achieved by popular vote. Instead, we rely on experts—a selection committee consisting of experienced cricketers. If popular mandate can't give us the best team that realises our national goal in cricket, why expect a different result in politics? Why not select our government by a similar procedure involving experts?

So, to reiterate the conundrum: democratically elected governments in our times are neither efficient nor wise. They show a propensity to fail at achieving their national goal: a high quality of life for all people. Then why not abandon democracy? Or at least introduce an eligibility criterion, restricting the vote to those with formal education? Won't education help in identifying the best political representatives? A democrat need not reject this argument. She may respond that this need not entail abandoning universal adult franchise but the distribution of education to all. This seems a decent solution. Sustainable democracies require a high rate of literacy. The more educated we are, it might be claimed, the better we become at choosing the best people to run our government.

But this argument is flawed. Literacy and education by themselves do not create good citizens or yield mature democracies. Many people, though formally illiterate, are politically astute and even possess qualities of good citizenship. Conversely, many educated people are prone to being self-obsessed, undemocratic and even authoritarian. Primary, secondary or even higher education by itself does not guarantee good citizenship.

The solution then is not just education per se but universal education of a certain kind, one that is focused on improving the quality of our democracy. Our current education system does not focus on education *in* democracy or what we might call democratic education. Nor does it build on elements of democratic culture embedded in our traditions.

Core Elements

What then are the core elements of democratic education? For a start, it requires the cultivation of democratic virtues. For instance, the ability to imagine and articulate a minimally common good. This requires that we distinguish what is merely good for me from what is good for all. And since each of us may develop our own distinct idea of the common good, it entails finding an overlapping common good. Relatedly, an ability to handle difference and disagreement and to retain, despite this difference, the motivation to arrive at the common good through conversation, debate, dialogue and deliberation.

The ability to imagine and conceive a common good is inconsistent with what the Greeks famously called 'pleonexia', the greed to grab everything for oneself, to refuse to share anything, to not acknowledge what is due to each person and to have no sense of reciprocity or justice. It follows that the idea of the common good cannot be developed without some sense of justice. Democratic education requires training in not succumbing to pleonexia. Also crucial is a spirit of compromise, of moderation, and a willingness, within acceptable value parameters, of mutual give and take. None of this is possible without other general capabilities such as listening patiently to others, being empathetic to the plight of others and having a commitment to continuing a conversation with people despite disagreement.

More important is the ability to participate in a particular historical narrative or, as the Canadian political theorist Jeremy Webber puts it, a 'commitment to a particular debate through time'. Members of a political community become better citizens when they relate to critical issues through historically inherited terms of debate, a continuing narrative, a specific ongoing conversation. The reflection of that debate in political decision-making is central to the members' feeling of engagement and participation. For example, there is a particular way in which the question of religion has been framed in India, as also issues of nation, caste and gender. Individuals become effective and meaningful citizens only by learning the terms set by debates around these specific issues. Since a useful entry to them is available through rich debates in the Constituent Assembly, a familiarity with them is a crucial ingredient of democratic education in India.

It also follows that democratic education involves a basic understanding of our society and its history, of its multiple cultural, intellectual and religious traditions, which set the terms of specific debates. I am frequently appalled at my own ignorance of the historical trajectory of our complex social problems and saddened to find that my highly educated friends do not know that a constitutional minority in India is not just a numerically small group but one potentially disadvantaged by virtue of that fact. Some mistakenly believe that religious minorities have reservation in jobs and in institutions of higher education; massive illiteracy continues to exist about the atrocious nature of our caste system; many continue to think that 'secularism' is a wholly Western concept, as if 'religion' is not. Only a proper democratic education can remove these misunderstandings and flaws.

What then is democratic education? Conceived broadly, it is a historically specific enterprise determined by the inherited vocabulary of specific political languages and the terms of debates in a particular community. It is designed specifically to enable conversation on issues central to a particular community, to strive for agreement where possible and to live peacefully with disagreement where it is not. In short, it involves social and historical awareness and key democratic virtues.

Many of these understandings and virtues can be inculcated by a good liberal arts education. The National Education Policy 2019 recognises this but alas insufficiently. And as far as I can tell from my skimpy reading, it has virtually nothing to say about how this relates to democracy. So it appears relatively innocent of the more specific requirements of democratic education. Without proper democratic education, I am afraid we will continue to perpetuate bad democratic practices, allow unhealthy scepticism about democracy to grow and eventually imperil it.

15

The Right to Protest in a Free Society

At the end of 2019, we witnessed unprecedented public protests in our country. Thousands and thousands assembled on the streets to demand that the government rethink the Citizenship (Amendment) Act and the National Register of Citizens. Such public protests are the hallmark of a free, democratic society, whose logic demands that the voice of the people be heard by those in power and decisions be reached after proper discussion and consultation. For this, the right to freedom of expression, association and peaceably assemble are necessary. Any arbitrary restraint on the exercise of such rights by, for instance, imposing Section 144 in anticipation of violent disruption of public order shows the inability of the government to tolerate dissent. It shows not the propensity of people to riot but rather acknowledges the incapacity of the government to discuss, deliberate or listen. An unreasonable limitation on protest is an affront to the very people in whose name a government is allowed to temporarily govern.

One must be grateful to the courts for having reiterated that the right to protest is fundamental. An innocent student of the Constitution may examine it and find that the word 'protest' is missing. He may read the relevant articles of the Constitution (particularly Article 19) altogether non-politically. For example, the right to free speech and expression may be taken to mean that everyone has the right to express their opinion on, say, a film or on the condition of the city they inhabit; the right to associate to mean the right to form self-regulating clubs, professional associations or societies; and the right of peaceful assembly to mean the right to have a picnic in a park or to participate in a religious festival, such as the Kumbh mela. Important as these rights are—in authoritarian, illiberal states even these rights are not guaranteed—this view is too narrow because in a democracy each of these embody active not passive citizenship. They constitute our political freedoms. The right to free speech and expression transforms into the right to freely express opinion on the conduct of government and the right to association becomes the right to associate for political purposes, for instance, to collectively challenge government decisions and to even aim, peacefully and legally, to displace the government. This is the basis of our multi-party system, where opposition parties are valuable adversaries, not enemies, and compete healthily for political power.

Finally, the right to peaceably assemble allows political parties and citizen bodies, such as university-based student groups, to question and object to acts of government by demonstrations, agitations and public meetings and launch sustained protest movements. In short, each of these rights have two interpretations. In the first, these rights are free from government interference and are exercised largely by people for private purposes in a classically liberal, non-political public space. In the second, rights are associational and are exercised to influence or gain power and, therefore, fundamentally political. These political rights are basic to a democratic society.

The constitution of any country gets its substance not just from the letter but also from the historically distilled lived experience often referred to as its spirit. The second interpretation, therefore, flows directly from our history. Undoubtedly, the background of our Constitution is formed by our anti-colonial struggle, within which the seeds of a political public sphere and our democratic constitution were sown. The Indian people fought hard and long to publicly express their views on colonial policies and laws, to dissent from them, to shape minds and form public opinion against them, to speak to and against the government and to challenge it. People not only signed writ petitions but also staged dharnas and held large public meetings, peaceful protests and demonstrations and even, for instance, in Gandhi's satyagraha, launched civil disobedience movements. None of these are literally found in the articles of our Constitution but are presupposed by it. That is why the preamble states that we are a democratic republic.

This cluster of inter-related political rights (expression, association, assembly, petition and protest) is meant to ensure that even when the government works in our interests, we don't passively sit back and allow the government to conduct business as usual. We act as watchdogs and constantly monitor their acts, for even such governments can falter, and then it is up to us to recognise and rectify their mistakes through consultation, meetings and discussion. However, another serious situation can easily arise. An elected government may stray from the constitutional course, go against the interests of the people, become unresponsive and refuse to listen. Here, pressure against the government must be built by still stronger public methods. Protests may take the form of street assemblies—the occasional, temporary gathering of a group to parade or demonstrate or become a sustained movement, which is necessary to complement or reinforce more conventional forms of politics. Remember Potti Sreeramulu starving himself to death in order to draw the attention of the Madras state government to the urgency of creating a new Telugu-speaking state of Andhra or the Chipko movement in which Gaura Devi, Chandi Prasad Bhatt and many others began to hug trees to prevent the then UP government from awarding contracts to commercial loggers? Such protest movements are particularly important for those outside the mainstream or who are not educated formally. After all, any disaffected person, no matter how illiterate or powerless, can shout a slogan, hold up a placard, go on a silent march and oppose the government. Meetings around a table rarely involve as many people as street protests do. It is not for nothing that Abraham Lincoln called 'the right of the people to peaceably assemble, a constitutional substitute for revolution'.

It is amply clear that democracies everywhere are founded on two core political rights. The first, the right of every citizen to freely elect their government, and when dissatisfied with its performance, to vote it out of power in a legitimately held election. (Article 326 of the Indian Constitution.) This remains the only proper constitutional procedure to get rid of a government and rightly so. Indeed, peaceful transfer of power is one of the great strengths of democracies. But short of displacing it, as long as it is done peacefully, any form of public action to challenge its proposals or decisions is also constitutionally legitimate, forming the second core of political right: to politically participate not only during but between elections.

The right to protest, to publicly question and force the government to answer is a fundamental political right of the people that flows directly from a democratic reading of Article 19. If so, one is left speechless at the way in which some governments sidestep issues, duck questions and wilfully obstruct any attempt to discuss. They habitually take decisions secretively and foist them on an unprepared people, and when challenged, campaign and canvass in order to retrospectively justify their opaque, midnight decisions. Will, for instance, the BJP government that promised '*sabka saath, sabka vishwaas, sabka vikaas*' demonstrate its legitimacy by really listening to everyone, especially its critics, or will it continue to vilify all opponents as traitors or anti-nationals?

16

The Politics of Enmity

Indian elections have become less violent over the last three decades. The credit for this must go not only to institutions such as the election commission but also to the political class. Yet there is another disturbing tendency, potentially replete with violence, that has been growing during the same period: to view political opponents as enemies to be annihilated. One gets a flavour of this in slogans such as 'Congress-mukt Bharat', but more than in statements, it is present in the tone of some speakers, in their body language and in the ferocity in their eyes.

Friends and Enemies

The pro-Nazi but important legal and political theorist Carl Schmitt made the friend–enemy distinction as constitutive of politics itself. To be political was necessarily to work with a distinction between an extreme version of us and them or friends and enemies. Not only was this distinction the decisive criterion of the political, but even within this relationship, enmity had priority over friendship: those not on our side, or disloyal to us, are automatically, irredeemably enemies. In doing so, Schmitt reduced all politics to war. At least war is an ever-present possibility in politics, he claimed, and therefore a political person must conduct himself as if surrounded by enemies. Schmitt was exploiting a distinction perfected by some strands within Abrahamic religions that invented the idea of an 'extra-systemic other', a radical other with whom no conversation is possible or one who is outside one's semantic universe. Those who do not adhere to the doctrine defining the system are enemies to be fought. Internal dissent too is anathema, akin to betrayal and joining the enemy camp, signifying treachery. Felt as existential threats, both outsiders and deviant insiders must be 'converted', brought in line or altogether expunged.

This horrendous resource within these traditions, when deployed under certain conditions, has played havoc in large parts of Europe, leading to crusades, inquisition, expulsions of Jews and to the final solution at the concentration camps, and outside Europe, in the liquidation, for example, of native Americans. Some detect the same ideological underpinning even in the neoconservative war on Iraq. Perhaps, its most recent expression is in the violence exhibited by Islamist organisations such as the Islamic State. However, this mindset is no longer confined to strands of Abrahamic theology; it has crept into other religions and even been secularised. It is found in the twentieth century in both fascism and Stalinism and more pervasively in a host of ultra-nationalisms that have led to ethnic cleansing and genocide in several parts of the world, including Indonesia, Cambodia and Rwanda. This strain of exclusionary nationalism has permeated China where undercurrents of Han nationalism have virtually turned Tibetan Buddhists and Uighur Muslims into extra-systemic others or enemies. It has infected South Asian cultures too, causing the partition of the 'subcontinent', ethnic cleaning of Tamils in Sri Lanka and the expulsion of the Rohingya from Myanmar.

In India, the frequent use of the term 'anti-national' for those critical of the current dispensation smells of the same fatal disease. How to deal ideologically with this seems to me one of the great challenges of our times.

Enemies and Adversaries

A mentality inebriated with the friend–enemy syndrome is fundamentally undemocratic. Knowing the difference between an enemy and an adversary is absolutely critical in a functioning democracy. An adversary is someone one wishes to defeat in a temporary contest such as a legal combat or a game of cricket. To wish to trounce an opponent in an election is entirely legitimate. On the other hand, an enemy is someone to be destroyed permanently. Adversaries can be won over and turned into allies but enemies cannot be. A compromise with an adversary is acceptable, even praiseworthy. On the other hand, with an enemy, a compromise spells defeat, an unacceptable concession and a betrayal. The world of adversaries in a democracy does not involve a zero-sum game; no one loses everything or forever. There are no permanent losers or victors; each competitor wins some and loses some in a fair contest. But all rules of fairness can be abandoned in a fight with an enemy. In this hostile scenario, all politics is nothing but war.

It is often heard that in politics there are no permanent friends or enemies. This may well appear to be opportunistic in some contexts but it is the very stuff of democratic politics where everyone hopes that today's losers can be tomorrow's victors and vice versa. Everyone, not only active political agents but also ordinary citizens, is assured that no matter which party wins, the fundamental interests and liberties of all, the majority as well as the minority, are secure, and despite deep differences on many matters, everyone also shares something in common. This commonality can be our humanity, national ethos, Constitutional or shared civilisational values nurtured through history. For example, in India, the value of pluralism, acceptance and accommodation, of refusing to view the world in terms of simple binaries has faced challenges from time to time by narrow-minded, rigid, hierarchy-ridden, upper-caste practices (often misleadingly termed Brahminism because it was legitimated by scholarly Brahmins), close-minded religious orders that accompanied Afghan and Turk invaders and marauders, and ruthlessly exploitative colonialists. More recently, heartless multinational corporations have also damaged this ethos by mindlessly turning everything into a commodity to be bought and sold in the capitalist market. But exclusionary ultra-nationalists (as distinct from inclusive, moderate nationalists) must not be left out of this nefarious list. They too are hell bent on throttling our civilisational values and democratic ethos.

Protecting Our Civilisation

As groups grow in size, they invent rules to regulate behaviour, formulate authoritative norms, install a structure of authority and, above all, evolve some criteria of who is in and who is out or of insiders and outsiders. Let us even agree that there is no 'self' without the 'other'. But rules can be rigid or flexible, a challenge to norms can be tolerated or punished severely and the 'other' can be viewed as a temporary adversary in a healthy contest, someone with whom one can also have a fruitful dialogue or one with whom conversation is impossible (a permanent enemy). This idea that membership in a group comes with an enemy to be fought was a powerful resource in the doctrines of some religions and has slowly taken root in Asian religions, including modern Hinduism. It has now entered our democratic politics. If it stays there, it will utterly destroy the *atman* of our civilisation and the *astitva* of democracy. Everyone across religious differences must strive to fight it. All democrats, if they wish to save their cherished system, must defang it before it is too late.

17

The Legitimation Crisis of Indian Democracy

For people who have traditionally viewed the state as a spectacle and frequently turned their backs on it, Indians have rather swiftly become state-centric. We constantly talk and read about it, capture it in images and films, are lured by the magic of elections and its arithmetic, and many, including the poor, feel they have a claim on it; we expect the state to find a solution to most of our problems. This is foolhardy, because the state fails us persistently. But such is the power of the democratic imaginary that ordinary people continue to repose faith in the very idea of the state.

To be sure, the Indian state periodically suffers from an acute crisis of legitimacy (legitimation crisis). All democracies depend for their survival on public approval and consent. Legitimacy obtains when people justifiably feel that enough is being done by the state to deliver what they need and want. It is absent when the gap widens between people's own expectations and the actual benefits received by them. Legitimation crisis then manifests itself in the steady accumulation of public complaints and grievances and in growing discontent, widespread disillusionment and popular protest—when large numbers of people begin to feel that they are victimised by their political system.

Three Moments of Crisis

Several such crises of legitimacy are seen in post-Independence India. I don't want to go into specifics; instead, I draw attention to three distinct moments of the legitimation crisis of representative democracy in India. The first I call the crisis of *procedural* legitimacy. For long, our representatives were elected by a process that was neither free nor fair. Strategic violence often generated fear among ordinary people—booths were captured and women, Dalits, minorities and the poor generally prevented from voting or compelled to vote for a candidate not of their choice. The strengthening of the election commission and the deployment of Central paramilitary forces have, to a large degree, overcome this legitimation crisis.

However, a second crisis of legitimation was brewing simultaneously. The electorate hopes that those chosen by free and fair elections would accurately represent their interests and deliver on their demands. When this doesn't happen, democracies plunge into what I call a crisis of *representational* legitimacy. In India, people attempted to resolve this crisis by a politics of community-based identities. Different groups, particularly the Dalits and the OBCs, decided to vote for people from their own respective castes—those who they intuitively trusted and mirrored them.

But at least since 2011, the failure of 'mirror representation' has pushed India to a deeper questioning of the democratic system itself. Call it the crisis of democracy's *moral* legitimacy. A feeling of betrayal by members of one's own community is accompanied by severe dissatisfaction with the entire democratically elected establishment. People increasingly feel that while the Indian economy is growing rapidly with more money circulating in the system, most of it is diverted and landing mysteriously in the lap of a very tiny upper crust. All political parties seem tainted: the Congress, BJP, Bahujan Samaj Party, Samajwadi Party and even the Communist Party of India (Marxist). Ever since, the electorate has been desperately looking for some political agency outside the established order to fix the system.

Individual or Institutions

To meet this crisis, two distinct responses have appeared before us. One is messianic, which depends on a heroic individual rather than citizen-based institutions, and the other is dependent on the collective capacity of citizens to innovate new institutions. The first is embodied by Prime Minister Narendra Modi, who has projected himself as a larger-than-life figure: strong, decisive, ruthlessly efficient and an outsider to the establishment. Untarnished by the 'corrupt' capillaries of Lutyens' Delhi, he can unblock the arteries through which goods and services could flow freely from the State to the people.

The second response emerged from a movement for greater transparency and accountability—that all power wielders must be permanently subjected to inspection, investigation and monitoring. Existing institutions of checks and balances seem insufficient to limit the power of democratically elected leaders. Citizens must take matters into their own hands, be persistently vigilant, diligently oversee government and act as watchdogs. Representative democracy can survive only with more participatory democracy. This was the promise of the United Progressive Alliance's Right to Information Act and the movement that led to the formation of the Aam Aadmi Party.

However, with the apparent seduction of large sections of the people by the first response and the Aam Admi Party leadership increasingly uncertain about which of the two responses it exemplifies, several worrying questions have sprouted of which two are paramount: What demons might be unleashed if and when the first response flounders and which new leadership will bring the people back to the properly democratic path that strengthens our best institutions and helps invent new citizen's initiatives?

18

Subjects, Citizens and Maharajas

The massacre in Thoothukudi (Tuticorin) made me think of the political status of those who came out to protest against Sterlite Industries. Formally and constitutionally, they were Indian citizens. Or were they? Were they not aliens, the new *mlecchas*, a threat to the political order and the state? Or perhaps, they were neither citizens nor aliens but a subjugated people—subjects who were punished because they dared to be citizens.

The State's Wrath

What did the locals do to incur the wrath of the state? They were merely exercising their minimal citizenship rights when they were mercilessly beaten by the police or shot by snipers. They made public their grievance about the vulnerable environmental conditions—the contamination of groundwater and pollution-induced diseases caused by the Sterlite plant—under which they are forced to live. This discontent notwithstanding, the government, with the alleged connivance of the Tamil Nadu pollution board, granted permission to the industry to expand. In deliberately violating their rights, do they not treat them as their subjects rather than as citizens?

The distinction between citizens and subjects is important in political thought and practice. To be a citizen is, first and foremost, to belong to a particular political community. Citizenship gives us a sense of who we are and creates a special bond with other members—a fellow feeling that one might call civic friendship. This is why, along with family, linguistic or religio-philosophical groups, it is a source of commitment and obligation. But citizenship also brings us rights. To secure basic needs, citizens can make claims on each other and particularly on the state. Protection of life comes immediately to mind. That one will not be killed by arbitrary or intentional acts of others or by man-made disease or pollution is a fundamental human right. In large and complex modern societies, so much has come to depend on the state that it alone must help realise it.

Other rights without which survival is impossible are dependent on the state too: the right to food, water, clean air, shelter, etc., or rights that marginally improve the quality of our life, for instance, to safeguard our personal possessions, ease of mobility from place to place, public playgrounds, illuminated streets and protection of personal freedoms. All these exemplify what might be called passive citizenship rights—passive because we, their bearers, are essentially recipients. We receive these benefits if we follow the law and pay our taxes and are left alone to care for our families and do our jobs. But unlike other forms of the state, democracy also gives us rights that change the quality of citizenship. They enable active citizenship rights to publicly complaint or protest, to deliberate on issues of public good, to scrutinise and criticise public policies, to hold our governments accountable, to form public associations, to vote and to stand for public office.

Unlike citizens, subjects have none of these rights. Political participation is simply out of the question—subjects cannot vote, deliberate on public issues, complain, criticise or stand for public office. They have no claims on the state—not even to basic rights such as the right to life. If they get food, shelter or any other personal benefit, it is entirely on the goodwill of the state. Conquered people, the colonised, slaves and all those who live under the law made by others and designed to oppress them are obvious examples. Subjects live in a state meant for others. The state for them is not a political community but a source of oppressive power. They are located within but do not belong to the state, nor do they identify with it. Subjects are bereft of civic friendship. All they have is a nameless, non-political relationship with other subjects.

A Continuum

So, can we call the Thoothukudi protestors subjects of the Indian state? That may not be entirely accurate either. Perhaps, rather than view citizenship and subjecthood in terms of a binary, it is best to see them as part of a continuum. On the citizenship–subjecthood continuum, the Thoothukudi protestors are barely citizens and mostly subjects. Better still, this continuum should be viewed more dynamically; large numbers of people in our democratic nation keep sliding from citizenship into subjecthood. Just as they begin to acquire minimal citizenship rights, they are thrown back to being subjects by an economic or political tornado in their lives. This is a normal circumstance of persons under conditions of domination—whenever oppression increases, people lose their freedoms, cease to be citizens and become subjects. Those generally without wealth or power are always on the edge of being subjugated. In fact, this is true of most of us; citizenship or subjecthood is not a fixed location but a constantly shifting position. When out of fear of government reprisal, the educated middle class shuts up, it turns into subjects. If you want to experience subjecthood, just step in for a moment into any local municipal corporation office. You will instantly feel like a hapless subject of a powerful, opaque empire.

However, there are some among us who are neither subjects nor citizens except perfunctorily. They command such enormous resources of power and wealth that they treat the entire apparatus of state power as their private instrument. Some heads of corporations, business magnates and politicians behave like and indeed are today's imperial rulers, reincarnating reckless maharajas of yesteryears who may exploit, oppress and dispossess others at their own sweet will.

Thoothukudi tells us that we are still a deeply divided political unit—most of us are largely subjects, some are citizens and a tiny group are maharajas, who can even use public force as private army to kill if it serves them or their friends.

19

Enter the Passive Subject, Exit the Active Citizen

Something new seems to be emerging in India. A decade ago, democracy was thriving. People with scant interest in politics increasingly felt a pressing need to become more vocal in the public domain. Remember the first decade of the twenty-first century? The Congress-led coalition government was compelled by activists to grant everyone the Rights to Information and Education and to launch MNREGA. The dastardly rape and murder of Nirbhaya turned thousands of young women and men into political activists. Citizen journalists emerged, capturing acts of injustice and sending them to television channels that routinely put the government in the dock. And who can forget the anti-corruption movement that virtually paralysed the government, catapulting into power not only the BJP but also the newly born Aam Aadmi Party.

In 2013, when we seemed to be on the verge of a democratic revolution, the active citizen appeared to have a bright future. Young men and women left lucrative jobs to join the movement for a new political future for India. They hoped to launch new parties accountable to the people and committed to providing them what they really needed. Yet, in one fell swoop, the political climate in the country seems to have changed. The active citizen is now viewed as a villain and pejoratively called an 'Andolanjeevi'. Those who only the other day personified active citizenship, today, in power, appear to shut the door on it. Not only active citizenship but the very idea of citizenship has plunged into crisis. Rightly or wrongly, some are ready to forego even their rights as passive citizens and prepared to accept or tolerate political subjection. Since subjects are rightsless people who live passively within the jurisdiction of their ruler, I am inclined to see this current moment as marking the rebirth of a new political subject.

Active and Passive Citizens

It is important to understand what this means. Bringing out the contrast between three key terms may help us do so. Take active citizenship first. By definition, citizenship here is a matter of doing. An active citizen is able to (a) vote, (b) publicly discuss the common good and use legally available means to influence public policy and the law and, if needed, criticize, modify or even repeal them and (c) run for public office.

This is in sharp contrast to passive citizens, who rarely act in the public domain. They are either unable or unwilling to vote. They either cannot or couldn't be bothered to take a stand on public issues. Standing for public office is the last thing they imagine or want. They are mostly content with receiving things from the state—precisely why they are passive. Citizenship here reflects what a person gets, not by what they do, regardless of whether this condition is forced upon or chosen by them.

But why still call them citizens? By virtue of two qualities. First, they still belong to a political community. They continue to be card-carrying members of a state that gives them an official identity. Second, they retain some basic rights—the right to protection against violence and those who need it and the right to a minimal package of subsistence goods. Moreover, while they make few demands of their own, they can complain when they fail to get what the state promises. Passive citizens are closer to being political subjects but are not quite so.

The Loyal Subject

At least two features distinguish political subjects from passive citizens. First, passive subjects don't have any rights. They live by the grace of the ruler and get protection and other benefits by being loyal to him. This dedication does not entail that subjects devote themselves to further only the personal interests of the ruler. They could easily subordinate themselves to a project of common good as long as it is defined by the ruler. Second, citizens never equate the state with current rulers. No democratic ruler can call the state his own. However, political subjects identify the state with the ruler, as does the ruler himself. Belonging to the state means becoming a ruler's subjects.

Unlike a democratic body of equal citizens, the relationship between subjects and their ruler then is unabashedly hierarchical. Though the subject's condition is a mixture of subordination and servitude, he gratefully accepts it because of the protection provided by the ruler. He interprets the wishes of the ruler as commands and has no appetite for rebellion. The gratefulness on the part of the subjects is matched by the exuberant munificence of the ruler. When a subject receives a small, negligible portion of the state's treasury, he believes it is charity flowing directly from the ruler's personal largess. Overawed by him, the subject cannot but be deferential to the ruler. Disobedience would amount to shameful betrayal.

I suspect that a substantial part of our political climate now approximates what I have described here. This is why I see the emergence of the new political category 'labharthi' as the rebirth of a new political subject. A labharthi is a passive recipient of meagre resources—a beneficiary of the ruler's generosity. Labharthis, no longer rights-bearers, are the exact opposite of ever-demanding, rights-conscious active citizens. In the 2021 assembly elections in Uttar Pradesh, the prime minister rightly went to them with the expectation that they would vote for him. Hardly abnormal in this environment. He instinctively knew that those who had eaten his 'namak' (salt) cannot betray him. Namak halals do not easily turn into namak harams, do they? Political subjecthood, nowhere on the horizon in 2013, is back now with a vengeance.

The Citizen-Subject

I may have given the impression that today's political world is neatly divided between rulers and their passive, loyal subjects. I do not intend this crude portrayal. There exists an extremely large group of people who are neither rulers nor passive subjects. I would classify them as a hybrid called citizen-subjects, for they are a mix of passive citizens and active subjects—active because they surrender aspects of citizenship and embrace subjecthood of their own volition. They are citizens because they see themselves as belonging to a state that in part is independent of the ruler. But what matters most to them is a private life of consumption, for which they are not dependent on the state. Even their life and personal property are protected by paid security guards. Since they make few demands on the state, active citizenship is of little value to them. Such people are happy to be passive citizens. They may even be indifferent to who the ruler is. This makes them starkly different from labharthis, ever grateful subjects whose very survival depends on a particular ruler's generosity.

Yet, they depend on this very ruler–state to protect them from external aggressors and perceived internal enemies. For this purpose, they abandon their identity as citizens and choose to become political subjects—willing, unquestioning and loyal supporters of the ruler and his pet common projects. Here, state-dependent labharthis and state-independent consumers converge. Both share a world in which some of their common benefits flow from the largess of the ruler and from the public display of loyalty to him. Alas, just when the passive subject was beginning to be seen as a relic of the past, it has made a stunning comeback. And upon re-entering our political world, it has severely compromised our democracy and made citizenship virtually redundant.

20

Can Electoral Politics Learn from Cricket?

How important is it to win? It is pointless to ask this question in the context of competitive sports such as cricket or in electoral politics where one enters the fray in order to win. But is winning the only point of these practices? Must we win at any cost?

Not Just about Winning

If the only purpose of playing cricket is to win, a quick and easy way is to have a five-over match. A few athletes with muscle power but clueless about the art of bowling, batting and fielding would give you a win with their slap-dash cricket. However, five-day matches are valued because the very best skills of the two contesting teams are expressed only in games of long duration. A win without a proper contest between two highly skilled teams is deeply unsatisfying. It takes the joy out of the game and brings little respect. In short, an important purpose of playing cricket is achieving excellence and deriving aesthetic pleasure.

Equally important is to win the game fairly. Consider this. A match is delicately poised when Sachin Tendulkar is wrapped on the pads off a ball clearly pitching outside the leg stump. The entire Australian team appeal vociferously, the home crowd in Sydney roars and the umpire raises the dreaded finger. A great batsman falls victim to a dubious decision and India loses the match. The whole country feels bitter and the ties between the two teams, indeed two nations, get strained. This is not hypothetical. Until the late eighties, Test matches were routinely dogged by controversy over home umpiring. Not that umpires were necessarily biased, but on occasions, for instance, under pressure from the home team and the crowd, they were forced into wrong decisions. Fairness in the game received a big boost when neutral umpires were introduced by the ICC to prevent endless carping, mutual distrust and recrimination.

From then on, there has been continuous effort on the part of the cricketing fraternity to check biases and minimise human error. Match-fixing is severely punished. Technology is used to strengthen impartial decisions: Snickometer, hotspot, ball tracking, zoom videography and reviews of umpiring decisions are now commonplace to prevent a cloud of suspicion over the winner. Clearly, we play cricket to win, but (a) a slam-bang approach that does not test the full range of skills makes the win look worthless and (b) an unfairly achieved win is hollow.

Besides, fairness and excellence are linked. Generating conditions that suit a team can help it win a few matches at home, but soon enough, its weaknesses are exposed. Flat-track bullies can score tons of runs at home but fail in seaming conditions. A good team must learn to play under different conditions and resist the temptation to nudge the curator to doctor home pitches. A team wins consistently and rises to the top only when its premier batsmen negotiate good quality spin and pace with equal ease, and such skills do not develop without 'fair pitches'.

In important ways, elections can be legitimately compared to competitive sports. Political parties enter the contest in order to win. But the whole point of choosing political winners is lost if the electorate is unable to properly evaluate or assess the past or future performance of political parties. In short, a major purpose of elections is to test the full range of skills of contesting political leaders—their ability to efficiently deliver on promises, to build consensus among different groups, to be open to criticism and know that criticism is not tantamount to personal insult, to not conflate private interest with the common good, to be sincere and truthful, etc. If elections cease to be an arena where political skills are publicly examined and assessed and are instead used by politicians by rhetorical flourish and spectacular demagoguery to hoodwink people into believing that they are the best, then, like wins in slam-bang limited-overs cricket, electoral victories become pointless. This is not to say that rhetorical or communication skills are unimportant, but if they deflect from substantive issues of welfare or obstruct the assessment of the full range of political skills, democratic elections lose much of their point.

An election won by unfair means is even more vacuous. Till the eighties, rigging and booth capturing were not uncommon. But once the election commission acquired greater constitutional authority and autonomy, seat fixing became difficult. Despite its flaws, the introduction of the electronic voting machine has further bolstered free and fair elections in India. But much work still remains to be done. Why?

The Electoral Hotspot

Electoral victories are still marred by the subtle deployment of unfair tactics. For instance, majoritarian pressure compels institutions such as the election commission to sidestep neutrality and overlook the violation of existing laws. It is impermissible in India to seek votes by showing explicit or implicit hostility towards or excluding particular religious groups. Why then did the EC fail to spot this in the 2017 assembly in Gujarat?

Second, some leaders of the BJP have distorted tactless remarks by politicians of other parties and mischievously given them a divisive and casteist twist to boost their party's electoral prospects. The electoral hotspot—our television cameras—clearly showed the intent to mislead but our EC kept mum. Our moral technology to detect and punish unfair electoral practice remains a distant dream. Cricket has taken many steps forward towards excellence and fairness. Electoral politics has a lot of catching up to do.

21

Democratising the Good Life

Modern life is unthinkable without an intimate family life, a satisfying job and the pleasure of buying and consuming things we want. Production (work), reproduction and consumption are an integral part of the contemporary idea of the good life. This was not always so.

The Monistic Conception

In much of human history, such life was considered too lowly and contrasted with other infinitely 'superior' ways of living. For instance, many human societies in the past put the highest premium on a life spent conquering, safeguarding and ruling territories and their populations. Courage in the battlefield was therefore the greatest virtue. The life of great warriors (Karna and Arjuna) was the stuff of which legends, myths and epic tales were made. In other societies, such as Athens, proper human fulfilment was possible only by participating in the political life of the city republic.

Other communities found the greatest value in a life of contemplation. The highest ideal was to have a life of the mind, penetrating the mysteries of the self and the world and identifying hidden structures that hold the universe together (for example, parts of the Upanishads, Aristotle and, in his own way, the Buddha). Relatedly, once the source of everything was discovered, which in some cases was identified with God, a life spent in the service of God and in complete devotion was man's highest virtue.

It is one thing to give importance to such lives (of political rule/participation, intellectual pursuits or religious devotion) and quite another to make any one supreme as if one alone is really worthy. Indeed, most single ideal-loving or monistic world views not only created a hierarchy between different conceptions of the good life but treated ordinary life as having no worth at all. A life of production and reproduction—namely one deployed on the field (sowing, ploughing, harvesting, digging, weaving, tanning, etc.) or household chores (cleaning, cooking, washing and raising children, generally by the lot of women)—was inferior, falling outside society's conception of the good life. In these societies, even healing, accounting or trading were seen as lowly. Second, high ideals were accessible only to certain classes of people—men of high birth and people with pedigree. The really good life (of politics, religious devotion or the intellect) was unavailable to large numbers of people. Monistic conceptions went hand in hand with exclusivism.

Pluralising the Good Life

A challenge to this way of hierarchically arranging ideals (the monistic conception of the good life) was already articulated in ancient Indian texts, which judged it unwise to spend an entire life pursuing a single high ideal. Rather, one's life must necessarily incorporate different ideals, though not all at the same time—the idea of the good life must be pluralised. We must divide our entire life in stages, regulating each stage by a different high ideal. For example, each person first spends his life learning and cultivating intellectual and moral virtues, then lives a life of the householder (gets married, earns and raises children) and eventually devotes the rest of it away from society in pursuit of God or other-worldly goods.

Such a life combines multiple ideals, each of which has highest value and validity only in a given context and for a given purpose. There is no ideal that is good for all times, for all places and for all stages in the life of a person. Correspondingly, to lead a complete life, many virtues are needed—physical stamina, bodily health, courage, a modicum of detachment, critical self-reflection, empathy, a sense for something higher than humans, to name just a few. And another virtue necessary in the mix is the capacity to properly balance different ideals.

The realisation that a full life requires multiple ideals posed a decent challenge to the monistic view but did not fully dethrone it or challenge its exclusivism. For instance, it did not question the stigmatisation of certain kinds of manual work and workers. Indeed, the opportunity to divide life in this way was not available to the 'lower castes'. In more recent centuries, however, several profound changes in our thinking—though not yet fully accomplished in practice—could democratise the idea of the good life.

A Good Life for All

The first is the realisation that household work, raising children and manual labour are as worthy or dignified as intellectual work or political action. Second, without downgrading intellectual pursuit or political involvement, a vision of the good life must include the pleasures of ordinary life. Third, a life suffused with multiple ideals requiring a number of virtues cannot be the preserve of any one group of people but must be available to all. The valuable bits in what were once considered high and low must be combined and made accessible to everyone. A person living a life of the mind cannot afford to be indifferent to physical skills and stamina or to the world of politics. Likewise, a sportsperson, a policeperson or an army officer cannot neglect virtues of self-reflection—nor can those involved in politics. And while professional expertise and domestic skills are important for the householder, so are, say, civility and public reasoning. Therefore, our society—in particular, our educational institutions—must be designed to help each of us cultivate all of them. Fourth, the final choice to decide how to combine these different ideals in one's own life must lie with the person who leads it. Each person must work out what precise kind of life to lead. Freedom of choice is integral to the idea of a plural and democratic good life. We still have some way to go before fully pluralising and democratising the good life and will need to work hard to achieve it.

PART III

Our Rights, Our Values

22

The Importance of Rights

The eminent jurist Fali Nariman has frequently remarked that we are fortunate to have a charter of rights in the Indian Constitution: the right to life, liberty, equality, freedom of expression, association, religion, education and the rights against various forms of exploitation. Why is this so? What is it in the discourse of rights that is absent in other constitutional moralities? The short answer is that rights-based morality helps build a free and equal society. How so?

Underlining Moral Equality

Imagine two tracts of land equal in size bisected by a fence, one belonging to me, an ordinary man with modest means, and the other to a very rich and powerful man, say, a local politician. Over a period of time, I detect that the entire fence has shifted on my side of the land, substantially reducing its size and, correspondingly, increasing the size of the politician's land. To reclaim my land, I have two options. Recognising the asymmetry of power between us, the first is to plead with him to restore the status quo. I request, I urge, I implore, but I dare not challenge him. He is mighty strong, and if he resolves to usurp the entire land, nothing can stop him. So I supplicate with folded hands, hoping that out of pity he will give it back to me. The second is to demand that he returns the land to me because I have a right over it. I do not ask him for a favour or prostrate before him. I go to him as an equal, with dignity and self-respect, and demand what is rightfully mine. Moreover, since my right over the land is justiciable, I may seek the court's intervention in restoring the fence to its original position. So one of the functions of rights is to underline our moral equality—that no one is intrinsically superior or more powerful than the other. A person's moral worth is the same as that of anyone else's. The discourse of rights is a part of an egalitarian ethic, substantially different from the ethics of hierarchical societies.

Another way of putting it is this: by representing their viewpoints, rights assist the vulnerable and the powerless. By empowering them, they help overcome their vulnerabilities. And not only the poor and the powerless. We live under conditions where strong emotional ties are sundered, where bonds of affection and loyalty are easily frayed, where conflict is lurking round the corner, where enough power is concentrated in the states, corporations or communities to render all of us vulnerable. Rights help not only those who experience permanent vulnerability but also those who are sporadically threatened by it. Rights are protective guarantees when all else fails. They are 'fallbacks' that come into play when love and affection disappear (for instance, from family relations) or become impossible (as in a large society of relative strangers among whom love is inconceivable).

Interpersonal Relations

Rights have another advantage. They are grounded directly in ordinary interpersonal relations. The idea that human killing is wrong is part of virtually every ethic, God-dependent or not. What then is the difference between someone refusing to kill a person because God commands him not to and someone who refuses to do so because the person has a right not to be killed? It is this: in the first ethic, we don't kill primarily because of our obligation to God or because we fear his punishment. The moral value of the demands of others is secondary. In the other, we are constrained primarily because of what we owe directly to another person. We tell ourselves that regardless of whether God exists or not, we recognise that to be alive is such a significant interest of all humans that we have the duty not to deprive them of it. No matter how strongly it is in my interest to kill someone or even if my own god commands me to do so, I will refrain from killing because the other person's need to live puts me directly under an obligation not to kill.

A mother does not have to be told that she needs to feed her child because God commands so; she will respond instantly to the cries of her child. Analogously, humans must respond to each other's rights, to the impersonal demands of each other in formal settings. Once people learn the culture of rights, they understand directly without intervention from an external force what they owe each other. If a child has the right to education, the state must respond to this demand and fulfil it. If a person has the right to express her views, then all others must respond to her demand not to be prevented from doing so.

There is an irony in Mr Nariman's remark; its undertones betray a lament that currently rights talk seems ineffective and toothless.

But rights are important. They give voice to the powerless, address the vulnerabilities of all, help us meet demands we legitimately make on one another—which is why we are grateful to those who bequeathed them to us.

23

Basic Needs, Basic Rights: The Right to Minimal Decency

Three thoughts occurred to me in the aftermath of the horrific tragedy in Muzaffarpur, Bihar, where the systemic failure of public healthcare killed over a hundred children. First, like the constitutional principle of a basic structure, it is time to articulate an equally robust doctrine of basic rights. Second, these basic rights must be viewed primarily as positive—rights not against interference from the state (negative rights) but to the provision of something by it. Third, just as individuals are punished for legal violations, the government of the day must also be punished for violation of these basic rights. This punishment need not await the next round of elections but must be meted out immediately by the law itself. In short, defaulting governments must be held legally accountable. The systematic violation of basic rights must be treated on a par with the breakdown of constitutional machinery.

A Solid Necessity

But what are basic rights? How are they different from other fundamental rights? Basic rights flow from basic needs such as physical security and subsistence. Needs are different from wants. You may want a chocolate every morning but you don't *need* it. Heavens won't fall if you don't get it. But basic needs are different. Their non-fulfilment can cause great harm or even kill. The failure to get an antibiotic if you have a bacterial infection can hurt you very badly. Heavens *will* fall if you don't get it.

Moreover, wants are subjective. You cannot be mistaken that you desire that chocolate, but you may be misguided, even unaware, of what you need. You may not be able to tell if you need an antibiotic because your mind can't tell the difference between bacterial and viral infections. This determination is done by a more objective criterion. Needs depend on the way human bodies are constituted. They are a solid necessity. One cannot get on with life without them nor can they be fulfilled by substitutes. For us, nothing can take the place of water, food and air.

It is true that, though terribly important, basic needs are not what we live for. They don't make our life worth living. But anything really worth pursuing depends on the satisfaction of basic needs. If we are continuously thirsty, cold, hungry, ill or homeless, we will be incapable of even framing a conception of worthwhile life, let alone pursue it. Imagine the plight of those who queue up for long hours to get a bucket of water or a place to bathe, dress or defecate. People suffer if basic needs are met inadequately or are delayed. They are then denied a minimally decent life.

When basic needs are not fully met, we feel vulnerable and helpless. We grieve, cry for help or seek assistance. We complain and demand elementary justice from our community, especially from the state. Elementary justice requires that before anything else, the state does everything at its disposal to satisfy all basic needs of its citizens, particularly of those who cannot fend for themselves. We feel aggrieved when the state abdicates this responsibility.

Security and Subsistence

But what does the language of rights add to the idea of basic needs? First, a right is something that is owed to us; it is not a favour. So rights help the recognition of anything that satisfies basic needs as an entitlement. Basic rights are claims to the state to provide us with goods and services that satisfy our basic needs. Second, when something is identified as a basic right, it puts the state under a duty to enable its exercise. The state becomes its guarantor. For example, the right to physical security, the first basic right, is socially guaranteed when the state provides its people a well-trained, professional police force. When society and its government renege on its commitment to do so, we hold them accountable. It follows that basic rights are a shield for the defenceless against the most damaging threats to their life, which include starvation, pestilence and disease. As the philosopher Henry Shue puts it, it is 'an attempt to give to the powerless a veto over some economic, social and political forces that harm them'.

These rights are basic also because many intrinsically valuable rights can be enjoyed only once these rights are secured. Imagine that we have the right to assemble freely in public, but just as one begins to exercise this right, one is threatened with assault, rape or murder. Most people will simply retreat. Is not a threat to physical security or bodily integrity the commonest weapon wielded by goons, political thugs and oppressive governments?

The second is the right to minimum economic security and subsistence, which includes clean air, uncontaminated water, nutritious food, clothing and shelter. By showing the devastation caused by its absence, the Muzaffarpur tragedy amply proves that the right to primary healthcare is also an integral part of the right to subsistence. A straightforward link exists between malnutrition and disease. As Dr T. Jacob John explained in an article 'Averting Deaths in Muzaffarpur' in *The Hindu* on 19 June 2019, encephalopathy, the biochemical disease that results from eating litchi fruit pulp, occurs only in malnourished children. It is common knowledge that malnourishment lowers resistance to disease. A similar link exists between disease, unemployment and poverty.

Credible threats to these rights can be reduced by the government by establishing institutions and practices that assist the vulnerable, for example, by setting up hospitals with adequate number of doctors, nurses, beds, medical equipment, intensive care units, essential drugs and emergency treatments. For this, proper budgetary allocation is required, which depends, in turn, on getting one's political priority and commitment right. When a government fails to provide primary healthcare to those who can't afford it, it violates their basic rights.

Vulnerability and Accountability

To these two basic rights, I add a third: the right to free public expression of helplessness and frustration when basic rights are violated. The scope of freedom of expression is large and I don't think all of it can be deemed basic. But the relevant part of it is. The right to make one's vulnerability public—to be informed about acts of commission and omission of government regarding anything that adversely affects the satisfaction of basic needs, to critically examine them and to hold state officials publicly accountable—is a basic right on a par with the rights to physical security and subsistence and inseparably linked to them.

It follows that governments must make arrangements for people to demand that their basic rights be protected, to complain when these demands are not met, to report lapses and omissions of the government, point fingers at apathetic government officials, criticise the government for its failures and to do so without fear.

These three basic rights can be summed up in a single phrase: the right to a minimally decent life. This is a threshold right. There are no limits to the longing for a better life. A society may soar, strive for collective greatness, but the point of having a threshold of minimal decency is that our life must not fall below a certain level of acceptable existence. Anything short of a minimally decent life is simply not tolerable. It is precisely this that horrifies us about the callousness of the Bihar government in Muzaffarpur and governments in India more generally. They routinely abdicate responsibility for the suffering they directly or indirectly cause. This is the reason we must ask why governments are not immediately and severely penalised when they undermine the exercise of these basic rights.

24

Rights of the Vulnerable, Duties of the Powerful

Duties and rights are conceptually linked to one another. There are no rights without duties. If a person has the right to something, it necessarily implies that someone else has a corresponding duty to ensure that that right is not violated. For example, if an individual has the right to free speech, then it is the duty of the state to prevent its infringement. Or take the right of religious freedom of say, American Hindus; other groups, regardless of their numbers or social power, have a duty not to infringe on their religious rights. If they ever fell short of space for religious worship, the government should help fix that problem and facilitate the public exercise of their right. Isn't it a shame then that in Gurgaon when ordinary Muslims with no easy access to a mosque were prevented by Hindu extremists from praying in the open maidan, only a lone Hindu shopkeeper and a group of Sikhs felt duty-bound to help them offer namaz?[2]

If I have rights that impose duties on others, then others also have rights that enforce duties on me. Individuals have as many duties as rights. Any individual who demands a right and expects others to allow or facilitate its exercise must also expect that she is equally duty-bound to reciprocate. This is so simply because, like her, all others have rights too. We are all rights- as well as duties-bearing individuals.

I hope it's abundantly clear that rights entail duties, that rights cannot be exercised without the simultaneous performance of duties. Because of their grounding in rights, these (rights-based) duties cannot be pitted against rights. No opposition between them exists. To say here that we must focus on duties *rather than* on rights makes no sense. What then could really be meant by the proposition that we must move away from a rights-based to a duty-based perspective?

Duties against Rights

It should be obvious that the framework of rights and duties discussed above is grounded in egalitarian assumptions. However, the moment we drop this assumption, the whole picture of rights and duties is transformed. To be sure, the conceptual relation between rights and duties remains unbroken. Rights continue to entail duties, but in deeply hierarchical, inegalitarian societies, only a few people have rights while the majority have duties to ensure the proper exercise of the rights of these few.

In patriarchal families, the father alone has the right to take decisions. This puts all other members under a duty to abide by his decision. Remember Amrish Puri in *Dilwale Dulhania Le Jayenge*? He decides, without consultation, that Simran, played by Kajol, is to be married to the son of his friend in a Punjabi village. Simran has no

[2] *Hindustan Times*, 'Sikhs in Gurugram Offer Muslims Space in Gurdwaras for Friday Prayers,' 18 November 2021, https://www.hindustantimes.com/cities/gurugram-news/sikhs-in-gurugram-offer-muslims-space-in-gurdwaras-for-friday-prayers-101637176916887.html

choice but to obey to leave her home in London and settle in India. The mother, though sympathetic to Simran, is also duty-bound to not object to the father's decision.

The same is true of caste-ridden societies. It is a misconception that the Hindu *varna vyavastha* has only duties and no rights. The duties of Shudras and Atishudras to serve people of higher rank flow from rights possessed exclusively by upper castes. A hierarchical caste system distributes rights and duties unequally. Only a few have the most important rights, the right to be served, for instance; the larger population has corresponding duties to ensure that these rights are exercised without hinderance. Any infringement on the rights of the upper caste, especially the Brahmin, according to the Manav Dharmashastra, brings heavy penalties to the violator, sometimes even death. Similarly, in many Islamic societies, rights and duties are gender-specific and unequal. It is men's right to have their testimony in court weigh twice as much as women, who are duty-bound to comply.

In absolute monarchies, the king (the shahenshah) has unrestricted rights and all others have corresponding duties, which increase as we go down the ladder of political hierarchy. Those at the bottom have the maximum number of duties towards the maximum number of people, all ranked higher than them. Talk of priority of duties over rights are rampant in inegalitarian societies. When people are asked to forget about rights and think more about duties, the subtext is that they should forget about caring for their *own* rights and concentrate on their duties towards the few. In hierarchical, inegalitarian societies where power is unevenly distributed, duties are often seen in opposition to rights.

Careful attention to the structure of rights and duties in inegalitarian societies reveals its deep connection to social and political power. Those in power have rights, those without it have duties. A transformation from a hierarchical to an egalitarian order does not produce a power-free order. Instead, such change generates, at least in principle, a democratic distribution of power. And it is this equality of power that ensures a system of equal rights and duties. Indeed, in egalitarian polities, more power means more duties. The powerless have rights, the powerful have duties. For example, it is the duty of the state to ensure that there is no poverty, disease or unemployment. In this context, any move to shift the focus from rights to duties and to complain about undue emphasis on rights breeds the suspicion that democracy is being undermined and hierarchy reintroduced through the backdoor.

Duties beyond Rights

However, one can't altogether deny the importance of a moral discourse that asks people to attend to duties. For, quite simply, duties that do not oppose rights exist, and they do not flow from rights but go *beyond* them. Let's take an example. A surgeon performs an operation. He does his job efficiently and believes that once done, he is under no obligation to be present in the hospital or talk to the family of the patient. Now consider another surgeon who, after performing operations, feels compelled to interact with the patients and placate the anxieties of their families. Abandoning an impersonal stance, she brings warmth to her interaction. This act of the second surgeon flows from duties that are integral to the surgeon's character, to the goodness of her heart, to her personal virtues, to her commitment to warm social relationships and does *not* flow from any right of the patient. To be sure, patients and their families have the right to a surgeon's full attention when she is performing the operation. A failure to do so would mean an obvious violation of the patient's right. But no right of the patient or his family is violated if the surgeon doesn't go the extra mile to personally reassure the patient and his family.

A society with people who take such virtue-based, solidarity-infused duties seriously is much better than one where such duties are not valued. If that is the case, it is good to ask people to go beyond rights and think also of their duties towards others and, more generally, towards society. We all have a duty to build a tolerant society or to remain vigilant against the potential wrongs of our elected rulers. But these duties are moral and non-justiciable. Many such duties are mentioned in our Constitution: to preserve composite culture, to develop scientific temper, to safeguard public property, to protect India's sovereignty and integrity, not to destroy natural environment, etc. None of them are legally enforceable but they impose an obligation on all citizens, especially those who occupy public office, to go beyond the call of rights-based duties.

25

Are Minority Rights a Good Idea?

It has become part of middle-class common sense that something is deeply flawed with minority rights in India. If how a society treats its minorities tests its civility, then minority rights could be a source of pride. But for most people, these rights have begun to signify an irritating weakness, caving in to a tantrum-throwing smaller group and demonstrating the majority's failure to exercise absolute control over society.

Every right granted to the minority, they claim, is a privilege unavailable to the majority. First, a minority is set apart from the rest and then given what is taken away from the majority. The majority's loss is the minority's gain. This, it is felt, is unfair because it creates blatant inequality between the two. How then can an equality-loving Constitution tolerate minority rights?

Rights are legally recognised special interests of a person that put others under a duty not to interfere with them. If I have the right to religious freedom, others must not interfere in the choice and practice of my religion. Some of these rights are given to groups rather than to each individual because only groups—individuals taken together—can perform certain activities. For example, a language can be spoken, a religious practice performed and a tradition sustained only by a group, not by an individual in isolation. Thus, linguistic and religious rights are granted only to groups, empowering them to ward off wrongful interference by other groups. They are meant to compliment individual rights, not to compete with them, and must not be used to restrict the freedom of individual members of groups they strengthen.

So, what rights do linguistic and religious groups have? Only three rights, none of them socio-economic or political, exist for them in India: the rights (a) to establish and administer educational institutions of their choice (Article 30); (b) to conserve their distinct language, script or culture (Article 29); and, especially for religious groups, (c) to manage their own affairs in the strictly religious domain and to establish and maintain institutions for this purpose (Article 26). But why are these rights available only to minorities? Why this special 'privileged' treatment of minorities?

Two Different Arrangements

Consider the following two arrangements. In the first, a separate entrance to a hall is designed to let in only certain very important persons—the new maharajas and maharanis—so that they are not forced to rub shoulders with ordinary folks. They are treated differently because they are believed to be superior to the commoners and to possess some unique qualities that others lack. By bestowing privilege to a few, this arrangement reinforces existing hierarchies.

The purpose of the second arrangement is entirely different. Here, a separate entrance is required to meet specific needs of persons who are disadvantaged in one way or another: old persons, pregnant women, parents with young children, people with broken or irreparable damage to their legs. By preventing an existing disadvantage from begetting another disadvantage, the second arrangement strengthens equality by helping society to treat everyone as equals.

These rajas and ranis could easily take the common entrance but they won't; it is beneath their dignity. Here, a special entrance protects a privilege denied to all others. On the other hand, disadvantaged persons won't take the common entrance because they can't afford to; the risks are too high. By providing access to a benefit that others already have and procure routinely, the special entrance here fulfils an urgent need. Egalitarian societies cannot tolerate the first arrangement and cannot do without the second.

Granting rights to linguistic and religious minorities is not a privilege akin to what the maharajas get in hierarchical societies but an egalitarian response to a potential disadvantage. For example, in Maharashtra, Marathi-speaking people do not need a right to their own language. Plainly, they have the power to legislate that their language is the medium of instruction in all schools. This puts, say, Tamil-speaking residents in Maharashtra at a potential disadvantage because their children may never be able to properly learn their own mother tongue. However, they can demand that in schools run wholly by them, there is no law to prevent them from teaching in their mother tongue. Once they have this right, all Marathi speakers have a legal duty not to interfere in its exercise. In possessing such a right, the Tamils are not taking anything away from the Marathi speakers. They are only securing for themselves what the majority already has. Similarly, by possessing rights to their religious practices, Muslims and Christians secure for themselves what the majority Hindus already have—the free exercise of their religion.

Just as ordinary, able-bodied persons do not require a separate entrance, socially and politically powerful majorities don't need special rights. And just as persons with a physical disadvantage need a special entrance to be able to do what ordinary persons do routinely, numerically smaller and less powerful groups need separate cultural, linguistic and religious rights. This gain for the minority is not at the expense of the majority. The minority gains what the majority already has. There is nothing wrong then in the idea of minority rights. In diverse and egalitarian societies, it is always good to have them.

26

Situating Plurality in an Egalitarian Frame

A German proverb proclaims that a man is what he eats. And, I might add, even more emphatically, he is what he does not eat. Indeed, a man is also what he wears, speaks, believes, worships and what he does not; the smells he strongly likes, the kind of music he listens to, the colours that entice him and which of these he is averse to. This list can multiply, and multiply differently for different people. Human diversity is rich and immense.

India's own diversity is among the richest: countless culinary habits, dress, customs and musical traditions; more than 200 different dialects and languages; religious and doctrinal diversity—the ritual-oriented Vedic practices, the teachings of Buddha, Mahavira, Zarathustra, the Torah and Guru Nanak, the religiosity in the Puranas, the Quran, the Bible and the great varieties of animism and atheism.

Hierarchical Plurality

In the past, this deep diversity existed within a framework of inequality. This was not unusual but true of virtually every agrarian, pre-industrial society endowed not only with a highly complex division of labour but also with an intricate network of social distinctions. Indeed, cultural differences often marked and strengthened a stable, rarely questioned hierarchy of roles and ranks. Differences in speech, dress, manner, food or appearance were deeply intertwined manifestations of minutely arranged, culturally nuanced social hierarchies, which were visible indicators of differential rights and duties in a highly unequal society. They performed another important function: by diminishing ambiguity and friction, they helped place everything and everybody in their proper place. They reduced conflict and maintained existing relations of power. Not everyone could speak, dress and eat as they pleased. Sociocultural boundaries were not easy to cross. Our past is a system of hierarchical plurality.

A succession of egalitarian waves has challenged this system. The most obvious pointer here is the opposition to caste and gender hierarchies. Rights and duties do not vary today from one caste to another or between men and women. The right to equality enshrined in the Constitution of India is not merely a negative right against discrimination but also a positive right to be treated as an equal. Every individual is entitled to equal respect and concern simply as a human being. It is not legally possible today to have one set of laws for men and another for women. Article 15 sounds the death knell of the old order: 'The State shall not discriminate against any citizen on grounds only of religion, race, caste, sex, place of birth or any of them.' It adds that none of these will be the basis for subjecting any citizen 'to any disability, liability, restriction or condition with regard to (a) access to shops, public restaurants, hotels and places of public entertainment; or (b) the use of wells, tanks, bathing ghats, roads and places dedicated to the use of the general public'.

Not only has the degrading practice of untouchability been banned but temples have long been thrown open to everyone regardless of caste. Caste is no longer a barrier for any job, even for the highest offices of the land. This legal installation of equality could not but begin undoing the inseparable, culturally nuanced distinctions that accompanied differential status and power relations. Indeed, when it speedily dismantled some of them, an illusion was created that we might be able do away with all cultural distinctions and give rise to a new system where either cultural differences are insignificant or people can live by one culture alone.

Contesting Homogeneity

This expectation that egalitarian social, economic and political movements will make cultural differentiation irrelevant or totally flatten our cultural landscape has proved to be mistaken. A complete system of universalised, abstract equality has not come into existence. The expectation that we would have a culturally homogenous society is belied too. We do not have a monocultural social system in India. Although infinitesimally small cultural differences that mark social hierarchies have disappeared or are on their way out, new, larger cultural configurations have replaced them. We have relatively more homogenised but distinct languages (among them, Bengali, Oriya, Assamese, Gujarati, Marathi, Hindi, Sindhi, Urdu, Punjabi, Tamil, Telugu, Malayalam, Kashmiri and Kannada), religions (not only Islam, Christianity, Zoroastrianism but also Sikhism, Buddhism, Jainism and, of course, the massively internally plural Hinduism), regional cuisines and literatures. Even large caste associations vie for equal recognition, each refusing subordination to the other. These cultures are unlikely to disappear. One way or another, cultural differences are here to stay.

Besides, can one publicly claim today that one language—say, Bengali or Hindi—is superior to Tamil or Punjabi? Can one claim that Christianity is superior to Hinduism or Islam? Indeed, by granting community-specific cultural and religious rights, our Constitution is among the first to endorse an egalitarian, multilingual, religiously plural and multicultural system—a system where no religion-, culture- or language-based group can say that it is superior to others.

Old Practices, New Illusions

India being India, nothing here is firmly entrenched. Hierarchical plurality still colonises large swathes of our land. Hopes of a complete system of abstract equality might now be entertained only by a handful of cosmopolitan intellectuals, but dreams of a culturally unified society, with or without social equality, are found aplenty in our public discourse and streets. The melodrama of how our Constitution—that (wisely) only partially endorses both abstract, culture-neutral citizenship rights (individual rights to education, belief, public employment, voting, etc.) and some multicultural rights (Articles 26–30)—contests these systems of old practices and new illusions is still being played out in our country. Alas, it is hard to tell how, when and even whether it will end.

27

Collective Honour and Individual Dignity

In many parts of our country, inter-caste marriages are frowned upon and inter-religious marriages are virtually taboo. Young couples in our villages sometimes pay a heavy price for such transgressions, with some even killed because their act is seen to dishonour their communities. The furore around the film *Padmaavat*, based on Sufi poet Malik Muhammad Jayasi's legendary allegorical tale *Padmavat*, betrays this same anxiety about a community's honour. The film is believed to have insulted a martial caste and violated the honour of the Hindu nation.

What sense are we to make of such community-related honour? Honour is a form of respect. To have honour is to be entitled to high respect—to be judged positively by a standard that many others fail to meet. To have collective honour is to be entitled to positive regard by others by virtue of belonging to a particular community. Indeed, the real recipient of such honour is the entire community. Honouring a community means judging it to be better than others. This concept of honour can be interpreted to yield an achievement-oriented conception of individual and collective honour, as when a person is awarded the Jnanpith Award or a Nobel Prize or the Indian team is elevated to the first rank in test cricket. But it can also lead to another conception of honour that is tied to rigid, inegalitarian practices and is at play in resentment against inter-caste and inter-religious marriages.

Honour and Hierarchy

In this other conception, individuals are defined almost wholly by their membership in hierarchically related communities and groups are viewed as naturally superior or intrinsically inferior (e.g., men vs women, upper castes vs lower castes, high-ranked vs low-ranked religious communities). Honour here is not earned but grounded in a hierarchically arranged world believed to be an incontrovertible fact. All performative acts (practices) are then meant only to reiterate this hierarchy, to continually demonstrate that one group is better and higher than the other and deserving of more respect. Honour is encoded in social norms and becomes the direct expression of status within a hierarchical set-up. Each group is expected to behave by the honour code between superiors and inferiors. One honours a superior community by not marrying any of its members. If the superiority of a community is inscribed in the bodies of its women, how can inferiors touch them? If a member from an inferior caste marries someone from a higher caste, he treats his superiors as equals, thereby violating the social code and dishonouring the entire community. And because the identity of one person in a community is deeply intertwined with that of the other, any member can claim to be offended by the marriage and act on behalf of the entire community to avenge the 'wrongdoing', and, thereby, repair the damaged code of honour.

This troubling notion of collective honour appears to dominate all the headlines these days. But mercifully, it coexists with and is challenged by another form of respect that I have discussed in Chapter II which also has little to do with achievement, appears to exist independent of community and challenges hierarchy by pointing to certain qualities shared by all humans.

The Dignity of Individuals

Whatever the current mood in the country, one outstanding feature of our age is that each and every one of us can legitimately aspire to a radical improvement in the material conditions of life. Underlying this yearning and its necessary public expression is a silent transformation in our self-understanding. To some degree, we have all begun to see ourselves also as individuals. This is not to say that we have ceased to define ourselves in terms of some or the other community, or that seeing ourselves as institutional role players (as a father, mother, husband or wife) is no longer important. But the social and communitarian dimension of our lives is now lived alongside, and sometimes in tension with, our lives as individuals. We believe that the life of each person matters because of our common capacity to create and lead a life of significance. We each have a point of view of ourselves, our life and the world. In a very important sense, our life is first and foremost our own and has also to be lived individually. This fact alone entitles us to a basic respect, which has little to do with community. In the English language, there is a word for this: dignity. Each one of us has dignity merely by virtue of our humanity. This is a kind of deep personal honour we are born with, and one that must be recognised as such. This notion has deep roots in the great renunciatory traditions of this land but was given fresh impetus in the last two centuries by equality-centred social reform movements, the anti-colonial struggle, struggles for gender equality and, above all, by a movement against caste hierarchies led by the greatest Dalit leader of our times Babasaheb Ambedkar.

India is living through a deeply interesting but troublesome transition where older ideas of collective honour are vying with new articulations of individual dignity. In this clash between two forms of respect, inegalitarian forms of collective honour are more likely to be pushed out of our society as social and political democracy deepens. But since humans can neither live without communities nor live entrapped within them, both collective honour and individual dignity will be needed in future. And would it not be good to see a form of collective honour flourish in our society that is consistent with individual dignity?

28

The Virtue and Practice of Toleration

It is increasingly felt by many that we are moving towards a fiercely conflict-ridden world in which toleration would be needed badly. But what does toleration mean?

Perhaps, it is best to begin by making a distinction between toleration as an individual attitude and toleration as a social practice. Toleration exists in society where it is a prized personal attribute—a virtue. But it is also present where persecution, violent confrontation or bloodshed have somehow been kept at bay. For instance, where in the aftermath of civil war convenient arrangements of cohabitation have evolved, fostered by sheer fatigue with violence. In short, toleration as virtue is not always necessary for emerging practices of toleration. Indeed, a tolerant society may well exist, at least temporarily, even amidst pervasive attitudes of intolerance.

Four Conceptions of Toleration

What then is toleration as an attitude? There are at least four different ways of understanding it. First, to tolerate is to refrain from interference in the activities of others, even though one finds them morally reprehensible and has the power to stop them. Formulated in seventeenth-century Europe during and after religious wars, this toleration is an attitude of forbearance preceded by psychological turbulence and anxiety; a person with more power eventually puts up with what he intensely dislikes in the less powerful. An example from our society might help. If cow vigilantes and their powerful backers are not publicly provoked by the beef-eating habits of Dalits, Christians, Muslims and people from the Northeast, they will have learnt toleration. Indeed, many do tolerate this habit among Northeasterners. Call this negative toleration.

A second conception of toleration also exists. Two groups may find each other's activities morally abhorrent and have equal power to interfere but both refrain from doing so because the cost of the ensuing conflict is far too high. They may reluctantly accept an arrangement of coexistence. This attitude of resignation is toleration mandated by balance of power, known among specialists as modus vivendi toleration.

The presence of diversity and disapproval is common to all conceptions but difference in form and intensity of disapproval yields two other variants. In the third, considerations of power are less relevant; instead, people refrain from interfering in each other's activities largely out of indifference. Disapproval exists but is mild and not acted upon. In large, complex societies, the business of living one's own life is so time-consuming that a concern with others is simply too onerous. People don't really care about what others do, as long as it is not done directly or deliberately in their face. All they wish is to keep out of each other's way. This is toleration as an attitude of live and let live, a feature particularly of post-industrial, individualist and liberal societies.

Finally, a fourth, mildly patronising conception, distinct from the other three, has been around for centuries. It is best understood in contrast with negative toleration in which others are reluctantly accepted against a background of prior hatred. Negative toleration manifests as privatisation of moral hatred. No such hatred is presupposed in the fourth conception. Take the following examples: we often put up with the blemishes of our children that we would probably not condone in others and we choose to overlook a fault in our loved ones that we would not excuse in any one else. We endure deep difference in the world views of fellow citizens because we value fraternity. This has a religious version too. We might be strongly committed to a world of gods and goddesses but still be willing to acknowledge monotheists and atheists as fellow truth seekers who are also in some ways pursuing a common goal of ethical self-realisation. We may disapprove of their beliefs and practices and be critical of them, yet we could view them as alternative manifestations of our own self or as exemplifying a common human religiosity. In all such cases, we put up with disagreeable traits of others, even if we have some power to interfere, simply because overall we have positive feelings for them. Here, one tolerates not despite hate but rather because one loves the other. A mixture of love, friendliness and fellow feeling is the background that sustains this conception. Call this positive toleration—one that encourages moderately critical respect. This is not quite recognising others as equals but still an admirable stance towards others. It's a virtue.

Toleration for Our Times

Clearly, of all four, positive toleration is most desirable. But, would it be wise to push it as a universal ideal in all contexts and for all times? I don't think so. Which form of toleration is best suited then for our time when intolerance is part of religious or nationalist piety for many? Recall the distinction between toleration as a practice and as an attitude. In complex, diverse societies inhabited by people with varying temperaments, dispositions and upbringing, we might not share the same tolerant attitude but still manage to agree on common practices of toleration. Those consumed with passion, verging on the fanatical, may be persuaded to cultivate negative or modus vivendi toleration. Those with a more empathetic disposition may well cultivate the virtue of positive toleration. And the many in between should easily be satisfied with an attitude of live and let live. To expect everyone to cultivate the virtue of toleration is unrealistic today. But is it not our good fortune that uniformity in tolerant attitudes is not necessary for a tolerant society?

29
What Emperor Ashoka Knew about Free Speech

Should members of one religious community have a right to freely criticise other religious communities? Why not? Indeed, they must. Should this right be absolute? No right is absolute, but if our speech never upsets other groups, then why have it as a right? So, does discussion on the subject end here? No, because having a right is different from exercising it. So we need to ask if there are circumstances when it is wise not to exercise but waive it instead? And if we feel compelled to criticise others, in what form must we do so? Should there not be some informal social norms or an ethos that helps us judge when and how to exercise the right to criticise other groups?

Message for the Ages

One thinker who squarely addressed the issue of norms of free speech was Emperor Ashoka 2,300 years ago. For a start, there was great religio-philosophical diversity in his time (Vedic Brahmanism, Upanishadic philosophers, Jains, Ajivikas, Buddhists, to name just a few groups). These included those who made ritual sacrifice central to their ethic and those who didn't, those who believed in gods and goddesses and those who did not, those who thought ritual sacrifice was sufficient for a good life and those who differed, those who believed in the theory of karma and others who didn't, those who evaluated karma negatively (to act is to acquire demerit) and those who did not, those who affirmed and those who denied radical asceticism and those who linked self-fulfilment to compassion towards others and those who did not. This deep diversity must have generated conflict, particularly because Ashoka tried to ensure that all these groups lived together, sharing the same public domain, rather than separately in ghettoes.

What form did conflicts take? In Ashoka's time, writing was virtually non-existent. Everyone lived in a vibrant oral culture. The entire complex of art, philosophy and religion, poetry, our deepest metaphysical thoughts, acts honouring gods and goddesses, were spoken, composed, recited, sung, chanted and heard. Words were believed to have magical potency. They could beckon gods to help us tide over problems, create something out of nothing, empower or disempower others, turn them into stone or even kill them. They could be a weapon or an elixir, soothe or cause grievous hurt, bring us together or pull us apart.

In such a strong oral culture, social conflict frequently took the form of verbal duels between adversaries in intellectual combats. Moreover, vitriolic reciprocal name-calling existed alongside fulsome expression of self-praise and excessive bragging about one's own prowess.

Artful Management of the Tongue

If words fall off the tongue effortlessly and tumble out inadvertently—worse, carelessly—it is imperative that unguarded speech be checked, that words be enunciated with great care and thought in public. And that is exactly what Ashoka advised—free speech must be regulated by *vācāguti* (the artful management of the tongue), a social norm of a specific kind of *samyama* (self-restraint). While coexisting religious communities might invariably find each other irksome, this negative response, Ashoka argued, must not be privatised or repressed. It should be expressed in the public domain but only upon meeting certain conditions.

To begin with, speech critical of others may be freely expressed only if there are good reasons to do so. Second, even when good reasons exist for criticism, one may criticise only on appropriate occasions. And finally, even on an appropriate occasion, one must never be immoderate. Critique must never belittle or humiliate others. Only moderate criticism on appropriate public occasions is justified. Thus, there is a multilayered, ever-deepening restraint on negative speech against others—self-restraint for the sake of others.

With this, Ashoka had evolved an original norm of civility, but he did not stop here. He further asserted that one must not extol one's religion/philosophy without good reason. Undue praise of one's community is as morally objectionable as unmerited criticism of the other. Moreover, even when there is good reason to praise one's own perspective, it too should be done only on appropriate occasions, and even then, never immoderately. Excessive self-glorification is a way to make others feel small.

Indeed, blaming other groups out of devotion to one's own world view and unreflective, uncritical self-praise, argued Ashoka, damages one's own community. By offending and thereby estranging others, such speech undermines the capacity for mutual interaction and possible influence. Thus, there must equally be a multi-textured, ever-deepening restraint on oneself—self-restraint for the sake of one's own self.

A Shared Ethos

For Ashoka, our duties towards others cannot be neatly separated from the virtues we cultivate in ourselves. Our moral concern for others can't be hived off from our ethical regard for ourselves. So if Ashoka were alive today, he would argue that a crucial precondition for exercising one's right to free criticism of other groups is a robust ethos of self-restraint and self-criticism. A social norm of self-reflective civility in public speech is a perfect antidote to the mutual estrangement between communities now creeping into our society.

30

Development Matters—So Does Identity

It is sometimes claimed that once ordinary people benefit from economic development, they automatically set aside issues related to their identity. Such a view was found not only in materialist theories that gave primacy in human life to economic factors but also among leaders of social and political movements. Nehru, for instance, is believed to have assumed that as India makes economic progress, religious identity would matter less and communal conflict would disappear. It is possible that some well-intentioned citizens share the same premise. Our own governments sometimes try to give the same impression. Give Kashmiris an economic package, prospects of more jobs, better healthcare, high-quality consumption goods, etc., and they will forget their specific identity and assimilate peacefully into the 'mainstream'. 'Development' shall trump identity.

Cultural and Ethical Framework

'Identity' is a much misused and abused term. We misunderstand it, misconstrue its significance and maliciously politicise it, but it refuses to go away. Why? Undeniably, we are biological creatures with basic material needs. But we are also expressive creatures, image builders, story makers, concept inventors and live in a world saturated with images, representations, myths, stories and philosophies. Over thousands of years, multiple imaginary worlds have been fashioned, each of which is the collective possession of different societies. These imagined narratives shape our material needs, making them complex, elaborate and distinct. All humans do not have the same food and sartorial preferences. They design their dwellings differently. They even use their bodies and tongues differently to communicate with one another. In short, our material needs, suffused with imagination and saturated with concepts, are filled with intricacy and nuance.

Moreover, we have developed non-biological needs and dispositions. We reflect on the world and on ourselves. We develop a sense of who we are. We have implicit or explicit answers to the question 'Who am I?' This is partly answered by our culturally mediated material needs: we are, for example, what we eat and do not eat. But equally important for this answer is an ethic that distinguishes the good from the bad, right from wrong, what is worth striving for and what is not. With the help of this, we get a sense of where we stand in this world and what stand we take on it. In short, we are also defined by our specific stand on what happens to us after we die, and, say, on our position on the place of women in society.

So we cannot live a proper life without a framework of culture and ethic—the source of meaning and worth in our lives—or without other people—a community—with whom we share this framework. If this identity-endowing cultural and ethical framework is so crucial to each one of us, how can economic development alone satisfy us? This un-substitutable need for selfhood will not disappear just because one's biological needs are fulfilled.

So, not only are identity-related needs extremely important, but these needs are satisfied by a *particular* socioculturally informed ethical framework. Why not any such framework? Good question. The answer is simple: we are born into a specific framework, are initiated into it in our childhood and, before long, it makes us who we are. It provides humans with features that define them. These form the core that remains relatively constant even as everything around changes. Moreover, these constitutive features matter more than anything else. A wart on the body may be permanent but it won't matter if it is removed. However, take away fish from Bengali cuisine and all hell will break loose. Tagore's songs in middle-class Bengali homes have the same status. To many Tamils, the same is true of the worship of Murugan; the relic of Muhammad in Hazratbal to Kashmiri Muslims; the Kamakhya temple to the Assamese. These specific, enduring, valuable beliefs and practices are identity constituting, anchoring people in the world, making them feel at home and giving them succour.

All this is true. But it is equally true that identity-related issues invoke fear. They are prone to being abused. They can even become dangerous. How so? This happens when a relatively enduring character of an identity begins to be viewed as immutable and incontestable, and derived from a single permanent source. An identity is then seen as defining us categorically, once and for all, in an all-or-nothing manner like something inscribed in our DNA. Anything that disturbs or threatens the structure of our sociocultural DNA unhinges and enflames us, forcing us to die, or even to kill, for it.

Identities in Flux

These conclusions about the nature of identity are troublesome but not inescapable for at least three reasons. First, although our identity-constituting beliefs, feelings and values are given in childhood, we become self-reflexive as we grow older and frequently begin to question, revise and even reject them. They must endure but they don't have to be immutable. Second, as we grow older, we enter different groups, begin participating in more than one sociocultural framework and develop multiple identities. These identities move in and out of focus depending upon context. It is doubtful if human beings will flourish—even survive—if they were entrenched exclusively within one framework, bound to one single, permanently embedded identity. Third, each of these identities is itself derived from multiple sources. Consider Jammu and Kashmir. Three thousand years ago, Kashmiri culture was Vedic like the rest of the north-western region, which included present-day Pakistan and Afghanistan. It then probably acquired a layer from Greek settlers and definitively from the teachings of Buddha. By the middle of the first millennium, it imbibed a strong strain of Shaivism. Later, highly syncretic Sufi currents and still later, large chunks from modern

Islam entered the region. Kashmiri identity is a palimpsest that unfolds layer by layer like an onion. It would be absurd to reduce it simplistically to monolithic ideas of Hindu or Islam. These are useful simplifications in ideological or political battles but truly speaking, half-truths or even lies. The core of Kashmiri identity is a complex compound, flowing from multiple sources, not reducible to a simple, single element. What's more, this is true of every regional identity in India, of Indian identity in general and, indeed, of every group identity in the world.

What is the political implication of these observations? Modern socio-economic conditions require states to take care not only of people's material welfare but also their identities. But these conditions also foster ethno-nationalisms that insist on one state for every monocultural identity. Deep down this is a lie because it defies the intricacies of human cultures. So, is there a viable modern political system that protects the complexity of human identities and mitigates their rough, violent edges? There is. A decent federal system that allows a great deal of political autonomy to distinct cultural groups, protects important common (national) interests and enables fruitful encounter of regional cultures does that. Disturbing this federal arrangement for the sake of a simplistic idea of unity is not a smart thing to do. At worse, it paves the way for prolonged conflict that endangers development. Paradoxically then, we might well be undercutting development in the very name of development.

31

The Ideological Crisis of Liberal Democracy

Liberal democracy was born with a design defect. Though a decent response to the existing social, cultural and economic conditions in which it took shape, it had inbuilt conceptual flaws that sooner or later were bound to run it aground. The very idea is destined to malfunction.

Negative Liberty

For a start, the term 'liberal' in liberal democracy drew its nourishment from a particular conception of liberty that the philosopher Isaiah Berlin termed 'negative'. The core idea of negative liberty revolves around the existence of a private sphere where an individual may do whatever she wishes, free from interference by the state or oppressive communities or social institutions. Negative freedom is secured by limiting the capacity of the state or social organisations to impose constraints on individuals. This is an excessively private conception of individual freedom: humans are concerned only with the satisfaction of their desires, indifferent to the shape of public life or the character of the state.

I do not belittle this idea. In conditions where powerful Churches, caste organisations or the state is hell bent on controlling every aspect of a person's life—who to marry, what kind of a family life to lead, what opinions to hold and what to eat—negative freedom is a precious good.

Yet to delve further into the history of the idea of liberal democracy, these negative freedom–loving and liberal persons—the traditional middle class—soon realised that limited governments on their own cannot ensure their freedoms. These freedoms depend on certain kinds of state. Even governments restrained by laws but run by manipulative, self-serving, whimsical, power-hungry men can create political conditions that undermine these private freedoms. If so, lovers of negative liberty must, to some extent, take the reins of government in their own hands. Democracy is unavoidable. Obsessed with private freedoms and fundamentally disinterested in the art of government, they reluctantly invented a new form of government—representative democracy.

Self-government is demanding. Assembling, deliberating and arriving at informed decisions on important public matters takes time and commitment. How can people preoccupied with producing, buying, selling, consuming and running their own lives in pursuit of private happiness also commit to running a government? They can't. So they do the next best thing: find those inclined to make politics their private business to become their representatives. For vast numbers of hapless people who can't afford to get away from the daily grind of ordinary life and for those whose main purpose in life is the pursuit of personal happiness, there is virtually no time for public life or political decision-making. Their idea of political involvement is just too thin; the only time they can find for politics is during elections when they choose their representatives.

So, what is the basic flaw in liberal democracy? It is inadequately concerned with public activity, political liberty and wider community life. People almost wholly devoted to their private lives take virtually no interest in public institutions, which can be easily manipulated to serve the private interests of the rich and powerful. Their small political freedoms can be stolen from right under their nose. Since they cannot muster the time or effort needed to learn about the traditions and heritage of their communities, these too can be easily destroyed before their own eyes.

To redeem themselves and their society, they need a sense of togetherness that helps build a vibrant political culture, one that is not exhausted by family love or narrow community feelings of caste or religion. They need a commitment to a shared good that presupposes a strong sense of public spiritedness. In short, to better realise even their own personal goals, the negative freedom–oriented middle class needs to find the right balance between private benefit and public good rather than allow one to be trumped by the other. Conversely, indifference to public life means that nasty political worms would gnaw at it, adversely affecting even their private life. A stronger concern for the public good is a necessary condition for negative liberty. By itself, the idea of liberal democracy is both insufficient and deficient.

Forging Solidarity

Most societies realise this sooner than later. That is why liberal democracies worldwide have periodic bouts of public spiritedness borrowed from the republican tradition. People become active citizens by coming out on the streets, challenge the establishment, protest with purpose and show distrust for liberal democracy by questioning existing modes of political representation. They demand greater transparency and accountability in public life. They even show a strong will to take political decision-making in their own hands. But this deepening democracy can't just be a one-off event like the Arab Spring or the anti-corruption movement that preceded the 2014 general election in India.

Moreover, democratic solidarity is not the only way to overcome problems of liberal democracies. This function can also be performed by nationalism—the ethically informed, inclusive variant or dubious nationalisms such as the exclusivist, hate-mongering, national populism that is surging ahead today in different parts of the world.

However, forging solidarities, building public institutions, putting sustained pressure on governments to make informed, ethically grounded public decisions and ploughing through historical material to sculpt traditions need a lot of time and effort. Hate-mongering nationalism and populism, on the other hand, are manufactured easily and pay quick dividends. Spectacle prone, sensation-driven, playing on the fear, anger and frustration that grows in a crisis-ridden liberal democratic polity, such nationalist populism can be generated by the empty rhetoric of a demagogue supported staunchly by an unprincipled, profit-seeking mass media. The contemporary crisis of liberal democracy is life-threatening, indeed!

How have things come to such a pass? Whatever else globalisation has done, it has definitely reduced democracy to an electoral event and further deepened the privatisation of individuals. Liberalism in the era of globalisation has made people more self-obsessed, less capable of thinking about the common good or forging political solidarity and strengthened the grip of envy induced by feelings of relative deprivation. So far, new technology such as mobile phones and social media have only exacerbated this isolation of individuals. Rather than properly communicating with one another and trying to build a common mind on issues of common concern, all of us are busy expressing ourselves on Facebook or WhatsApp. Multiple discordant voices vie for public attention on social media, talking past one another or venting their personal anger, paranoia or hatred at an imagined enemy. Fierce individualism and nasty nationalism are fuelling each other. Caught within this diabolic syndrome, we risk losing even our hard-won negative liberties. Somewhere along the way, we have taken a wrong turn. Course correction and addressing the persistent crisis of liberal democracy will now require enormous collective effort and strong political will. And much hinges on whether the traditionally liberal, privacy-loving middle class will rise to the occasion and begin thinking of the public good.

32

The Trouble with Liberalism and Other Isms

Not long ago, an interesting debate ensued among eminent public intellectuals, sparked off by Harsh Mander's lament over the increasing invisibilisation of Indian Muslims in our public sphere.[3] Since one indication of this disturbing trend, cited by Mander, was an advice from a politician that before entering the political arena, Muslims might as well jettison their skull caps and burqas, the contentious discussion centred on what a correct and consistent liberal position on this issue entailed. Ramachandra Guha claimed that this counsel was 'forward-looking' because burqas in particular were 'antediluvian', inviting unambiguous liberal opposition.[4]

Mukul Kesavan and Apoorvanand claimed that its oppressive symbolism should have no bearing on citizenship rights, that our political participation cannot depend on sartorial habits dictated by religious affiliation.[5] Besides, a liberal offensive against religious orthodoxy must not rely on callous stereotypes about one another.

A Little Bit of Both?

I do not wish to engage in this debate, though I must confess that on this issue my sympathies are more with Mander and Kesavan than with Guha. I am interested instead in foregrounding a potential problem plaguing such debates, particularly the assumption that all ideologies including liberalism are tightly bound, self-contained

[3] Harsh Mander, 'Sonia, Sadly,' *The Indian Express*, 24 March 2018, https://indianexpress.com/article/opinion/columns/sonia-sadly-congress-muslims-party-sonia-gandhi-5100506/

[4] Ramachandra Guha, 'Liberal, Sadly,' *The Indian Express*, 24 March 2018, https://indianexpress.com/article/opinion/columns/liberals-sadly-indias-liberals-must-take-on-both-hindu-and-muslim-communalists-5103729/

[5] Mukul Kesavan, 'Liberal, Really,' *The Indian Express*, 28 March 2018, https://indianexpress.com/article/opinion/columns/muslims-in-india-hindu-bjp-comgress-religions-in-india-liberal-really5111181/ and Apoorvanand, 'Liberally Blinkered,' *The Indian Express*, 24 March 2018, https://indianexpress.com/article/opinion/columns/muslims-in-india-rss-hindu-rss-congress-bjp-narendra-modi-5106313/

systems comprising principles or values wholly distinct from and in permanent rivalry with other ideological systems such as communitarianism, socialism or conservatism. For instance, liberalism dictates that freedom of individuals must override the demands of community, an article of faith for communitarians. Also, liberals and communitarians can never intersect; any apparent convergence is proof that one or the other ideologies has been grossly misinterpreted. How can someone, without contradiction, be both liberal and communitarian?

In fact, liberalism has no timeless, fixed content—an unchanging core. The different doctrines or principles that fall under the rubric 'liberalism' share only a family resemblance. Each of them is as different from the other as are members of a large extended family. Some liberalisms are single value doctrines (monists); others try to combine different values (pluralists); some single value liberalisms insist on liberty as the core value; others, equality. Multi-value liberalisms give due place to both—some even to community (fraternity). Some are out and out value-individualists; others combine them with values of community; some think that the hallmark of liberalism is toleration; for others, it is individual autonomy; some, idolising a free market, demand that the state keep its role to the minimum; others demand state intervention for social welfare and justice. If there are many liberalisms, there invariably exist many ways of being liberal, and therefore no one course of action dictated by liberalism exists. The question 'What is required by liberalism?' has no single answer. Likewise, the answer to the question 'What is to be done?' cannot be extracted from a simple query about what liberalism or any other *ism* requires.

Second, the family of doctrines that fall under 'liberalism' exist in a field where they interact with contending ideological families, which they shape and are shaped by. This is partly why they evolve and have a history. In some historical contexts, some forms of liberalisms are difficult to distinguish from conservatism, and in others, from socialism. A doctrine that fell under 'liberalism' in the past can today, for many liberals, fall outside. Most of these perspectives develop at some time under conditions of hostile competition but at other times through conversation and dialogue. Consider liberalism and communitarianism, or community-oriented religious pluralism. They are engaged in a continuous and frequently converging debate. When they mutually criticise each other, they also learn from and refine each other.

A rhetorical, antipodal approach blinds us to such convergence. Only if one believes that liberalism is complete as it is, can one dismiss religious or non-religious communitarianism. But doing so is to commit the mistake of treating a living tradition of thought as a dead dogma. When one views them as rigid, self-contained systems in mortal combat and search for total victory, one exaggerates differences between and disregards differences within communitarianism and liberalism.

Breaking Boundaries

In short, many of these doctrines not only share a family resemblance but, to carry the metaphor further, sometimes marry each other, producing offspring that sometimes resemble one parent and sometimes the other. Good thinkers attempting to offer a solution to a problem or thinking self-reflectively through existing predicaments do not bother to consult the fossilised handbook of a particular ideology to find out whether the proffered solution is dictated by it. Wise thinkers who contribute to a debate do not persistently cross-check to see if they are crossing an ideological frontier. They do not needlessly think through an ideological prism, and when they do, they allow dead ideology to do the thinking for them and become dogmatic gatekeepers of ideological fortresses.

It is a bad practice to follow ideological diktats—to worry more about ideological consistency than about concrete issues at hand. Strangely, to do so is to fall into the trap of self-indulgent, expressivist politics (obsession with 'how am I'—my singular commitments—expressed in politics) rather than how to harness our collective power to make a valuable difference in the world and to engage ethically with complex situations involving others. Fruitful moral thinking is contextual and value-pragmatic. Moral integrity does not mean ideological consistency or being soft on one principle to accommodate another, which is a sign of moral opportunism. Real ethical lives dip into different ideological currents. Living ideological traditions are flexible, yielding the possibility of multiple morally legitimate practices. Ethical people should not have to always ask if they are living up to a core value identified with an *ism*. Doing so often leads to moral blunders or outright stupidity.

PART IV

Our Religious and Secular Ideals

33

Recovering Gandhi's Religious Vision

Gandhi was suspicious of many things modern, including modern Hinduism: a new nineteenth-century religion sharply demarcated from others and a fitting rival of Islam and Christianity. Why? Because he viewed himself as a sanatani, an adherent of a way of life that started long, long ago but, unlike the ancient that is dead and gone, continues to live today.

Ineradicable Diversity

Central to this seemingly everlasting Hindu imagination is its deep plurality, reflected in its acceptance of the coexistence of three basic ethical forms: one dependent on multiple gods and goddesses, one on a single god and one entirely independent of god, gods and goddesses (for example, truth seeking). For Gandhi, this religio-philosophical plurality is the inevitable and healthy destiny of humankind. 'There is endless variety in all religions … and interminable religious differences,' he said. 'Some go on a pilgrimage and bathe in the sacred river, others go to Mecca; some worship him in temples, others in mosques, some just bow their heads in reverence; some read the Vedas, others the Quran … some call themselves Hindus, others Muslims.' For Gandhi, there is not only diversity *of* religions but also diversity within them: 'While I believe myself to be a Hindu, I know that I do not worship God in the same manner as any one or all of them.'

Given the inescapability of deep religious diversity, he argued, 'The need of the moment is not one religion for the whole of human kind, but mutual respect, equal regard and tolerance of the devotees of different religions.' This moral–practical attitude of equal regard for all religions is entailed by an epistemic grasp of the deeper, more fundamental unity of all religions. 'The soul of religion is one, but encased in a multitude of forms. Wise men will ignore the outward crust and see the same soul living under a variety of crusts.'

The basic reference of all religions is the same: God or Truth. 'All religions are true and all have some error in them and that whilst I hold by my own, I should hold others as dear as Hinduism and make no distinction between them.'

Inclusive Monotheism

Gandhi's *inclusive* (belief in one God that encompasses all gods) rather than exclusive (belief in only one True God, while holding all others as false) monotheism flows directly from Indian polytheistic traditions, a trait they share with other religious traditions of the ancient world (Greek, Latin and Pre-Islamic Arab religions). The implicit theology of these religions allows for translation of gods.

In virtually all cultures of classical antiquity, each god performed a function based on his cosmic competence: gods of love, war, knowledge or craftsmanship. Likewise, each god embodied an entity of potentially cosmic significance: gods of fire, rain, earth, time, sun, moon or sea, and there were primal gods who create, destroy, preserve and so on. Virtually, every god or goddess in one culture could be related to gods and goddesses of another culture. For example, the Goddess Parvati of one Indian regional culture is related to the Goddess Durga of another region by viewing both as benign and fierce forms of the primal Goddess Devi. This way, differences—benign/fierce—continue to be viewed as irreducible yet translatable. This is a theology of recognition in which the gods and goddesses of each culture are recognised within the background of a common semantic universe.

One feature of inclusive monotheism then is that 'all worship the same God although under different names'. Gandhi illustrates this by a striking verse from the Guru Granth Sahib in which Nanak says that God may be called by the name of Allah, Rahim or Ram. Such an ecumenical perspective permits multiple attachments. If different names refer to the same god, then why not embrace all?

Two more things follow. First, 'to revile one another's religion, to make reckless statements, to utter untruth, to break the heads of innocent men, to desecrate temples or mosques *is* a denial of God.' Second, 'it is wrong for anyone to say that his God is superior to that of another's. God is one and the same for all.' At one level, there is a fundamental unity among all religions, and precisely because of it, they must be regarded as equal. If so, movements of conversion or purification are pointless. 'The real Shuddhi movement consists in each one trying to arrive at perfection in his or her own faith.' In such a plan, a person's character is the only test. 'What is the use of crossing from one compartment to another, if it does not mean a moral enhancement?'

Toleration and Respect

For Gandhi, respect and toleration were related and virtually indistinguishable. This might appear strange. To 'tolerate', in the classical seventeenth-century meaning of the term, is to refrain from interference in the activities of others even though one finds them morally repugnant and despite having the power to do so. Here, one puts up with and even suffers the morally reprehensible activities of others. At best, the powerless other escapes interference of the powerful because the latter shows mercy towards them. This is hate-based toleration—I hate but still tolerate.

Gandhi's toleration is different. Parents often put up with the blemishes of their children, which they would not suffer in others. We choose to overlook a fault in our spouse that we would not excuse in others. We might endure religious differences with fellow citizens because we value fraternity. In short, we tolerate some disagreeable beliefs and practices of persons or groups because we identify with many of their other beliefs and practices. In all such cases, we put up with dislikeable states of others even if we have some power to do something about them simply because we have love or love-like feelings for them. Others are tolerated not despite hate but, rather, because they are loved—I love, so I tolerate. This is Gandhi's love-based toleration, which is entirely consistent with respect.

Unlike the hate-based conception of toleration that presupposes that oneness with significant others is achieved by abolishing the radical other and eliminating plurality, for this second Gandhian conception, oneness is attained by accepting all radical others as equally significant because they variously manifest one supreme being. Thus, to tolerate is to refrain from interfering in the life of others not despite our hatred for them but because we love them as alternative manifestations of our own selves or because we deeply care for some basic norm common to all of us. We may not be able to be what they are or even dislike some of their beliefs and practices, but we recognise that they are translations of our own selves or of God within each of us. This, Gandhi believed, binds us together in a relationship of lasting affection.

Gandhi's religious vision encouraged multiple attachments, multiple belongings and multiple religious identities. Is it not time that we challenge the idea of religion as an exclusive monolith, one for which the highest achievable social ideal is an opportunist, morally dubious hate-based toleration and recover the deep pluralism and love-based toleration at the heart of Gandhi's religious vision? Indeed, as religious rivalry, conflict and violence intensify, can we afford not to?

34

The Moral Ambiguity of Modern Religion

Modern religion is a complex phenomenon, and reasonable persons can only have an ambivalent attitude towards it. Invoking both love and hate, it can neither be unconditionally respected nor indiscriminately disrespected. Citizens can neither demand that the state keep completely out of religion nor that it arbitrarily intervenes in each aspect of it. Why?

Religion as Ethics (Religion A)

Let me draw you into a thought experiment: an eight-step speculative history of the religious and philosophical lives of human beings. Assume that in the very distant past we developed a capacity for transcendence, that is, to step back and look beyond life as we find it, to holistically examine our existence and the world, to dispassionately see its limitations and aspire to overcome them. A gap now emerges (Step 1) between what we currently are and what we could be at our best. In striving to overcome this gap, we search for a vision, both personal and collective, in terms of which we can chart a journey of self-cultivation or self-realisation.

One important condition for finding this vision or path is getting guidance, most likely from a wise and insightful teacher, one who has deep influence in shaping our character and practice and helps us go higher and dig deeper. Let us then imagine that people begin to follow his teachings (Step 2). They become followers of a path—a marga—towards self-realisation.

Over time, a fellow feeling—a loose sense of community among the followers—develops (Step 3), which is important because self-cultivation needs mutual learning, influence and reinforcement. Self-development is a guided, social activity. Teachers and other learners are crucial to it.

This loosely organised human endeavour—this gamut of practices, dispositions and character—can be called religion in one important sense. Call it ethical religion, or Religion A. Now, Religion A may be gods/goddesses-dependent (ancient societies such as India, Greece and Rome) or God-dependent (monotheistic religions such as Judaism, Christianity and Islam) or independent of God—faith in the rightness of human action and human rationality—as in the visions of an atheist/secular society in ancient Greece (Platonic) and India (Buddhism, Jainism, Mimamsa). From very ancient times, India was home to many variants of Religion A, even though it had neither a word for religion nor a distinction between religion and philosophy.

Religion as a Social System (Religion B)

Imagine now that over time the community of Religion A develops an institutional structure involving hierarchies of power and status (Step 4). Some of these hierarchies grow because a section within the community has taken upon itself the responsibility to systematise teachings and turn them into intellectual doctrines (Step 5). Given the new importance of doctrines, some within the bureaucratic structures become gatekeepers, maintaining strict rules of entry and exit (Step 6). Perhaps some of these are proselytisers, view each other as rivals fighting for individual allegiances and slowly begin to define themselves in opposition to one another (Step 7). They even break each other's heads over differences of doctrine or practice, and even the heads of some of their own who differ from the 'accepted' doctrines (Step 8).

Variants of Religion A, which have gone through Steps 4–8, have now become religions in another sense. Call them religions as social systems, or Religion B. What was once a loose community has now metamorphosised into a highly doctrine-oriented, bureaucratised, exclusivist structure. Alas, the pursuit of Religion A has for some time now been dependent on one's belonging to Religion B.

Now, because religion has come to be understood as an amalgam of both Religion A (teachings of individual or collective self-realisation) and Religion B (institutionalised, power-laden, status-ridden and doctrinalised), many reasonable persons are bound to develop a deep ambivalence to it. They may revere Religion A and find Religion B repugnant.

Modern Religion

Modern religion tends to be comprehensive, referring to both Religions A and B, and therefore is neither unambiguously good nor wholly bad. One can neither live without it nor relate to it without resistance and critique. The only sensible attitude towards it is critical respect.

This has broader political and state-related implications. Our politics cannot be conducted without drawing upon the resources of one or the other Religion A. Hence Gandhi's statement with which even Nehru agreed: 'I can say without the slightest hesitation that those who say that religion has nothing to do with politics do not know what religion means.'

But equally, Religion B cannot meddle in politics without vitiating it. Furthermore, morally sensitive citizens can neither endorse a strict separation between the state and modern religion nor allow the boundaries between them to become so porous that the state wilfully destroys people's freedom to choose and practise Religion A. This is why they must insist that the state keeps a principled distance from all religions—keep off Religion A and intervene when morally necessary in Religion B.

35

Religion and the Indian Constitution

Checking political tyranny, protecting the basic interests of dissenting minorities and saving all citizens from taking decisions now that they might regret later are important objectives of all liberal–democratic constitutions. But the Indian Constitution goes further—it attempts a comprehensive social transformation: to affect a social revolution.

Religion appears to be the main target of this attempted transformation. If so, how does this transformative potential of the Constitution impact a society saturated by religion?

To answer this question, let me return to the distinction made in the previous essay between an individual's ethics of self-fulfilment and social norms of everyday conduct. By the first I mean a framework for meaningful living and dying, say, a full life in this world, swarga (heaven) in another world, or freedom from recurrent births and deaths (moksha or nirvana) or obeying the commands of God.

By social norms of everyday conduct I mean rituals and ceremonies of social interaction, but primarily norms governing interpersonal relations—with whom one should or should not interact, who one should or should not marry, with whom one should or should not dine, who is to perform which job in society, etc. Ethics of self-fulfilment and norms of social conduct may be so tightly connected that they form one single system. Or the connection between them may be so loose that they are seen to constitute two separate systems.

Ethics and Social Norms

In the Abrahamic traditions, the connection between ethics and social norms was sometimes forged so tightly that they became part of a single deeply connected system. And the term 'religion' was invented to refer to this whole. Thus, if a person chose to be, say, a Latin Christian, he instantly became part of this entire system. Adopting a particular set of Christian beliefs on salvation went hand in hand with taking part in specific Christian rituals and ceremonies and entering a web of unequal social relations with non-Christians. It would be wrong and impermissible for a person with Christian beliefs to participate in non-Christian social rituals or tolerate pagans.

For this reason, a religion-centred social revolution in Europe meant (a) breaking the monopoly of Christianity and presenting options other than dominant Christian ideas of self-fulfilment—pluralisation of ethics; (b) loosening the connection between ethics and social norms, freeing social norms from Christian ethics and building norms of social equality that transcended religious identities—secularisation and (c) fighting a Church that blocked secularisation and pluralisation.

By contrast, the connection between ethics and social norms remained very loose in the Indian tradition. Because social norms and power hardly ever dictated the choice of ethics, there was greater innovation, and so ethical frameworks proliferated. There were always many ethical frameworks to choose from. People could move freely from one framework to another, and sometimes, without any discomfort, participate in several. And yet, precisely because social norms existed independently of ethics, this very ethical flexibility went hand in hand with great rigidity within social norms. This is so because hierarchical and fixed caste relations lay at the core of these norms. Ironically, they even complemented each other; as long as one remained within the caste system, one could choose any ethical framework or any path to self-fulfilment. A person could find fulfilment in a loving relationship with Krishna, in achieving swarga or in liberation from the cycle of rebirth and at the same time follow common norms governing unequal social relations. A person may quit a this-worldly Vedic ethic in order to lead an ascetic Jain life but all the while continue to belong to the Vaishya caste and therefore remain enmeshed in hierarchical caste relations. This was true even for those who became Christians or Muslims; they chose a modified Abrahamic ethic but remained entrenched in the caste system.

'Religion' in India

Given that the term 'religion' was invented to refer to a single system, it was not easily applicable in the subcontinent where ethics and social norms do not cohere into one single whole. Yet such is the force and sway of the term 'religion' that it has been simultaneously used to refer to two relatively distinct and independent systems of ethics and social norms. This has generated many problems and much confusion.

Consider the following simple example from the natural sciences to grasp the absurdity of this profound misnaming. The term 'water' refers to a single entity composed of two distinct elements, oxygen and hydrogen. Where the two gases are deeply connected to form a single compound, the term 'water' is appropriate, but we rightly use two distinct terms 'hydrogen' and 'oxygen' for each when the two remain disconnected from each other. How utterly erroneous it will be to call them 'water' when they exist separately! Calling distinct systems of ethics and social norms in India by the common term 'religion' is equally insane. But then once a term grips the popular imagination, it is difficult to dislodge.

Some scholars have tried to get out of this hole by using 'religion' in two different senses—ethical religion and social religion. (Roughly captured in the previous essay by the distinction between Religion A and Religion B.) Though not entirely satisfactory, we might accept this and say that in India a profound pluralism of ethical religions exists. Yet, followers of different ethical religions participate in much the same caste-ridden social religion.

How does all this help us understand the relationship of our Constitution to Indian religions? Unlike Europe, where people have to fight for pluralisation of ethics, in India we do things differently. First, we strive to conserve the immense pluralism of our ethical religions and act against any attempt at religious homogenisation or exclusion. The Indian Constitution performs this 'conservative' function. Second, by preventing a tight connection between social norms and ethical religion, the Indian Constitution also ensures that we do not have 'Religion' as originally conceived, something as totalising as Latin Christianity had been or Saudi Islam now is. Finally, the main objective of the Constitution is to destroy what is at the core of India's dominant social religion—its deeply hierarchical caste system. This last feature alone marks it as an instrument for social revolution.

36

What the Courts Miss in the Constitution

Consider the January 2017 Supreme Court judgement in *Abhiram Singh v. C.D. Commachen*, pertaining to Section 123 (3) of the Representation of the People Act, in which one of the learned judges, Justice T.S. Thakur, correctly notes that the courts must remain sensitive to India's constitutional ethos to which secularism is integral. Citing S. Radhakrishnan and several court judgements, Justice Thakur then expounds the meaning of secularism: a secular state must not identify with any one religion or be controlled by it. It is neither pro this or that god nor anti-god.

This is spot on because such identification accords privileged recognition to one religion, which violates the principle of equality. After all, one implication of any privileged recognition is lesser recognition of other religions, reducing them to secondary status. This is blatantly discriminatory. Besides, such privilege encourages other forms of disabilities in the non-religious social and political domain, inducing a vicious cycle of discriminations that cannot be tolerated in democracies. This, the judge concludes, 'necessarily implies that religion will not play any role in the governance of the country ... [The] encroachment of religion into secular activity of the state is *strictly prohibited*.'

Flip Side of the Same Coin

A second feature of Indian secularism, the judge says, is that it does not reject religion. A secular state does not entail the denial of 'reality of an unseen spirit or the relevance of religion to life or that we exalt irreligion'. On the contrary, the state must guarantee everyone the freedom to practice, profess and propagate their religion. This is the flip side of the same coin. The prohibition on 'mixing state power and religion' entails that the state is under obligation to not encroach upon the free exercise of religion. In short, a state is secular if religion and state power are 'kept apart', strictly separated from each other, and this separation is required to protect inter-religious equality, non-discrimination and the fullest possible exercises of religious freedom.

Though partly correct, this interpretation misses the truly distinctive feature of Indian secularism. While the judgement fittingly rejects the identification of a secular state with any one particular religion or non-religious philosophy, it injudiciously concludes that this implies that neither religion nor state can play any role in each other's affairs. But the Indian Constitution allows the state to play a legitimate role in the affairs of religion. Likewise, it permits religious considerations to sometimes enter governance. Unlike the rhetoric and ideology of the American wall of separation, in India, legitimate principled intervention of the state in religion and vice versa is constitutional. The two are distanced but not completely separated.

Religion in Governance

For a start, state intervention does not always prohibit but rather facilitates the free exercise of religion. The recognition of a religious community is a positive act on the part of the state. Granting rights to religious minorities (Articles 25 and 26) is a form of state intervention. Thus, religious minorities can set up and maintain their own educational institutions, something large religious communities routinely do without the need for special rights. Moreover, all religious groups, small or large, have equal opportunity to avail of subsidies by the state to run their schools and colleges. Similarly, the Indian state decides which special days associated with religion are to be declared national holidays. All such decisions are based on religious considerations and are integral to governance. Therefore, to say that religion does not play any role in the governance of the country is simply wrong.

Second, if hierarchical caste structure and patriarchy are intrinsic to the doctrine and practice of religions, then the constitutional ban on untouchability, the opening of temples to all Hindus regardless of their caste and gender and the past/future judicial reform of Hindu/Muslim Personal Law demonstrates that the state can legitimately impinge on religion. It can do so also if religion or caste-based communalism disrupts social harmony. Indian secularism is hostile not to religion but to caste- and religion-based communalism. The same values—freedom, equality and social harmony—that prohibit the state from encroaching upon religion also allow it to intrude in it and permit the entry of religious considerations into the state.

In short, a distinctive feature of Indian secularism is that it rejects the 'wall of separation' but demands that the state keep a 'principled distance' from all religions. It requires that the state has a value-based engagement with or disengagement from religion. Indian courts must endorse and espouse principled distance and drop the tired rhetoric of strict separation.

37

Should the State Leave Religion Alone?

The Sabarimala judgement and its aftermath have brought the issue of state intervention in religion back to the table: should governments leave religion alone instead of interfering in it? There is no simple answer to this question. Much depends on what one means by religion.

In one sense, religion refers to that aspect of human life where we relate to the transcendent through personal belief or collective practice. This transcendent entity can be seen either as existing within human persons or outside them in the highest possible realm. Religion then largely consists of spiritual exercises by which one digs deeper or goes higher. A mind-boggling variety of ways to carry out these exercises exist—god-dependent, gods- and goddesses-dependent or entirely independent of god. Let us just call this religion faith. (In the previous essays I called it ethical religion or Religion A.) To the question should governments leave faith alone, the answer simply has to be a resounding yes. Not that government's interference is always unwarranted. For example, if collective rituals involve human sacrifice, then state should intervene. The point is that there must be a general presumption that governments must not interfere in faith.

Intervening in Organised Religion

However, it is commonplace that as faith communities become large, they feel the need to be rule-bound; in order to become stable and self-sustaining, they institutionalise themselves. But institutionalisation often involves the introduction of hierarchical relations of power and status. Some people in this relation have more power and status and are 'more equal' than others. They systematise beliefs surrounding spiritual exercises into explicit doctrines. They insist on doctrinal purity and lay down strict but spurious rules that split followers into the 'normal' and the 'deviant'. They fix violent and exclusionary penalties for the deviants and thereby manufacture gated communities with robust notions of who is inside and who is outside. Concepts of heresy and infidelity are generated, and a whole society infested with persecution comes into being. In this second sense, religion refers to institutionalised faith communities, such as the those headed by a church, math or sangha. Now, spiritual exercises cannot be undertaken without belonging to such strongly institutionalised religion (also termed Religion B). Should the state allow discrimination, exclusion, marginalisation, humiliation, oppression and persecution by elite-controlled religious institutions or instead ensure that those within the faith community lead a free, dignified life? My view on this is crystal clear. A government must, albeit with great care and sensitivity, intervene in organised religion to prevent any practices of domination within it. It should also inhibit any attempt on its part to dominate members of other religious communities.

There is, however, a third sense in which the term religion is used, one that refers neither only to faith nor to powerful institutions that order and control it but instead to historically transmitted traditions, indeed to an entire way of life. Thus, people frequently say that Hinduism is not a religion in the conventional sense but is rather a way of life. But if religion is a whole way of life and if this entails the breakdown of the very distinction between religion and society or religion and culture, then all relations of hierarchy and domination that are found in society are also subsumed under it. In this conception of Hinduism as a way of life, caste or gender hierarchies are as religious as they are social. Caste domination or gender violence then becomes integral to Hinduism. How can a state that has accepted freedom and equality as one of its founding principles turn a blind eye to these oppressive practices within the Hindu way of life? In short, if religion is conceived as a way of life, then the state is duty-bound to intervene in religion. Here, the answer to the question 'Should governments leave religion alone?' must be an even more categorical no.

Keeping a Principled Distance

It is because religion is a complex and morally ambivalent phenomenon that there cannot be a single, emphatic yes or no answer to the question raised above. In my own work over decades, I have consistently maintained that a strict separation between state and religion is not desirable. The state can neither take the view that it will control all aspects of religion nor that it will have nothing to do with it; that no matter what happens, it will always keep religion at an arm's length. The state must keep, what I have called, a principled distance from all religions.

What does it entail for law and public policy in relation to religion? On the principled distance view, there is absolutely no need for a state to have any law or public policy pertaining to matters of faith untainted by control, hierarchy or exclusion. A state must not interfere in what faith we have and how it is practised. Faith in god, gods and goddesses or in god-independent human qualities such as reason must remain free from interference. But equally, a just, egalitarian and freedom-sensitive state cannot abandon its obligation to remove the residue of intra- or inter-religious domination from society. This is why laws that prohibit triple talaq or lift restrictions on the entry of women into temples such as Sabarimala must be enacted. Customs that demean or humiliate women must go.

I have consistently argued that this is precisely how secularism is conceived in India: not as a political perspective that permits authoritarian control of religion by the state nor as one that encourages a libertarian hands-off approach towards it but as one that promotes a nuanced and flexible policy of value-based political or legal decision on whether or not to intervene in religion. This principled-distance variety of secularism is the unique ethical stance of the Indian Constitution, a gift from India to the rest of the world.

38

The Inner Complexity of Popular Religiosities

Using one's institutional status and spiritual halo to grab and boorishly display power, fame and wealth is bad enough, but in recent times, more and more 'gurus' are coming out as sexual perverts embroiled in horrific exploitation of their own followers, raping women and castrating men. It came as a relief, therefore, when the Dera Sacha Sauda chief, Gurmeet Ram Rahim Singh, also accused of murdering journalist Ram Chander Chhatrapati for exposing his misdeeds, was convicted for rape and sentenced to twenty years in prison.

Reassuring as this was, it was also deeply distressing to read that he hobnobbed with and was patronised by various political parties. Not long ago, the Central government had afforded him the use of VIP airport lounges meant exclusively for prime ministers, presidents and heads of foreign government. Worse, ministers of the Khattar-led BJP government of Haryana had bowed before the chief.[6] Furthermore,

[6] PTI, 'Haryana CM Manohar Lal Khattar Admits There Were Lapses in Handling Dera Situation,' *The Economic Times*, 25 August 2017, https://economictimes.indiatimes.com/news/politics-and-nation/haryana-cm-manohar-lal-khattar-admits-there-were-lapses-in-handling-dera-situation/articleshow/60226072.cms?from=mdr

the BJP government in Haryana betrayed its own brand of 'vote bank politics' when, despite knowing that they were armed with weapons and explosives, it allowed Singh's followers to congregate in large numbers a day before the verdict.

Shameful and shocking as all this is, the Dera Sacha Sauda case also raises other issues, demonstrating, if one is prepared to keep one's eyes and ears open, how socially complex and ridden with deep moral ambiguity such social phenomena are. A straightforward, unbiased examination of any such organisation goes straight to the heart of issues of religious diversity and institutionalised religious domination.

Forms of Religious Diversity

Take the issue of religious diversity. Two forms of it commonly come to my mind. First, diversity of religion—the existence in society of a populace professing faith in distinct, well-demarcated Hindu, Christian, Jewish or Islamic ideals. Second, diversity within religion. Here, what immediately appears before us is what can be called horizontal diversity—when a religion is internally differentiated because its core beliefs and practices are differently interpreted, especially by competing elites, for example, Protestants, Roman Catholics, the Greek Orthodox among Christians; Shias, Sunnis, Ismailis, Ahmadis among Muslims; and Vaishnavites, Shaivites and Shaktas among Hindus.

What is less noticed is that religions are characterised by another kind of diversity—call it vertical diversity. This occurs when people of the same religion engage in diverse but hierarchically arranged practices. A religion might mandate that only some of its members engage in certain kind of practices and others be excluded. For example, caste-ridden Hinduism makes a distinction between pure and impure practices. Practices performed by certain castes are pure and members of other castes or women are excluded from them. For instance, women or Dalits may not be allowed entry into the inner sanctum of temples and in many cases even into the precincts of an upper-caste temple. But such marginalised or dissenting sections of society do not cease to have religious or spiritual lives. They invent gods (or pantheons that include spirits, ancestors and deified heroes), identify gurus, develop forms of worship of their own, often away from the eye of and, sometimes, in tension with caste-laden Hinduism. Song-based devotionalism among women of virtually all castes and yogic or meditation-based practices of individual salvation among 'lower castes' provide examples of such diversity.

Vertical diversity brings home a point that ought to have been made at the very outset. Every form of diversity, including religious diversity, is enmeshed in power relations. If so, endemic to every religiously diverse society is an illegitimate use of power whereby the basic interests of one group are threatened by the actions of another. It further follows that inherent in religiously diverse societies is the possibility of both inter- and intra-religious domination (discrimination, marginalisation, humiliation, exclusion and reproduction of hierarchy). In short, domination can develop between religions (between, say, Hindus and Muslims), within religions (sectarian domination of say Shias by Sunnis) and even within faith practices of the marginalised (domination of women among OBCs, Dalits or tribals).

The Case of Dera Sacha Sauda

To come now to my main point: what we saw in the case of Dera Sacha Sauda is a highly pernicious form of intra-religious domination—oppression of followers, female and male by their own guru. No condemnation is strong enough for what had happened. But a cursory glance at the history of their formation shows that such organisations frequently grow out of resistance to inter- as well as intra-religious dominations.

Dera Sacha Sauda, from what I have gathered, was formed in 1948 by an ascetic spiritual seeker Mastana Balochistani. It apparently grew from resistance to the totalising claims of mainstream, organised Hinduism, Sikhism and Islam. The Dera's simple teachings emphasise the recitation of sacred words, meditation and the achievement of individual transcendence. The devotees are asked to practice forms of asceticism and avoid self-indulgence—to abstain from ritualism and from making monetary religious donations. Facilities of drinking water and *langar* (community kitchen) are provided in their ashrams. They are inclusive and have not only Sikh but Christian, Hindu and Muslim followers, many of them from Dalit and working-class backgrounds. Singh clearly abandoned the original milieu of Mastana's religiosity, replacing it with the sickeningly glitzy world of fame, power and wealth, but during his satsang gatherings, he sat beneath Hindu, Sikh, Muslim and Christian symbols and attracted the marginalised.

Such folk and guru-based religious orders, at least at their birth, valorise individuality and personal freedom, are egalitarian, focus on mental and physical health and this-worldly happiness for all. In doing this, they reproduce the fluidity and flexibility of ancient and popular Hinduism. It would be wise not to dismiss or overlook this aspect of these organisations—that they are part of a religiously plural landscape and, at their best, resist intra- and inter-religious domination. Also, that they are a bulwark against the homogenising practices of large, powerful and totalising religions, unless of course they are co-opted by them. So, even as we take stock of Gurmeet Singh's crimes, it's important to understand the role of folk and guru-based religious orders.

39

Constitutional or Party-Political Secularism?

Few countries in the world exist where secularism is more bitterly contested and perhaps even fewer countries than India where the term has been persistently misused and abused. No other term in India has been continuously battered and evacuated of meaning or significance. The cacophony that surrounds secularism may well be the price that it has to pay for becoming an integral part of our country's public and political discourse.

A couple of decades ago, Indian secularism was unfairly charged by its opponents for being anti-religious. It was subsequently labelled as a pro-minority doctrine. In recent times, we have been advised to choose between secularism and development, as if secularism was an anti-development ideology. And in July 2017 we saw the bizarre spectacle in Bihar where secularism and corruption were viewed as blood brothers; the champions of secularism, mired in corruption, are arresting the growth of an economy perched to take off and soar high, it was claimed.

How has secularism come to such a pass? This is a complex story, which I cannot even begin to narrate here. However, I will speak of a small but important conceptual episode within this tale: the degeneration of constitutional political secularism to what I call, for want of a better term, party-political secularism.

European and Indian Secularisms

What are these two secularisms? To understand India's constitutional secularism, it is best to contrast it with European conceptions. The break-up of Latin Christendom in Europe generated religious wars. Elimination and expulsion of religious dissenters produced predominantly single-religion societies. Each European state closely aligned itself with one or the other dominant church in society. Thus, England became Anglican, Scandinavia became Lutheran, Spain and Italy became Catholic, Denmark became Calvinist and so on. Over time, however, the church was seen to become too politically meddlesome and socially oppressive. A movement for 'un-churching', or curtailing the power of the church, was set in motion. A battle ensued between the state and the church in which, by and large, European states prevailed. European states separated themselves from the dominant church. Thus, the separation of state and church became the defining feature of European and, later, American secularisms.

In India, the situation till at least the twentieth century was completely different because there had not been any attempt to liquidate religious diversity. The state has always found ways of dealing with all religious groups. Hardly any state existed that did not patronise all existing religions. Under modern conditions, this practice developed into a defence of religious pluralism. The state had to respect all religions and treat them non-preferentially. Respecting religions often entailed the necessity of the state to keep off all religions. On other occasions, it meant that the state positively contributed to enhancing the quality of religious life, for instance, by giving subsidies to schools run by religious communities. At the same time, quasi-religious institutions such as caste continue to be oppressive, particularly to Dalits and women. This demanded that the state intervene wherever religion was hierarchical and coercive. Hence the ban on untouchability and the reform of gender-discriminatory personal laws.

India's constitutional secularism requires that the Indian state be neither wholly respectful nor disrespectful of religions. Critical respect for all religions is the hallmark of Indian secularism.

Furthermore, it enjoins the state to keep a value-based or principled distance from all religions: to interfere or refrain from interfering in religions depending entirely on which of these strategies best promotes freedom, equality and fraternity.

The Growth of Opportunism

But in the last forty years or so, we have developed another secularism—what I call party-political secularism, an odd, nefarious 'doctrine' practised by political parties, particularly the so-called secular forces. This secularism has dispelled principles from the core idea and replaced them with opportunism; opportunistic distance from all religious communities is its slogan. It has removed 'critical' from 'critical respect' and reduced the idea of respect to making deals with the loudest, most fanatical, aggressive sections of every religious group. Thus, political parties keep off religion or intervene as and when it best suits their party or electoral interests. This has led to the banning of *The Satanic Verses*, the unlocking of the Babri Masjid/Ram Janmabhoomi Temple, the curtailing of women's rights in the Shah Bano case and to deals with the likes of Bukhari. Instead of respecting the best in religious groups, political parties hobnob with those least deserving of respect. Party-political secularism means that political institutions such as the state and political party keep an opportunist distance from the notorious and highly politicised sections of all religious groups. This is also a fertile ground for majoritarian Hinduism, whose spokespersons can question all the deal-making and opportunism of 'secularists' without self-examining their own equally unethical practices.

Alas, electoral politics has sidelined or corrupted our constitutional secularism. To be fair, electoral politics breeds opportunism. If one's only aim is to win, to do so by any means is always tempting. But it is here that we need the courts, a free press, an alert citizenry and civil society activists to move in and show a mirror to these so-called secular parties and tell them what they can and cannot do. I am not blaming political parties alone. This is a collective failure. It is on all of us to stop the proliferation of the misuse and abuse of a secularism that was fashioned collectively by Mahatma Gandhi, B.R. Ambedkar and Jawaharlal Nehru.

40

How to Rescue Genuine Secularism

One word conspicuous by its absence not only from the 2019 election campaign but perhaps from the entire political discourse in recent times was secularism. Prime Minister Narendra Modi brought it back in his victory speech. Most political parties in the last thirty years practised a *naqli* (fake) secularism, he said. His great achievement, he implied, was to have unmasked these fake secularists and single-handedly dismantled secularism. Until now, for Mr Modi, fake secularism has been the handmaiden of minority appeasement. The next day, however, he spoke of winning back the trust of the minorities, who, he said, have been deceived and cheated by other parties. With this, fake secularism was given a different meaning; it does not pamper but cheats minorities. In other words, it does not satisfy their real needs but only gives the illusion of doing so. Here, Mr Modi acknowledges that Muslims are a deprived lot. So what according to him is an *asli* (genuine) secularism? The answer, he said, is the inclusion of minorities in '*sabka saath sabka vikas*', which is translated by his party as 'justice to all, appeasement to none'. To this he added '*sabka vishwas*', winning the trust of all.

Fears of the Minority

On the treatment of minorities by other parties, the prime minister is partly right and partly wrong. Wrong because the insecurity among minorities is created largely by some of Mr Modi's own political supporters. Lynchings in the past few years and the fear that such random violence creates are only the tip of this gigantic iceberg. Right because when in power most non-BJP parties have done little more than provide security. Now, the condition for feeling safe and secure must not be underestimated. Freedom from fear is important, and to live in the fear of being lynched only because you are a Muslim is a very real unfreedom indeed. Yet, political parties have not helped Muslims with their *vikas*. Some have even pampered the orthodoxy within their communities and have done little to bring them out of their ghettos. So this secularism is partly fake because it has often meant tolerating minority communalism and hobnobbing with the most selfish and conservative spokespersons of the multiple Muslim communities of India.

It is very sad indeed that in the election campaign these 'fake secularists' failed miserably to speak up for Muslims. Perhaps, they were terrified that if they spoke of the legitimate interests of Muslims, they would be immediately branded as pro-Pakistan, anti-national or anti-Hindu. Yes, 'fake' secularism has failed the minorities and the people of India, but the BJP and its supporters, particularly the so-called fringe, must take a lot of blame for that. This needs course correction and the nation would be grateful to the prime minister if he began that process.

But is the secularism propounded or implied by the prime minister genuine? At least in theory, '*sabka saath sabka vikas*' gets one thing right: no individual citizen should face discrimination on grounds of religion. Basic amenities, good health, education, housing and employment should be available equally to all regardless of their religion. If he succeeds in this endeavour, he would make great strides towards realising secularism.

However, secularism combats not just discrimination and other worse forms of inter-religious domination such as exclusion, oppression and humiliation. It is equally opposed to intra-religious domination, that is, the domination over women, Dalits and dissenters within every religious community. For instance, the fight against the hierarchical caste system in India, quite like the struggle against the church in European history, is integral to the fight for secularism, a point noted by both Ambedkar and Nehru. Equally important for secularism is opposition to religious fanaticism and bigotry. Neither of these is explicitly captured by '*sabka saath, sabka vikas*'.

Misunderstanding Secularism

That Indian secularism is not anti-religious is widely understood, but not that it is simultaneously against both forms of institutionalised religious domination. How did this misunderstanding develop? First, the struggle against inter-religious domination (a defence of minority rights, opposition to majority and minority communalism) became separated from the fight against intra-religious domination (religion-related patriarchy and caste domination, fanaticism, bigotry and extremism). This then jettisoned the intra-religious dimension from the meaning of secularism, and much to the detriment of its overall value, secularism began to be identified—by both proponents and opponents alike—exclusively with the defence of minority rights.

This opened the door for viewing secularism first as a tool to protect the interests of Muslims and Christians, of no relevance to Hindus, and then for twisting it to appear as pro-Muslim and anti-Hindu. The strength of Indian secularism—its advocacy of minority cultural rights—was easily made to appear as its weakness and the burden of its defence, which, rather than be shared by all citizens, fell on the shoulders of minorities and 'pro-minority secularists'. This is unfair. Secularism is needed as much to protect Hindus from intra-religious domination, 'fringe elements' as well as proponents of religion-based caste and gender hierarchies as much as to protect minorities from their own orthodoxies and extremisms. Asli secularism plays that role; naqli secularism protects fanatics and legitimises gender and caste-based domination.

Secularism today has other problems. One is its intellectual failure to distinguish communitarianism from communalism. Communitarianism simply notes that an individual is at least partly defined by his or her religious/philosophical commitments, community and traditions. Therefore, it is entirely appropriate to claim that one is a Hindu, Muslim, Sikh, Christian, atheist, etc., and to take legitimate pride in one's community or be ashamed of it when there is good reason to be.

Communalism is different. Here, one's identity and the existence and interests of one's community are viewed, even defined, as necessarily opposed to others. It is communal to believe or act in a way that presupposes that one can't be a Hindu without being anti-Muslim or vice versa. Communalism is communitarianism gone sour. It is to see each other as enemies locked in a permanent war with one another. Every decent Indian national should be against communalism. But no one should decry legitimate forms of communitarianism. It is simply wrong to conflate communitarianism with communalism.

Attention must also be drawn to another problem of Indian secularism. Our education system often fails to distinguish religious instruction from religious education. No publicly funded school or college should have religious instruction, which is best done at home or in privately funded schools; but reasonable, decent education should include elementary knowledge of all religious traditions. A deeper understanding of these traditions is vital for it would enable students to discern their strengths and weaknesses and identify what in them is worth preserving or discarding. But Indians come out of their education system without any critical understanding of their religio-philosophical traditions. As a result, a defence of our own religious traditions or critique of others is shallow and frequently mischievous. This too is fake secularism.

What Is to Be Done?

What then must be expected from real, genuine secularism? Justice to all citizens, affirmation of all reasonable religious identities, rejection of majority communalism, careful defence of legitimate minority rights only when accompanied by a robust critique of minority extremism and a critical appraisal of religions with a deeper, empathetic grasp of their traditions. The government's primary business is to prevent religion-based violence, oppression and discrimination. Perhaps, those outside the government should attend to its other functions. Together, we may just rescue our genuine secularism.

41

Secular Hindu, Secular Muslim

Though 'secular' and 'religious' are conceptually related, people differ on the nature of this relationship. For some, 'secular' means 'anti-religious'. If so, nothing can be both secular and religious. To be secular, a state must be anti-religious. Likewise, a secular person must oppose religion. Strictly speaking, on this view, a secular Muslim or a secular Hindu is a contradiction in terms. How can one be anti-religious if one holds religious beliefs? At best, a secular Muslim, say, is a person who has given up his Islamic faith but remains Muslim culturally.

This view runs into problems because it presupposes that religion is unambiguously bad in a world where a large part of humanity continues to be religious. A secular perspective so conceived is largely irrelevant in societies such as India. Therefore, some Indians propose another conception: 'secular' means 'multireligious'. A secular state respects all religions by impartially facilitating them, funding their schools, valuing their respective traditions, etc. But this view too runs aground. It presupposes that religion is an unambiguous good despite much evidence that it generates conflict and oppression. Why then should states support religion? Besides, how can a person not be partial to his own religion? How can we ask Jains to show equal respect to, say, Islam? Now, there are healthy traditions in India that happily allow people to have multiple attachments and to respect virtually every faith. We know that Hindus go to gurudwaras with much reverence and that Hindus and Muslims visit dargahs with equal devotion. But such multi-faith loving individuals apart, it is unfair to expect people to be deeply religious as well as (impartial) secular.

A Viable Conception

I therefore wish to challenge these views and offer an entirely different conception of the secular: neither anti-religious nor naively multireligious, it means 'against institutionalised religious domination', a term I have already used in my other essays. But a more detailed explanation should help.

No one likes to be forced, controlled or dominated by another. None of us really likes to do things we do not want, particularly when they are blatantly against our own interest or good. Yet the exercise of power is rampant; not only are people forced to do things they would not otherwise do but they almost appear to do them willingly. Why? Fear plays an important role here. We submit because we know that refusal, defiance or disobedience begets the wrath of the powerful. Often, this lesson is learnt the hard way. Someone from among us is terrorised, even killed. Images of past brutality leave us with no choice but to do as we are told.

Though economic, political and status-related motives are usually behind such acts of domination, frequently the motive is religious or religion-related. Consider the following: a woman is burnt at the stake on allegations of witchcraft; a man is stoned to death for heresy—holding beliefs or opinions contrary to religious orthodoxy; a woman is not allowed to enter a temple because she is menstruating and hence considered 'polluted'; a man believed to be an 'untouchable' is humiliated and killed for riding a horse, a privilege available only to the upper castes.

Common to these outrageous real-life instances are: (a) persons are prevented from doing what they want—they are excluded, marginalised, oppressed or humiliated on religious or religion-related grounds; and that (b) both victims and perpetrators are from the same religious community. Call this intra-religious domination.

Take another set of examples. A Muslim father kills Ankit, a Hindu, for loving his daughter; churches are attacked by intolerant Hindus or militant Muslims; Hussain is unable to rent a house in a Hindu-dominated building; Akhlaq is killed because he is alleged to have eaten beef/killed a cow. Here we have (a) discrimination, oppression or sheer violence on grounds of religion but (b) both victims and perpetrators come from different religious communities. Call this inter-religious domination.

No to Hostility or Oppression

I wish to argue that 'secular' should mean not against religion or a simple-minded acceptance of all religions but 'opposition to institutionalised religious domination'. I say this because in Europe it connoted opposition to the church, a classic instance of intra-religious domination, and in India, rejection of caste or gender hierarchies, repudiation of religious extremism (intra-religious domination) and, in addition, protection of a religious community from the power of another (inter-religious domination). A secular perspective then demands that in a multireligious society, a state be designed to impartially reduce inter- and intra-religious dominations. Furthermore, it may help people develop a form of respect proper for their own religion and that of others. For this to happen, states should be impartial rather than be partial to a particular religious community (Hindus or Muslims) or a section thereof (male and/or upper castes).

But, more importantly, this view does not make a similar, virtually unrealisable demand of impartiality from religious persons. It allows persons to be partial to their own religion and yet be opposed to any aspect of it that perpetuates intra-religious or inter-religious domination. A practising Hindu or Muslim can oppose any attempt by co-religionists to dominate people of other faiths. Likewise, a Hindu is not any less Hindu if he opposes extremism within or religiously grounded caste or gender oppression. A Muslim can, without contradiction, fight violence in the name of Islam or women's oppression. Indeed, the more attached one is to a religious community, the more sensitive he is to its infirmities and greater his resolve to stem the rot within it. Such a person is partial to his own religion but precisely for that reason wants to expunge all that is oppressive or degrading within it. This is how a person can be deeply Hindu, Muslim, Sikh or Christian and yet be staunchly secular.

42

The Significance of the Term 'Secular'

What value is added by the term 'secular' to liberal democracies, that is, states that safeguard liberties of individuals and political freedoms of citizens? For some scholars, virtually nothing. Why? Because, while secularism is against discrimination only on the basis of religion, a 'liberal democracy' is against all forms of discrimination. The term 'liberal democracy' subsumes 'secularism'. Why bother with 'secularism' then? Why not commit ourselves to the priorities of a liberal democracy instead? This is a fashionable view in Europe. Even some Indian scholars argue for the sufficiency of Articles 14–16 and 19 of the Constitution.

Discrimination and Recognition

This view is inadequate, if not wrong. The word 'secular' is important. Those who claim the sufficiency of liberal democracy must think again. True, their claim has had some validity in Europe, but it is losing relevance there too. However, in places like India, it is a virtual non-starter. Why? Let us first get a handle on Europe's specificity. Secular states did not emerge in Western Europe in the immediate aftermath of the religious wars. These wars were stopped by the establishment not of a secular but a confessional state in which people were forced to embrace the religion of the king. Those who did not comply faced death or expulsion. Every European society from then on became religiously homogenous—England became Anglican; Scandinavia, Lutheran; France, Catholic. Over time, some dissenting groups were tolerated, but not without paying a price for their dissent. For example, although they were permitted to have their own church, it had to be hidden away in small bylanes. Even the rich were forced to build small chapels within the premises of their homes. Dissenters lived under the threat of persecution and daily harassment. The tolerant states of early modern Europe were a far cry from the liberal-democracies modern European states aspire to be.

Once other religions were eliminated or tamed, a struggle began against a politically meddlesome and socially oppressive church. The demand to separate church and state (which later came to be called political secularism) was supported by those who favoured free markets, private property and personal liberties. The moment this separation was sufficiently achieved, it began to be taken for granted and slowly receded into the background. In this sense, secularism lost its political and social salience in these religiously homogenous societies. The fight for a liberal state seemed sufficient.

Centuries later, when the general ethos in Western Europe witnessed the further decline of Christianity, the term 'secular' found itself linked to a humanist world view for which religion, whatever its private benefits, was potentially a public problem. While becoming increasingly less salient, it was etched in the bitter collective memory of these societies as the source of discord from which they had mercifully escaped. Religion, already on the defensive, faced greater devaluation and marginalisation. No one wanted religion-grounded recognition. With this, the idea of separation of state and religion lost its normative value further. These liberal states, where religion was no longer significant, granted formal equality to all citizens and called themselves liberal democratic.

But what if Europeans had to institute a liberty-loving, equality-caring state as soon as religious wars erupted? What if there was not much of a time lag between religious wars and the growth of a serious commitment to the values of liberty, equality and fraternity? Had this been so, demands for ending the religious persecution of dissenters and preventing religious homogenisation would have been immediate. How else could a state live up to the ideals of liberty and equality? Moreover, the dynamics of a multireligious society is such that religion would not have lost its salience. Then, instead of getting rid of religious dissenters and minorities, a general consensus might have been sought to prevent their domination by the majority religious community. Had multiple religious identities been part of the social climate, a commitment to equality would have compelled European states to give impartial public recognition to all religions. Such states would be secular precisely in the sense that Indians conceived it—something with which to fight not just religious fanaticism and intra-religious oppression but also the domination of one religion by another. They would have been forced to call themselves not just liberal (subsuming within it secular in the European sense) but also secular in the sense defended by Gandhi, Nehru and Ambedkar, where it designates impartial public recognition to all religions. My point then is that the greater the salience of religion and depth of diversity in society, the larger the prospect of intra- and inter-religious dominations and the more pressing the need for a state—given its commitment to liberty, equality and impartial recognition—to call itself secular.

Also, if religion-related bigotry and denial of recognition is present persistently, then it is hard to forget or ignore it. People potentially affected by them need to be repeatedly told that the state is there for them. The function of the term 'secular' is to do precisely that—to reassure anyone threatened by religious or religion-based exclusion, discrimination or misrecognition that the state is committed to preventing all this. To drop the word 'secular' then undermines confidence in the impartial character of the state.

Why Use a Specific Term?

The point can be made differently. Why lump together all forms of discrimination and oppression under the same general term? If the term 'secular' focuses on one specific kind of domination, why not to use it? Isn't decluttering our world and helping us focus on particular features an important function of all concepts? Why not call a flower 'red' when you have a distinguishing word for it? What point would be served by simply calling it coloured? To be sure, in some contexts, this might be sufficient. For example, if our purpose is to differentiate it from all white flowers, the use of the term 'coloured' is adequate but not if one coloured flower is to be distinguished from another. Likewise, 'secular' helps focus on institutionalised religious domination and to demarcate it from other kinds of domination based on class, gender, ethnicity, etc. Secularism implores us to resist it.

In religiously homogenous societies, particularly where the importance of religion has weakened, liberal democratic states tend to be relatively indifferent to the term 'secular'. However, in religiously strong and diverse societies such as India, the term 'secular' is indispensable. It cannot disappear from public and constitutional discourse. Is it surprising then that after a few years of exile, it resurfaced in India?

Here, we cannot follow European habits but must embrace both liberal democracy and a form of secularism that fights religion-based misrecognition. Indeed, even Europe is changing. After the migration of workers from former colonies, Europe's new religious diversity has brought religion-based recognition to the fore. Therefore, in Europe too, demands for an impartial secular state (in the Indian sense) will become louder.

43

The Future of Indian Secularism

Our public discourse is resounding with triumphalism on the one hand and laments the death or defeat of secularism on the other. It seems as if the bhoomi pujan has burnt its bodily remains, and if anyone cares to claim it, the ashes of secularism will be buried near a dargah or immersed in the Sarayu. As a child of the republic founded in 1950, one part of me wishes to join the lamentation. But the other part, nudging me to contemplate this moment, asks: does anything in India ever die? Silenced, yes; forced temporarily to go underground, maybe; transmigrate to another bodily form under a different name, possibly. But death? Gone forever? No!

Three years ago, on 6 August 2017, I had written in a short essay for *The Hindu*, included in this volume, called 'Constitutional or Party–Political Secularism?' The basic premise of the article is that secularism has paid a heavy price in our country for being at the centre of public and political discourse. It has been persistently misused and abused. Distinguishing it from constitutional–political secularism, I called this abused entity 'party-political secularism'.

Respect and Critique

It is worth repeating that constitutional secularism is marked by at least two features. First, critical respect for all religions. Unlike some secularisms, ours is not blindly anti-religious but respects religion. Unlike the secularisms of pre-dominantly single religious societies, it respects not one but all religions. However, given the virtual impossibility of distinguishing the religious from the social, as B.R. Ambedkar famously observed, every aspect of religious doctrine or practice cannot be respected. Respect for religion must be accompanied by critique.

It follows that our state must respectfully leave religion alone but also intervene whenever religious groups promote communal disharmony and discrimination on grounds of religion (an inter-religious matter) or are unable to protect their own members from the oppressions they perpetuate (an intra-religious issue). Therefore, and this is its second feature, the Indian state abandons strict separation but keeps a principled distance from all religions. For instance, it cannot tolerate untouchability or leave all personal laws as they are. Equally, it may non-preferentially subsidise schools run by religious communities. Thus, it has to constantly decide when to engage or disengage and help or hinder religion depending entirely on which of these enhances our constitutional commitment to freedom, equality and fraternity. This constitutional secularism cannot be sustained by governments alone but requires collective commitment from an impartial judiciary, a scrupulous media, civil society activists and an alert citizenry.

Advent of Opportunism

Party-political secularism, born around 40 years ago, is a perverse ideology embraced by all political parties. This secularism has jettisoned all values from Indian secularism and replaced them with opportunism. Opportunistic distance (engagement or disengagement), mainly opportunistic alliance with some of the worst elements of religious communities, particularly for the sake of immediate electoral benefit, is its unspoken slogan. Indifferent to freedom and equality-based religious reform, it has removed critical from the term 'critical respect' and bizarrely interpreted 'respect' to mean cutting deals with aggressive, visible, conservative and politicised sections of religious groups—unlocking the Babri Masjid/Ram Janmabhoomi Temple for puja and forsaking women's rights in the Shah Bano case, etc. It has even been complicit in igniting communal violence. This party-political 'secular' state cosying up alternately to the fanatical fringe of the minority and the majority was readymade for takeover by a majoritarian party. This was accomplished by removing the word 'all' and replacing it with 'majority': respect only the majority religion; never criticise it but recklessly demonise others; and ridding the state of the corrupt practice of opportunistic distance not by restoring principled distance but magically abolishing distance altogether. This is untrammelled majoritarianism masquerading as secularism, one that opposes 'pseudo-secularism' without examining its own equally unethical practices.

Today, Indian constitutional secularism is swallowed up by this party-political secularism with not even a little help from the Opposition, media and judiciary. Yet I hesitate to pronounce the death of constitutional secularism. Grounded in millennia-old pluralist traditions, it cannot easily be brushed aside. Instead, I prefer the word 'setback'. Brakes have been suddenly applied to this largely state-driven political project of dealing with inter-religious issues such as communal harmony. It has come to a screeching halt or has broken down. Does secularism then have a future?

Two Crucial Moves

I suggest two crucial moves to kick-start the discourse and practice of secularism. First, a shift of focus from a politically led project to a socially driven movement for justice. Second, a shift of emphasis from inter-religious to intra-religious issues. I invoke the name of two great leaders B.R. Ambedkar and Jawaharlal Nehru to make my point. B.R. Ambedkar dispassionately observed that when two roughly equal communities view each other as enemies, they get trapped in a majority–minority syndrome, a vicious cycle of spiralling political conflict and social alienation. This was true in the thirties and the forties. Today, feeling extremely vulnerable, Indian Muslims appear to have opted out of this syndrome. When this happens, the syndrome implodes. The result is neither open conflict nor harmony, simply an exiled existence for Muslims in their own homeland.

B.R. Ambedkar also claimed that when communities view each other as a menace, they tend to close ranks. This has another debilitating impact: all dissent within the community is muzzled and the much-needed internal reforms are stalled. If so, the collapse of the syndrome unintentionally throws up an opportunity. As the focus shifts from the other to oneself, it may allow deeper introspection within multiple dissenting voices to resurface, create conditions to root out intra-religious injustices and make its members free and equal. After all, the Indian project of secularism has been thwarted as much by party politics as by religious orthodoxy and dogma.

Europe' Example

Here, Europe's example will help. The fight against the oppression of the church was as much a popular struggle as it was driven by the state. Europe's secularism provided a principle to fight intra-religious oppressions. Nehru understood this. For him, secularism was not only a project of civic friendship among religious communities but also of opposition to religion-based caste and gender oppressions—an endeavour at the heart of our own socially driven freedom and equality-oriented reform movements in the nineteenth century. For the moment, the state-driven political project of secularism and its legal constitutional form appear to have taken a hit. But precisely this 'setback' can be turned into an opportunity to revitalise the social project of secularism. Since the Indian state has failed to support victims of oppressions sanctioned by religion, a peaceful and democratic secularism from below provides a vantage point from which to carry out a much-needed internal critique and reform of our own respective religions and to enable their compatibility with constitutional values of equality, liberty and justice. A collective push from young men and women untainted by the politics and ideological straitjacketing of the recent past may help strengthen the social struggle of emancipation from intra-religious injustices. Those who most benefit from upholding these constitutional values—the oppressed minorities, Dalits, women, citizens sick to death of zealotry or crass commercialisation of their faiths—must together renew this project.

Inter-community Relations

I am not suggesting that we must hereby ignore inter-religious issues. But having itself produced disharmony, it is surely beyond the capacity of the current state to restore communal harmony. But distance and the freedom from mutual obsession give communities a breathing space. Each can now explore resources within to construct new ways of living together. The issue here is not simple retrieval of older, failed modes of religious toleration. The political project of secularism arose precisely because religious toleration no longer worked. Needed today are new forms of socio-religious reciprocity, crucial for the business of everyday life and novel ways of reducing the political alienation of citizens, a democratic deficit whose ramifications go beyond the ambit of secularism.

If a critique of religion is to come at least partly from within, then its idiom must also draw from local religiosities and the multiple languages in which they find expression. A critique purely from outside, one which is not partly immanent, will not work, nor can popular democratic struggles be taken over by middle-class vanguardism. However, such struggles too need support from intellectuals. But to be effective, these intellectuals should already have learnt from a wide variety of cultural traditions, both natal and those outside their immediate ambit. Only then will their voice carry weight and be heard.

PART V

Deep Issues That Matter

44

The Mimetic, the Mythic and the Theoretical

One of the least understood functions of critical reflection is to reconcile conflicting viewpoints and find common ground between positions that appear to be polar opposites. One such opposition exists between the secular and the religious. Since religion is usually associated with myth and ritual and the secular with science and reason-directed theory, I wish here to question the polarity between myth and ritual on the one hand and science and theory on the other.

To do so, I take help from the work of the evolutionary psychologist Merlin Donald. He argues that over time, sequentially, human beings have developed three distinct cultural capacities by which to understand the human and non-human world. The first such capacity, called mimetic, developed almost two million years ago, stored directly in skills and is largely performative. Here, we use our bodies not only to communicate with each other by expressive gestures (anger or joy on our face, head movements to say no, eye brow to express surprise or displeasure, etc.) but also to collectively enact past, present and future events (the coronation of the king, the *shraddha* ceremony for ancestors, wearing white clothes at mourning rituals, etc.).

The second capacity that developed 100,000–250,000 years ago is our ability for grammatical language and to construct oral narratives. To tell stories, folk tales and moral fables; to freely use our imagination to make sense of how we and our world originated and what might happen to us when we or our world dies; to imagine 'heaven' and 'hell' and utopias or dystopias on or beyond earth. These are fact-defying, imaginative constructs, replete with fictitious events, fantasy, archetypical figures, heroes and villains. Donald calls this capacity mythic.

Finally, the third capacity developed 3,000–5,000 years ago, with which we are able to step back and look beyond what we experience and conceive a world outside or deep within us, a world unearthed by disengaged reason, free of our own personal, subjective properties—an objective world. It is a form of abstract thinking that takes us beyond our immediate context and allows us to think with a greater degree of generality. Dependent on the written word, it encourages us to think about thinking: to discern the internal structure of arguments and unearth the assumptions and presuppositions of our thought. This is thinking with controlled imagination—with constraints of evidence and rational argument. In short, it is the world of science, argumentative philosophy and abstract reasoning, which Donald calls 'the theoretic'.

Compartmentalising Our Lives

That these three capacities can sometimes work against each other is not in question, but what creates polarity between them is an ideology that makes them mutually exclusive, which claims that each succeeding capacity is superior and properly emerges when the previous, inferior capacity is abolished. Thus, a move to a higher theoretical stage of reason-based science and philosophy necessitates leaving behind the lower mythic and mimetic stages. A theoretic culture is achieved by eliminating the vestigial elements of the mythic and the mimetic.

Despite this ideology, some of us try to resolve this conflict by compartmentalising our lives. This has taken two forms. One is found in the lives, for instance, of some scientists, engineers, doctors and economists. In their research or techno-professional life, they allow the supremacy of hard-nosed reason. In their personal, social and political life, they let religious myths and rituals rule. The other is found in educated, anti-religious and secular-minded persons. They dismiss myths and rituals as features of a bygone era and live most aspects of their life as if governed by reason alone, but they allow the mimetic to survive in sport, theatre and dance and the mythic to endure in novels, poetry and films, in art and entertainment.

But such solutions are patchy and unsatisfactory. They continue to be mired in deep misunderstanding. In fact, as Donald tells us, these three capacities have emerged sequentially—one came after and on the shoulders of the other but without destroying its predecessor. It modified, not replaced it. Moreover, they are not hierarchically related. Each makes a distinctive and complementary contribution to human understanding. The truth is that all of us, regardless of whether we are religious or secular, partake in all three cultures—mimetic, mythic and theoretic. Each one of us deploys these three cultural capacities to varying degrees. The modern mind remains a complex mix of mimetic, mythic and theoretical elements.

Take the mimetic, for instance. We have wedding rituals to reinforce mutual commitment and commemorative rituals such as keeping a two-minute silence at 11 o'clock on 30 January each year to *not* forget Gandhi's sacrifice. Why? Because rituals play a crucial role in underlining the collective significance of an act or bring stability in human interactions that are ephemeral and may otherwise fall apart. Have you ever seen a singles tennis match ending without the ritual of players hugging each other or shaking hands to express that their rivalry is over and they are friends once again? Modern, secular lives are also governed by myths. Our popular culture is mythic; it cares two hoots for reason or evidence, fictitiously connects disparate events and influences us by heroic exemplars, such as the mythical angry young man. Why, even 'scientific' economics generates myths such as that of the rational economic man!

In short, secular rationalists—theoretically minded scientists and professionals—would do well to acknowledge the continuing hold of myths and rituals in their lives. But equally, those immersed in religious myth and ritual must value not only scientific reason but also the social uses of reason in clarifying meaning, unearthing beliefs and pictures that have receded into the background, finding or generating common ground for discussion and mutual understanding for reconciliation.

45

Are Rituals Still Important?

For many contemporary Indians, religious ritual is simply a part of daily life. On the other hand, many others won't want to be caught performing a ritual; they feel uneasy. An impression that rituals are entirely redundant, optional extras at best, is a pervasive feature of modernist consciousness that treats them as vestiges of a premodern, archaic past to be left behind as we become more educated and rational. This is partly because of the association of rituals with religion and mostly because of the belief that they can't survive the test of reason; they are meaningless, empty of content, needlessly repetitive and time-consuming; they sprout superstition and involve nonsensical mumbo jumbo. Moreover, they seem to reinforce a collectivist mentality that gives little room for individual freedom and innovation. This critique of ritual is not without precedents. Indeed, it has a long history.

In ancient India, even dissenting Brahmins questioned rituals when they became elaborate and expensive; the loss of simplicity and economy derailed them from their original purpose. Later, Upanishadic thinkers indicted them for their inanity; they were vacuous unless they related to knowledge hidden from common sense, that is, what later came to be viewed as the deeper relationship between Brahman and Atman. An even more radical critique of Vedic ritual was launched by Jains and Buddhists, who questioned the materialist motivations behind them. What use are rituals performed in order to procure this or that worldly good? Two of India's greatest sons Gautam Buddha and Ashoka shifted the moral axis away from rituals to kindness and compassion towards all living beings. Proponents of bhakti challenged the ethical centrality of rituals and even social reformers such as Dayanand rejected the excessive ritualism in Hinduism.

The Significance of Rituals

Two things follow from this. First, if a rational critique of ritual was already present in the ancient world, then we can no longer divide our social universe as being ritual-oriented in the past and reason-oriented in the present. Second, this long history of critique shows that rituals survive criticism. No matter how hard we try, they can't be jettisoned. Why then, despite rational criticism, do rituals continue to play an important role in human life?

Consider this: We are not satisfied with receiving our university degree certificates by post or an SMS. We voluntarily take part in a highly theatrical ceremony with differently codified dress for those who bestow university degrees and those who receive them. We reiterate our resolve to keep our country independent by unfurling the national flag every 15 August and celebrate our Constitution through the Republic Day parade. We have memorials to not forget our loved ones when they are no longer with us. We continue to have rituals of healing, rituals to mark rites of passage such as attaining puberty or getting married, death rituals, rituals to mark the entry into the country's Test team, as when a cap is handed over by a senior cricketer to one making his debut. We even have simple rituals of ordinary social interaction such as rituals of greeting.

It is because we are not mere machines or biological organisms but expressive creatures; we do not express ourselves only in oral and written speech but directly in bodily performances, that we continue to abide by existing rituals—the Hindu wedding ritual of going around the fire has been prevalent virtually uninterrupted for over 3,000 years—or invent or adopt new ones.

All these formal acts and utterances are reiterated and performed publicly, theatrically, so that all relevant people can participate in them. Many rituals break away from the routine of daily life to emphasise that certain events are special. But most of all, it is because rituals are the most economical way of reducing the fragility of social life (nothing in social life is permanent!)—establishing and consolidating social facts so that we continue to have them. Neither words nor rational argumentation can do this job as efficiently as rituals can.

Furthermore, even skills learned with meticulous attention to rules soon assume the form of ritual-resembling habits. By virtue of reduplicative practices—consider how tennis strokes are perfected by constant repetition—they become unavailable to consciousness, and precisely for that reason become far more efficient. It is their very thoughtlessness that helps achieve this. Ironically, we ignore the importance of rituals only when we shut our eyes to our daily life. We can throw out one ritual for good reason, but soon enough, for a different and equally good reason, another one occupies the space left vacant by its departure.

Two Filters

So rituals and ceremonies that involve skills and modes of action learnt painstakingly by our ancestors and transmitted inter-generationally to become part of collective memory and cultural repertoire are necessary. The question then is not whether or not to have rituals but what kind of rituals to have. I suggest all rituals must meet two criteria: one ethical and the other aesthetic. The aesthetic requires us to align our rituals as close as possible to other forms of memetic activities—dance, music, drama, etc. I won't say much else here except by pointing to the vast difference between V.V.S. Laxman's wristy stroke play and the stodginess of Geoffrey Boycott or the ugly heaves of a tailender. The ethical is even more important. It first compelled us to abandon human and animal sacrifice and continues to demand that we jettison any ritual that legitimises domination. So, reason must question, say, wedding rituals that reinforce hierarchies between men and women but it will never succeed if it questions the very idea of ritual.

46

Why Language Matters

The frequent emotional outburst and sense of indignation expressed by Tamil speakers against the perceived threat of the imposition of Hindi compels us to ask why does language matter so much to us? Why are we deeply attached to a particular language? Why do we identify with it so strongly?

According to one theory of the nature and importance of language, it is an instrument by which we describe the world outside it. We have ideas in our heads, and language, consisting of signs—marks or sounds—is needed only to communicate these ideas to others. Our mental representations are private but become public once words are used to designate them. We convey our thoughts to others in and through words. If this is the only function of language—to designate, describe and communicate things and thoughts that exist independently of it in order to make them public—why would anybody be attached to a particular language? Can't this job be performed by *any* language?

So this account fails to explain our deep attachment to a particular language—our mother tongue. It doesn't explain the emotional intensity with which people fight for their own language. Is there an account of language that can?

Objects and Relations

The 'constitutive theory' by the well-known philosopher Charles Taylor does. According to this theory, pre-linguistic humans had already begun to express themselves, but when they became language users, they changed fundamentally. Language helped them articulate explicitly what was earlier somewhat vague and inchoate. It changed the nature of their thought. Language makes certain features of an entity more salient than others, pushes some into the background while foregrounding others. As we fix our attention only on some features, we draw boundaries and make distinctions, no matter how rough, fluid or porous. We contrast them with other things. To take a simple example from the English language, when we sit at a table, we use a material object with a flat top with one or more legs that serves a range of purposes such as eating, writing, meeting and so on, which is different from, say, a bench or a stool that might look similar but fulfils different purposes. These particular purposes and activities are part of the meaning of the term 'table', crucial to learning how to use it. None of this is possible without a certain kind of reflective, focussed awareness, which literally brings into existence a piece of wood *as* a table. So the word 'table' brings a new thought, a new social object and a new set of activities into being. Without that term or its equivalents, the sociocultural object, table, would not exist. It is in this sense that words, thought and the world are constitutively linked.

Just as the objects that surround us are linguistically constituted, so too are our relations with one another. For instance, learning the use of the words 'teacher' and 'student' is to learn a whole gamut of social relations crucial to the practice and institution of education. It also helps constitute how those performing these roles (teachers and students) may stand in relation to each other—formal or informal, friendly or withdrawn, casual or serious and so on. Furthermore, language constitutes not only a web of power-laden or power-free social relationships but also new emotions. For example, anger experienced by non-linguistic animals is different from indignation, which depends on a grasp of what is just and unjust. To admire someone is more than just being attracted to her; it is to see her as having exceptional virtues or achievements. We don't just desire things or are repulsed by them but also evaluate, by a standard, which desires are worthy and which among all worthy entities are of even higher worth. This recognition of a standard—the distinction between correct and incorrect or morally right and wrong, a specifically human characteristic—is also constituted by language. In sum, unlike the purely physical, chemical or biological world, the human world is word-laden and shot through with language. We are, as Professor Taylor puts it, language animals, living in a dimension—the linguistic dimension—in which other animals do not.

The Attachment to One Language

Another feature of language to which the constitutive theory draws our attention is its strong communitarianism. Word meaning is created and recreated in speech, conversation and dialogue with others. It follows that a language would not exist or grow without a speech community, a community of language users. So Tamil is sustained by and grows within the specific community of Tamil speakers, so also Bengali or Hindi. And it is not just speech community that shapes and creates language but language also constitutes and sustains speech community. Since thousands of languages exist and are nourished by their speakers, different linguistic vocabularies imply different ways of constituting and experiencing the world, each having different feelings, concerns, sensibilities, aspirations and so on. Language makes us what we are; specific languages make us the specific creatures that we are.

So, our own language matters to us because it constitutes us and our world—our own specific way of being in the world. Language makes us at home in the world. In a manner of speaking, we dwell comfortably only in our own particular language.

Because the particular language we learn constitutes us and our world, our relationship with it simply has to be very deep. And we all feel a special bond with all those who speak the same language. Just imagine the alienation of, say, a rural Tamil speaker who lands unprepared in Texas, and imagine equally his relief and elation if he ever finds a Tamil-speaker there. Fifty years ago, Tamilians probably felt similarly in Punjab.

The constitutive theory explains the deep attachment people have to particular languages. It explains why a particular set of language speakers respond with indignation when faced with perceived threat to their language. They fight to defend it.

What does not follow, however, is that languages are self-contained entities. Instead, they are, as the sociologist Steven Lukes puts it, 'clusters or assemblages of heterogeneous elements with varying origins', dynamic constellations in a moving galaxy, intermixing, borrowing from one another, being shaped and in turn shaping one another. The demand for purity is an enemy of language growth and innovation. Consider the Sanskrit term 'puja'. It has been suggested that it may have *not* Indo-European but Dravidian roots, deriving from the Tamil word '*pu*' (flowers). How many of us know the Sanskrit word 'Veda', or 'vid', is linked to 'wit' and 'witness', the

English 'daughter' to *dugdha* (milk), or 'free' linked etymologically to the Sanskrit '*preeta*' (love)? Languages that now seem radically distinct from each other have evolved together over a long, interconnected global history.

One must remember the ease and dedication with which people born in one linguistic community embrace languages different from their own. Indeed, we can be attached to more than one language. Just think of the Hebrew–English-speaking Indologist David Shulman's love for Tamil and Telugu, not to speak of the passionate bilinguality of good translators. So while deep attachment to one's language is understandable, the pathological obsession with which people defend its purity, uniqueness and superiority is unwarranted, pathetic and unforgivable.

47

Private, Public and Political Morality

Though related, political, public and private moralities are not identical. They may come from the same source but they are distinct. This point has been noted in the Western tradition since at least Machiavelli. But its lineage in India is ancient.

Ethics in Three Domains

Take, for example, Ashoka, who can be interpreted as having spoken of dhamma (ethics) in three distinct domains. The first is interpersonal morality. Each of us has special obligations to our children, spouse, parents, teachers and relatives. We have a duty towards those under our special care, including the aged, 'servants', animals and, occasionally, strangers.

Second, intergroup morality in public life. Crucial here is the harmony between different religio–philosophical groups generated by the exercise of *samyama* (self-restraint). He particularly emphasised the importance of *vācāguti*—controlling one's tongue to be critical of other groups only if there is good reason to, only on appropriate occasions and always moderately, and also to praise one's own group only when there is good reason to, only on appropriate occasions and always moderately. Neither hate speech nor speech glorifying oneself was acceptable as part of public morality, a point very relevant in our times.

Ashoka then spoke of power-related political morality, specifying what rulers and the ruled owe one another. Subjects owe obedience to their king. But the ruler too owed something to his subjects: to ensure *janahita*, the good of all (including all living species), and *janasukham*, happiness not only in this life but also in the afterlife. To achieve this, rulers and their officials must display *damdasamata* and *viyohalasamata* (impartiality in meting out punishment and in politico-legal acts more generally). This sums up the core of Ashoka's political morality: a commitment to impartiality—to justice.

What then is the difference between private/public morality and political morality? In our personal life, for instance, while dealing with those with whom we have close daily encounters, such as our family, friends or 'servants', we can't help but be partial, and in the larger public domain too, where we face people with different religio-philosophical sensibilities, we can't entirely escape some degree of partiality to our own world view. By contrast, the political domain requires the impartial or just use of power for the good of all.

Family, Civil Society and State

Two thousand years later, the German philosopher Friedrich Hegel made similar points, although in a different way and in an entirely different context. He distinguished three spheres of human life: family, civil society and the state. The family, Hegel claimed, was the smallest community in which its members do not even distinguish themselves from one another. Their identities are fused. A family is bound by emotional ties, mutual love and affection. Members take pride in each other's achievements and feel a strong sense of shame at others' wrongdoing. Morality here is guided by unarticulated feelings.

The family is different from another sphere of life that Hegel designated civil society but more appropriately be called 'market society'. Here, each person acts as an individual with a sharply defined sense of her own interests, which are distinct from, compete and may even clash with the interests of others. No one is tied to the other by bonds of love or affection. Since there is no community but only an aggregate of individual interests, there is no commonly held ethic either. Competitive life is governed by coercive legal rules to regulate the pursuit of self-interest. At best, each individual devises her own subjective moral maxims.

Finally, Hegel spoke about a third domain where people once again see themselves as members of a large political community—as citizens of a state. Citizens in a political community must be bound together neither by feelings nor by self-interest but by a commitment to common values discovered by public reason—values such as political freedom, solidarity, shared traditions and cultural heritage. Morality in this domain requires that we overcome our loyalty to blood relations, not pursue only our private interests and commit instead to using power grounded in shared principles. Love and hate are largely imposters in this domain, where consensus is forged by the use of public reason. Its democratic version requires that we deliberate and, guided by values of openness, equal respect and justice, help each other arrive at impartial laws and public policies acceptable in principle to everyone in the polity.

Furthermore, those who wield political power must realise that what they do has enduring consequences affecting the lives of an incalculably large number of people. This brings with it enormous public responsibility that derives in no small part from the fact that they have at least temporary legitimacy to use force against ordinary citizens. They have, at their disposal, an apparatus of violence simply unavailable to heads of families or members of civil society. Powerful politicians, therefore, must show great care and sensitivity to the appropriate use of force and violence.

Private and Political Morality

One important implication of the difference between private and political morality is this: it is sometimes believed that moral scrupulousness in one's private life automatically guarantees high moral stature in political life. This simply does not follow. Those wielding public power may refuse to enrich themselves, their family or friends and resist from obtaining sexual favours. But such 'cleanliness' need not entail scrupulous political morality. What use is personal incorruptibility if the politician is partial to or discriminates against one particular community, abandons public reason, smashes dissent to concentrate power in his own hands, makes arbitrary use of force and lives in the illusion that he is greater than all the institutions that surround him? What if he begins to believe that he alone possesses the truth or knows the good of the entire community—and precisely because of the moral restrictions he has placed on his personal life, feels released from any restriction on the use of power in the political arena? In short, a person who is profoundly moral in his private life may brazenly violate all norms of political morality, undermining justice and public reason. Conversely, it is entirely possible that a person who has morally slipped in his private life (cheated on one's spouse, enriched himself, etc.) respects the integrity of public institutions, is acutely sensitive to the moral costs of violence, shows a deep commitment to justice and upholds reason-based democratic norms.

Don't get me wrong, I am not suggesting that politicians are free to abandon private morality. But we often find comfort in the illusion that there is one simple, seamless morality reflected equally in private and in public. In fact, most humans are complex moral agents. It would be wonderful if our private and political moralities were perfectly aligned and we achieved the highest moral standards in both. But in a non-ideal world, we can only hope that when people choose to lead a life in politics, they will at least follow minimum norms of political morality even as they fail to be scrupulously moral in their private lives.

48

Why Institutions Matter

There is much talk these days about the decline in our institutions. Aren't they failing to perform, being systematically undermined, even destroyed? On the one hand, people are heard lamenting that our courts are compromised, that our Parliament is dysfunctional or that our higher education is in a mess. On the other hand, it is also heard that as long as a powerful individual is getting things done, why care about institutions? The rules and procedures of institutions are cumbersome and time-consuming. If the same result is obtained with bypassing them, why bother? So, do institutions matter? If they do, why? What are institutions meant to do? What are they anyway?

I propose that an institution be seen as closely related to a social practice but not identified with it. How can we make sense of this rather opaque claim? Let's go step by step. What is a social practice? First, unlike an individual act, it is a practice that necessarily involves several people. No single individual has the power to sustain it. Second, unlike a one-off act, a practice is recurrent. Third, people jostling in a crowd have no collective purpose; indeed, they may be purposeless altogether. A social practice, on the other hand, exists for the realisation of a common need or purpose and therefore requires coordination and cooperation among individuals. A practice is necessarily sustained by a group. Fourth, a practice is skill-based and therefore must be learnt. And being collective, it involves a pooling together of skills. An individual throwing a ball against a wall is not engaging in a social practice but a fielder throwing it to a wicketkeeper in a match is.

To sum up, a social practice is an enduring, purposive and valuable activity of a group sustained by the pooling together of multiple skills. Without social practices, human life is neither possible nor worthwhile.

Sustaining Social Practices

Enough on social practice, but where does an institution figure in this? Like other human artefacts, practices are fragile and have a propensity to disintegrate without collective effort. They need to be collectively established by continual reiteration and renewal. But meaningful replication by groups requires mutual trust and expectations, best achieved by fixing roles and formulating rules enforced by someone in a position of authority. So when a social practice embeds roles and is governed by rules or norms that tightly bind a group together and organise it into a stable collective, we have an institution. Thus, cricket, education, medicine and governance are practices but cricket associations, universities, hospitals and government departments are institutions. We frequently use the term 'institution' both for valued social practices and for rule-governed, organised groups, but perhaps it is best to reserve the term for rule-governed organisations rather than for valued social practices.

And this gives a clue to why institutions matter: they help sustain valuable social practices. Besides, they unburden individuals by economising on time and effort. Since they evolve by collective effort over time, they embody social wisdom not immediately available to individual consciousness. Imagine if each individual was to take part in a practice as if it was starting from scratch, needing just his critical moral reflection to kick in! We would be left thinking endlessly with no time to act. This is why we minimise our thinking and outsource it to social rules and norms; it's also precisely why we need rule-bound institutions in the first place.

Institutional Morality

It follows that institutions give birth to a new, emergent morality: roles must be performed well, rules must be followed and those given the task of enforcing them must do so responsibly, fairly and impartially. Institutions give rise to a set of role-specific rights and duties. Only a surgeon has the right to use a knife on a patient's body; only professional judges can give binding judgements in court; only those with the required qualification have a right to teach in universities. No matter how great an individual captain is, cricket teams win only when each player performs as his assigned role requires and when rules are properly enforced by the umpire. Each social practice is sustained largely by its own specific institutional morality.

Breakdown and Renewal

When an institution breaks down or is deliberately attacked, at stake is the valuable social practice related to it. The practice of education suffers when universities are run by people with little understanding of academic norms and values. If the election commission turns partisan, the democratic practice of free and fair elections is severely jeopardised. Active citizenship is endangered when institutions of media abandon fair and objective reporting of processes and events or when political decision-making is done behind closed doors by people who misuse power. When a powerful individual bypasses institutions, the damage he causes to social practices is incalculable.

Institutions are corrupted when they begin to thwart rather than facilitate practices; they become hollow if disconnected entirely from practices that give them their point and begin to serve only themselves and their officialdom. For example, when a university administration consumes more funds for its salary and perks and spends less on the academic life of students and teachers or when politicians and bureaucrats forget why they occupy the political and administrative positions they do, which is to serve the people.

Of course, like individuals who constitute them, institutions also go to sleep! They suffer from lethargy and inertia. When that happens, they need to be reawakened and renewed, something impossible without collective self-reflection. If so, both for their own sake and for the sake of the practices they serve, institutions must not throttle this activity of self-reflection. From time to time, there should be collective deliberation about the purpose and importance of social practices and institutions and on why they matter.

49

Why Universities Matter: The Case of JNU

I proposed in chapter 2 that a nation be seen as a people in continuous conversation. I'm sure there are other places in the country where the Indian nation is forged daily. But for me, JNU was the pre-eminent site where this happened.

A Microcosm of India

In my early education in Delhi, I encountered students and teachers largely from Punjab and UP, and occasionally from West Bengal, Tamil Nadu or Maharashtra. But in JNU, every living minute of my years as a teacher between 1980 and 2005, I encountered scores of people from every nook and cranny of India. A university, by definition, is an ecumenical, all-inclusive institution, but how many universities manage to attain this ideal? JNU was able to do this by being hospitable to women and minorities and because of its sensitive admission policy that inducted candidates from virtually every region of India—aspiring men and women from economically deprived areas and those historically disadvantaged by their place in the caste hierarchy. JNU was a microcosm of India with all its beauty and warts.

An equally attractive feature of JNU was its democratic culture. Where in India would you find a university in which student union elections were held with only hand-painted posters and no money power? Political talk from one side was countered with more talk from the other. These often turned into verbal duels and intellectual fisticuffs but never physically violent. JNU elections were a lively festival of discussion, argument, polemic and discursive contestation that harvested alert, engaged citizens, many of whom found a home in national politics and went on to become public officials committed to the Constitution.

But, perhaps, the most enticing feature of the university was its academic programme. Teaching was a serious undertaking; no teacher dared miss a class. Classrooms overflowed with students, many of whom came voluntarily from multiple departments across disciplines. Large MA classes could last up to two hours with students concentrating on every word uttered by the teachers. Yet, if a point needed clarification or an argument some elaboration, a raised hand could gently, uninhibitedly interrupt the lecture; then the class would join in an exciting, unexpected conversation. The art of listening, conversing, discussing and debating would be taken to new heights. In smaller MPhil classes, neither the teacher nor students would want to leave the classroom until the caretaker arrived to lock the building. Even as some discussants left for home or hostel, others would trundle down to a nearby dhaba to try and unravel the mysteries of the social and political universe. I reckon most teachers earned the respect and affection of their students who, without being overawed, looked up to them for intellectual guidance.

Perhaps I am overstating my case and should nuance it. Undeniably, many students in their first semester were intimidated by students from metropolitan cities, fluent in English and with superior academic preparation. How much more anxious and daunted they must be in the presence of highly qualified teachers? This must be particularly true for Dalits and students from 'backward regions', who barely spoke English, and when they did, spoke with a heavy local tint. These students, struggling to keep their head above water, could manage a grade no higher than B-minus. However, by the end of the second semester, they grew in confidence, spoke up in class and improved their grades. Their transformation was exhilarating—a teacher's triumph no doubt, but also a victory of the culture of the university that encouraged learning from peers.

In the school and college where I studied, the brightest students were seen to produce results without hard work, as if by innate ideas or else by tuning into a satellite of knowledge from which ideas beamed directly to their brain at the speed of light! But in reality, knowledge production and acquisition are qualitatively different. Real ideas grow and are learnt with patience, hard work and commitment. Books and journal articles have to be read over and over again. One has to sweat it out in the library. The engagement with ideas has to move beyond the library and the classroom into small, intensive, friendly groups. Then, a retreat into monkish solitude is needed for transcribing research and to learn to throw away more words than one eventually keeps. A coherent piece of writing emerges after years of arduous labour. In the best universities of the world, scholars win respect and admiration by this dedicated effort. JNU competed with the best in the world because it taught everyone the value of such intellectual toil.

Original ideas germinate when research and teaching are creatively connected and when teachers test their burgeoning ideas on young productive minds that, untamed by disciplinary protocols, raise adventurous, hitherto unasked questions. For this cutting-edge research, teachers need the freedom to design and restructure their courses every other year. JNU gave us this opportunity. Moreover, impartiality was not conflated with impersonality. Anonymity was set aside and question papers were set and marked by the same teacher who taught the course—a new form taken by the *guru–shishya parampara*. In JNU, learning occurred in creative in-between spaces where a complex dialectic was at play between formality and informality, equality and legitimate hierarchy, friendship and civility, unilateral instruction and unregulated discussion.

Shortcomings

However, JNU had its share of weaknesses too. First, an unwholesome reliance by some on jargon, abstraction and ideology. Theoretical abstraction counted for more than lived experience; seductive ideologies mattered more than what the eyes could see and the ears could hear. What I say might ring untrue in the face of stories by JNU students on how they learnt the tools to grasp the social, political, economic and historical realities of their country. Yet, a tearing hurry to connect ideas to the interests of social groups, as if they are born to serve only one or another class, marred their understanding. Very often this led, on the one hand, to a failure to detect multiple possibilities in ideas and, on the other, to a disconnection from the real world.

To be sure, good academic research requires a degree of disconnection from the world, at least in phases. But eventually, researchers must find a way to reconnect. This is one of the big mysteries of JNU: how could this happen simultaneously—the connect and disconnect with reality? And while the production of knowledge is accompanied with intellectual waste, to have grounded a painfully self-righteous and incestuous politics on this undigested excess of abstractions was self-indulgent, delusional and exclusionary, unworthy of a great centre of learning.

My second issue is with the mindset behind a glaring omission. It took JNU forty years to launch a philosophy department, usually the mainstay of universities around the world. I guess this was due to the pervasive social scientism in the sixties, when JNU was established. Equally disturbing is the absence of a deeper collective study of Indian religions. We may more easily omit the teaching of what is called religion in the West but not what is 'religion' in India. For good or for bad, multiple religious cultures partly constitute the social reality in India. A refusal to engage with them is to get a partial, distorted picture of the Indian reality. This only plays into the hands of those who wilfully manipulate these profoundly plural religious experiences for their own nefarious political benefit.

50

The Artist in the Public Sphere

It is a truism that our actions are determined by what we believe ourselves to be—by our self-understandings. Each of us carries a picture of what we are—a model of ourselves that guides us through the world, shapes our motivations and makes us behave one way rather than another. If so, what are the dominant self-understandings of artists in our times, particularly in relationship to state and politics?

Not long ago, in strongly traditional, hierarchy-ridden societies, even great artists saw themselves as beholden to their rulers. Deference and submission were crucial ingredients in their mental make-up; after all, a ruler was the primary source of patronage. Today, two very different self-understandings of artists are dominant.

Two Kinds of Self-understanding

Most modern artists see themselves as producers of cultural or aesthetic values, which they embody in their work by using imagination and thought in their chosen medium. Since this complex process takes place largely in the study, the studio or the aangan, some artists see themselves as intensely private beings playing little role in public, except while performing or exhibiting their work. Deeply inclined to mind their own business, they may even develop a cultivated indifference to public issues. Yet as creators of aesthetic values, they are also their custodians. So when these values are threatened by the practices of the state or by oppressive social forces, even they, unless living in fear, don't stay quiet. Therefore, in relation to society and politics, they are watchdogs. The great, quietly conservative and Upanishad-influenced poet T.S. Eliot said succinctly, 'We should be vigilantly watching the conduct of politicians and economists for the purpose of criticising and warning, when the decisions of politicians and economists are likely to have cultural consequences.' When cultural values are adversely affected, artists must go public, Eliot suggested.

Alternatively, when general conditions necessary for the functioning of all cultural institutions are undermined and norms of minimal decency are violated, the outraged artist must confront the state, simply as an ordinary, decent human being. An obvious example is Rabindranath Tagore, who, after the infamous Jallianwala Bagh massacre, returned his knighthood. Remember how artists took to the street when in 1989 theatre activist Safdar Hashmi was bludgeoned to death by political goons? George Orwell put this point well: 'When an artist engages in politics [joins the resistance, fights fascists] he does so as a human being, but not as an artist.' The implication is that when artists eventually throw themselves into political struggle, they discard their social persona and return to basic humanity. When elementary moral sense is consistently violated, they join hands with others to fight it without insisting on their exclusivity or difference.

Pure Artist, Pure Citizen or Both

This first largely apolitical self-understanding developed in pre-democratic societies with little political liberty, where popular participation in political decision-making was virtually absent.

Without a proper public sphere, an attitude of indifference to state and politics was built into the self-understanding of artists. However, a new kind of artist with a second, very different self-understanding emerged in democracies where citizens entered a newly constituted public domain with views on the whole society. Such artists do not separate their social persona as artists from their political persona as citizens. They are always artist-citizens, acting sometimes as pure artists, sometimes as pure citizens and often as both. They belong to a newly evolved social category, the public intellectual, who, as the French philosopher Jean-Paul Sartre famously put it, necessarily 'fails to mind his own business'. Artists feel responsible not only for what happens in their own field but also for just about everything in the world and try to fulfil this responsibility by constant social and political engagement. Inextricably linked with the public domain, they feel incomplete without it and enter it to express themselves in the language they know best: the language of art.

And without always intending to do so, they enlighten their public. The greater an artist, the deeper her insights and the more she is expected to see further than most others, which enable people to understand what, left to themselves, they do not. Doing so through their work and example becomes an important part of their self-definition. They begin to hope that, mediated by public opinion, art may bring about a change in civil society and state institutions. So by gentle instruction or dialogic exchange, artists seek to mould public opinion too. They see themselves simultaneously as sophisticated pedagogues or co-participants in the production of a shared culture.

It is in this context that we should view the public acts of some of our artists. It is absurd to expect the Caranatic vocalist T.M. Krishna to be servile to the state or be indifferent to wrongdoing in society and politics. Artists like him simultaneously embody both kinds of self-understanding. Though their art demands that they be intensely private and get massive swathes of time to themselves, they speak out in public on moral decay, social injustice or political impropriety as decent human beings. Equally, as public intellectuals—as artist-citizens—they feel compelled to continually comment on society and politics through their art. They protest. They criticise the government of the day. They oppose social oppression. To be sure, acting on both self-understandings is not every artist's cup of tea. One's childhood and temperament strongly determine one's attitude to persistent public engagement. Equally, expressing oneself politically cannot be the moral obligation of every artist. But it cannot be anyone's contention today that the primary duty of the artist is to mind her own business or to confine herself to 'non-political' art. In doing what he does, Krishna is neither being an ideologue nor showing a narrow political bias. He is being true to his calling as a responsible artist.

51

Deep Sociability: Sharing Sacred Spaces

We live in dark times, perhaps among the darkest in living memory. Not a single day passes without news of rape or lynching, not to speak of treacherous lies, vitriolic rumours, venomous threats, fearmongering, hatred and violence. And then, apart from these human misdemeanours, there is the devastation caused by nature's fury. But amidst this gloom and destruction, one is also blessed to witness acts of exemplary courage, care and compassion.

Particularly heartening are some stories from Kerala during the devastating floods of 2018. Two groups of fasting Muslim youths reportedly spent the second day of the Haj pilgrimage removing post-flood slush and silt from temples in Wayanad and Malappuram. In Mannarkkad, the Sunni Students' Federation washed the Ayyappa temple. In Thrissur, where masjids were inundated with water, the Purappillikavu Rakteshwari temple hall was thrown open to Muslims to offer Eid namaz.

More heart-warming is the fact that such acts are not restricted to Kerala or to the present. In June, the Sri Krishna math of Udipi held an Iftar party in its premises. In September 2017, when the ground in Uttarakhand's Joshimath was submerged under rainwater, local Sikhs offered their gurudwara to Muslims for Eid prayers. The same year, religious organisations funded the Sikh-run Khalsa Aid to hold langars for Rohingya refugees on the Bangladesh–Myanmar border.

I can't but reach the reassuring conclusion that humanitarian ethics—a deeply compassionate response to extreme human suffering—is alive and kicking among ordinary Indians despite the violence and hate-mongering reported every day, and that every act of anger and animosity that is reported has its counterpart in an act of care and compassion that goes unreported.

The Springboard for Generosity

What is the deeper motivation behind such acts of kindness? Remember this: these acts are happening in a domain of human life filled with severe restrictions, where sectarianism is rampant. After all, Hindus have all kinds of conventional taboos in relation to Muslims. Despite this, why do they welcome them into their own sacred spaces? Muslims believe in one transcendent god. Why, then, help believers in multiple, false gods? Have people transcended their religion to feel part of one larger community, say, Kerala or India? Is the motivation stemming from a more catholic interpretation of their own religions? Or is human suffering so intense that people are moved to act kindly despite disagreement or past hostility? For, these are not instances of religious tolerance or religious acceptance; they are symptomatic of a deep respect for humanity. Sometimes, in moments of unspeakable tragedy, we get a glimpse of our own humanity—or, perhaps, our own divinity is revealed to us. Hence my question what is the springboard for such acts of generosity? What qualities help us shed prejudice, hostility, indifference, selfishness and transcend the boundaries between the self and the other?

The Magic of Empathy

One is the magical quality that each of us has to literally step into the shoes of another. We tend to think of our minds as coterminous with our bodies and therefore the boundaries of our bodies to be restricted to the physical contours of the biological organisms that we are. But the boundaries of our self almost never coincide with the body, except at our truncated worst or when we die. For the rest, we experience a continual, context-dependent contraction or expansion of the self—a self that encompasses our children, parents, best friends, co-workers, linguistic, religious or cultural community. And when faced with an unprecedented, superlative achievement by other humans or the most intense human suffering, we are propelled to completely identify with them. When that happens, we virtually become the other, seeing no difference between 'us' and 'them'. Boundaries collapse and we begin to feel each other's pain and joy as our own. Empathy is a fundamental human attribute and only someone who has gone through psychopathic training or sociopathic misfortune is left without any trace of it.

Deep Sociability

Apart from the emotive, experiential empathy, another trait more foundational, exists in human beings. I allude here to the philosopher David Wong's suggestive idea that desiring a constructive relationship with others, including with those who we don't fully comprehend or with whom we disagree, is one of the abiding, though not always dominant, motive in the psychological make-up of humans. This trait, what I call 'deep sociability', is good in itself. People value good relationships with others not only for instrumental reasons but also for intrinsic ones. They do not merely wish to cooperate with others for mutual benefit. They wish to be with others and do things together because they find it enjoyable, fulfilling and uplifting. This is why they also wish to be recognised and accepted by others. If so, disagreement on some issues, even on some important ones, motivates people to look for agreement in other domains. People have a capacity for unconditional sociability that compels them to set aside disagreement or minimise the significance of radical difference. Put generally, because we are born radically incomplete, we achieve completion only with and by others. So all our lives we strive for this other-dependent completion. Deep sociability is the motor driving us towards fulfilment. The best social philosophy and literature, both religious and non-religious, teaches us this. But often it is written in the simple hearts of ordinary folks.

52

The Necessity of Intellectual Virtue

The acquisition of knowledge is no longer the preserve of a few. The need for widespread literacy in modern societies as well as the development of public spheres have meant that the acquisition and communication of knowledge, including the understanding of radically different people and cultures, has to be democratised. Gathering knowledge through reading, writing and exchanging ideas is a general human need in contemporary societies.

In the past, those trained to acquire, preserve, nourish and transmit knowledge had to go through rigorous protocols. They had to learn the norms of knowledge formation: proper ways of collecting and assessing evidence, drawing sound inferences from data, formulating concepts and frameworks of explanation, cultivating empathetic understanding, etc. It is true that some forms of knowledge gathering and transmission that were normal earlier make us uncomfortable today. The elites spoke primarily to themselves, wrote for themselves, stealthily guarded the knowledge they 'owned', did not allow public dissemination and even punished anyone from outside the circle who tried to procure it. Yet, the crucial point here is the existence of fairly rigorous norms of knowledge acquisition in the past, as also an ethic of reading, writing, speaking, listening and sharing knowledge. There was great emphasis on intellectual virtues and punitive measures were put in place to check the corresponding intellectual vices.

Do Not Make Hasty Judgement

It seems to me that in the contemporary world of democratised knowledge acquisition, insufficient attention is paid to intellectual norms and virtues. What norms must exist for all those who participate in the 'life of the mind'? What virtues must be cultivated today and what vices must be avoided? There are many, but here I focus on just one: intellectual openness. It must surely be an integral part of our education, nurtured early in our childhood and ingrained so firmly that it remains with us as long as we are intellectually active.

But what is this quality of openness? Suppose a newspaper claims that the Indian economy is growing at 10 per cent, it is incumbent upon me, the reader, with no particular beliefs of my own on this matter, to check if this is true. Not much research is needed. Relevant facts—some supporting and others challenging the claim—are available on the internet. And if that information proves indecisive, it is easily obtainable from other reliable sources. Anyhow, the least I can do is not rush to believe or disbelieve this factual claim but to delay my judgement. I must eschew intellectual impatience or recklessness and keep my mind open.

Thus, one important feature of being open-minded is to refrain from making hasty or premature judgements. This intellectual virtue of hearing both sides, to be persuaded only by better evidence and argument, should be cultivated through education. Exercising intellectual caution and not getting easily swayed by hyperbole is an integral part of intellectual life. Sadly, this elementary virtue is neglected or forgotten today. Why else would rumours and fake news be so rampant and successful?

Set Aside Strong Conviction—Listen

Second, let's suppose that I am convinced that talk of global warming is humbug, that those pointing to its rising dangers are indulging in motivated, mischievous exaggeration. Let's further suppose that I am presented with fairly strong evidence that unlike previous ages when climate change was caused mainly by changes in the output of the sun, the current phase is largely man-made, caused rapidly by burning of fossil fuels, deforestation and synthetic substances such as chlorofluorocarbons. Here, the evidence provided challenges my strong belief. But I disregard it and hold on to my belief firmly. Isn't this a sign of close-mindedness? The intellectual virtue relevant here is to have the courage to temporarily set aside my strong conviction and listen to the opponent's argument. In this situation of a straightforward conflict of views, to give a fair, impartial hearing to opposing beliefs, arguments and evidence, to be open-minded in another sense, is what I am required to do.

Move beyond Your World View

A third form of open-mindedness is even more important—crucial for knowledge of other people and cultures. Our habits of reading, listening, seeing and understanding often get locked within a particular intellectual framework, which becomes our default position. It becomes naturalised—something taken for granted. We seem unable to think, read and write without it. For example, in some cognitive frameworks, anything good (a rich man's wealth) or bad (a poor man's suffering) that happens to an individual is either a product of his own personal choice or to do with some bad karma in previous life. No place exists in this framework for any idea of systematic harms caused by one group to another or by social, cultural and institutional biases built into the system. Such naturalised intellectual frameworks may also be influenced or defined by a particular culture, philosophy, religion or caste. So Hindus might think about the world with their own very Hindu assumptions and Muslims and Christians with their own. And each finds it difficult to move beyond to enlarge their respective visions, which is understandable. However, these frameworks can be the source of many prejudices, and because they are implicit and lying in the background, they can generate an invidious form of closed-mindedness. Only those who have opened up their hearts and minds can overcome the limitations of deeply entrenched world views. Alas, this open-endedness is least remembered when it is most needed. No society can survive normlessness in intellectual life. Neglecting intellectual virtues may not cause immediate visible harm but spell disaster in the long run.

53

Rational Temper and Moral Reasoning

Humans cannot survive without evidence and reason. If a majestic cobra unexpectedly appears in your vicinity, you better not ignore the evidence that it is a lethal, venomous creature and run for your life. Instrumental rationality is a primitive form of reason as old as human beings themselves. Rational inferences too are intrinsic to daily existence. Farmers can tell by examining the nature of the soil what will and will not grow in it.

Forms of Reason

So why are we encouraged to develop a rational temper when early socialisation already makes us rational? It's because we learn skills of evidence gathering, inferring and instrumental reasoning in the limited domain of our own experience, but modern life in industrialised societies can hardly be lived by these alone. To recognise and handle complex evidence and intricate deductive and inductive reasoning, sophisticated forms of instrumental reasoning based on formal education is necessary. A modern society's need for such rational creatures is insatiable. But is this all there is to human reason?

Two other forms of reason are even more important if we must move beyond survival to living our lives well. First, reasoning about valued ends. It is not enough to explore the best possible means to satisfy whatever we happen to want. We also need to reason about which desire we should pursue. According to the Canadian philosopher Charles Taylor, we are not weak but strong evaluators—not only with an ability to (weakly) evaluate if money is to be spent on satisfying this rather than that desire but also to ask what place money has in our life. In short, we (strongly) evaluate our desires by some standard of higher worth. Of what use is a prosperous life without friends, family and community or without dignity and self-respect, we might ask. The Buddha gave up an affluent, royal life to reason precisely about such ends of life: what makes life meaningful to us as individuals, as social beings and finally as humans inhabiting the world? Developing a rational temper is learning to reason about what makes life worthwhile and what we should really care about.

Second, equally important for us is contextual moral reasoning, found aplenty in ordinary practice but in need of more cultivation. Suppose your child is ill, your wife is out of town on work and you have an urgent meeting to attend. What would you do? I doubt you will put the health of your child and the meeting on the same scale of commensurability and do a cost–benefit analysis or look at your moral rule book and ask which of the two acts is dictated by some categorical imperative such as always place the highest value on your work or, alternatively, always put your child's health above all else. Single-value rules are absurd because neither of the values can easily supersede the other. To be sure, the health of your child is more important than a work-related meeting. But even so, a moral rule, if there was one, will have to be sensitive to the actual circumstances at that time. So if the child's temperature is, say, 100 degrees Fahrenheit and your attendance at the meeting is critical, you would probably leave your child behind with some reassuring words. But if the temperature was 104, you would face a dilemma; if the meeting is really urgent, you might request a trusted neighbour or friend to help you out. But if there is no alternative, you will probably skip the meeting with regret or postpone it.

This way of negotiating values is not only appropriate in personal life but offers a good model for public reasoning in society. Collective decision-making cannot put all preferences, regardless of their worth, on the same commensurable scale and then subject them to a cost–benefit analysis. A million people have both a little green patch and a personal gym and therefore the benefit of building a mall on the site far outweighs the cost of losing a public park. This reasoning is wrong because the larger environmental benefits of a public park must enter our reasoning as an independent, qualitatively different value and not as one aggregated desire that can be easily exchanged for another. Nor can we have an absolute, non-negotiable, single-value perspective to come into play here: our physical environment must always, no matter the circumstances, have greater value than all else. To my mind, single-value doctrines are as dangerous as a value-free, quantitative, cost–benefit analysis.

Exemplar of Moral Reasoning

So how should we proceed when reasoning about norms, laws and public policies of our society? We needn't go too far here because our Constitution serves as a prefect exemplar. At stake in the deliberations of the Constituent Assembly were multiple values: individual freedom, religious freedom of communities, equality among individuals and inter-religious group equality. The Constitution does not elevate one value, say individual freedom, above all others. Instead, it moves deftly through each of them. So, recognising the importance of inculcating specific religious values among children of smaller groups, the Constitution grants a fundamental right to minorities to found educational institutions (community-freedom). All religious groups, large or small, are, nevertheless, given the right to apply for state funding (equality between groups). However, a condition for accepting state subsidy is that a child, say, a Hindu, cannot be refused admission to a school run by, say, Christians (no discrimination on grounds of religion—individual equality). Finally, once a Hindu child is admitted to a Christian school, she cannot be forced to attend prayers in the chapel (individual freedom).

This approach of wading through values, accepting potential conflict between them without allowing any one to trump the others, finding the right balance and endorsing ethically sensitive compromises is the hallmark of sound moral reasoning. This art is an integral part of being rational.

54

Love, Respect and Critique

It seems counterintuitive to be critical of something we revere, to publicly acknowledge wrongs committed by the very nation to which we owe loyalty, to detect moral flaws in the character of children we love 'blindly'. Love, devotion, patriotism and even respect are possible only if critical judgement is suspended. Right? Conversely, flaws and blemishes surface only when what is mine ceases to be mine and I begin treating my family or community as any other. The best critiques depend on complete detachment.

I wish to argue, however, that this way of separating critique from love or attachment is mistaken. In an earlier essay, I proposed that we critically respect the religion or philosophy to which we owe allegiance. Here I would like to extend this attitude to the family into which we are born, the institution where we work and the country we call our home.

Our Country, Right or Wrong?

'Our country! In her intercourse with foreign nations may she always be in the right; but right or wrong, our country!' remarked Stephen Decatur Sr, an American naval officer, in the aftermath of the American War of Independence, exemplifying the kind of loyalty and commitment that precludes criticism. Possessive pronouns such as 'mine' or 'ours' are laden with strong sentiment and passionate commitment, but they need not compel us to react defensively at the slightest complaint of wrongdoing. Understandable it may be, but it is not the only response and certainly not the best. A more appropriate rejoinder is to reflectively evaluate the negative judgement and if, on deliberation, found valid, to act and set things right. Here's an obvious example: a parent sees or is shown some wrong done by her child or some defect appearing in his character. A foolish reaction would be to cover up or whitewash what the child has done and announce that the child committed no wrong. This myopically appeases the child, throwing the door wide open to future moral disasters. The wiser response is to resolve to set things right—to patiently sit with the child, understand his motivation and then launch a sensitive and sensible process of moral rehabilitation. What is true of our children is true of our religious communities and of the nation too. When a wrong done by our religious community (brutal rape of women from another community) or our nation (callousness to poverty or farmers' suicides) jumps to the eye, one can neither publicly defend this wrong nor hide one's head ostrich-like under the sand. The wrong has to be collectively and openly identified and set right.

It is by this logic that another American, Carl Schurz, a Union general in the American Civil War, amended Decatur's statement, investing it with another virtually opposite meaning: 'My country, right or wrong; if right, to be kept right; and if wrong, to be set right.' When our country behaves well and meets appropriate moral standards, we feel good, even proud; but when it behaves badly, it still remains ours and, for that reason, we have a special obligation to identify what is wrong with it and openly criticise it. It is simply mistaken to presume that the stronger our identification with a country, the harder it is to recognise or acknowledge its wrongs. Indeed, the closer our identification with a nation, the stronger the motivation to restore it to the right path. This desire to move it in the right direction propels us to a better understanding of what precisely has gone wrong. Love and attachment motivate us to undertake sharper, persistent critique. Indeed, the more things go wrong, the more severe our critique and more intense our desire to put things back on the right track. A critique does not require total emotional detachment.

Distance not Detachment

Although critique is possible without radical detachment, it does demand *some* distance. But distance from what? I believe that public criticism of whatever is ours—family, institution, religion or nation—presupposes the ability to disconnect not from the entire community but its rotten segments: persistent lies told by our children, the callous indifference to hierarchy and intolerance within our religions, the petty acts of power and manipulation within our institutions, the pernicious oppressions in our nation, etc. We move away from these decadent sites not to escape to some place wholly outside our community but to other, more morally defensible locations within it. We move sideways to wherever the morally right stance is still alive. This is not possible if we remain close to the beneficiaries of the rot or succumb to the base Machiavellian temptation to whisper in the ear of power wielders. A son cannot criticise patriarchy in his family or remove it if he kowtows to his oppressive father or himself benefits from the unfair burden imposed on his mother. But to be critical, he does not have to renounce his family either. Likewise, Indians do not become anti-national, or Hindus, anti-Hindu, when they justifiably criticise some of their unethical practices.

A final remark to reinforce my main point: a better grasp of what we are and a fair appraisal of how well we fare require a form of understanding available only from the inside, from particular locations within our religious, national or institutional community. A sustained connection with one's community is crucial to understanding what it is and should be. Only when such understanding is available can we arrive at appropriate and relevant critiques. Thus, a deep connection—some emotional and intellectual attachment (love, respect and commitment)—is an important condition for an appropriate critique. Critical respect is crucial to a vibrant living community.

55

The Social Value of Religious and Political Dissent

Dissent is not only the 'safety valve of democracy', as Justice D.Y. Chandrachud reminded us, but is also vital for meaningful social life. Societies stultify when everyone converges on a single opinion or when official stories go unchallenged. Flaws congeal and social rot sets in. Right or wrong and pleasant or unpleasant, views must be expressed and orthodoxies challenged because that is the only way to publicly identify and remove social, political and economic deficiencies.

Surely, it is not a hidden fact that vast numbers of destitute Adivasis and poor farmers are dispossessed of their lands by the greed of predatory corporates. It is an open secret that when normal channels of justice are unavailable, helpless victims are pushed to taking arms. Did not every other Hindi film, not long ago, show

how the merciless exploitation of innocent farmers invariably turned them into vengeful dacoits? Do we not realise that coercive violence by the state causes greater alienation among such hapless people, pushing them further and deeper into an endless cycle of reciprocal violence? Is it not the duty of every conscientious citizen to speak out against this injustice and, if necessary, to dissent from official discourse that paints them as monstrous enemies of the state? But alas, as an American judge put it some fifty years ago, 'It is an eternal temptation of a government to arrest a speaker rather than correct the conditions about which he complains', an observation that is particularly apt for those activists who are fighting for the fundamental rights of the poor and the marginalised.

Introducing Sedition

Power makes people short-sighted. In 1798, the American federalist party of rich property owners enacted the controversial sedition act that criminalised all criticism of the government. Their ostensible justification: growing tensions between France and the US. But oddly enough, all those persecuted under the act were members of the opposition belonging to the then far more democratic Republican. It is clear that the act was introduced only to prevent the Republicans from gaining power. A Republican Congressman was imprisoned for describing President John Adams as being swallowed up 'in a continual grasp of power, in an unbounded thirst of ridiculous pomp, foolish adulation and selfish avarice'. Predictably, the federalist greed for political power backfired. The imprisoned senator became a popular hero, and in 1801, a fellow Republican Thomas Jefferson became the new president. Myopic governments fail to see that criminalising dissent eventually extracts a heavy political price.

The social value of dissent is unmistakable. Dissenters are not renouncers or quitters; they never withdraw from society. They are engaged, connected critics, who oppose prevailing orthodoxies. Deeply committed to their society, they wish to see it flourish, which is precisely why they speak about its various ailments. Dissent is one of the most courageous acts of citizenship, for dissenters speak when most others are silent. They show what most others do not want to see. They stick out their necks aware of the danger that they will be misconstrued, stigmatised and deliberately accused of disloyalty. Dissenters refuse to be bystanders in a land with only a fleeting interest in its well-being. They dwell there and believe they have a huge stake in it. They are proud to belong but refuse the comfort of silence in the face of the unjust suffering of others. The dissenter is the ultimate patriot.

A Glorious Tradition of Dissent

I have no inkling of the history of political dissent in India but have a sense of its glorious tradition of social and religious dissent. The great Magadha intellectuals of their time, the Upanishadic thinkers and the Buddha can be viewed as religio-philosophical dissenters who challenged Vedic ritualism. The legendary Tamil poet Sivavakkiyar, deeply critical of caste hierarchy, also negated the idea of rebirth: 'The sound of the conch does not return to the broken shell, nor life to the broken body … the fallen fruit does not reappear on the tree and the dead are never, never, never, reborn.' Basavanna, the twelfth century Kannada poet and philosopher, rejected gender and caste discrimination. Kabir, Ravidas and Nanak refused to identify with contending religions of the day and laid a foundation for new paths to self-discovery and liberation.

The nineteenth century saw Dalit women openly oppose religiously driven patriarchy. Muktabai, a student of Savitri Phule, attacked caste-ridden Brahamanical ideology: 'Let that religion, where only one person is privileged and the rest are deprived, perish from the earth and let it never enter our minds to be proud of it!' Tarabai Shinde, comprehensively attacking oppression of women, ripped into the male tendency to incriminate women: 'People go about pinning the blame on women all the time, as if everything bad was their fault …. Is it true that only women's bodies are home to all the different kinds of recklessness and vice? Or have men got just the same faults as we find in women?'

All these dissenters were outstanding moral agitators, introducing social, intellectual and spiritual turbulence in public life. Some backlash from orthodoxy must surely have been there. Yet they expressed their views without fear of social repression or political persecution. But would they have survived harassment, public humiliation or imprisonment if they were living in India today? I wonder how even Swami Dayanand Saraswati, a major dissenter in his own right, would fare in our times. Is it not ironic and civilisationally suicidal that people are trolled, arrested and even killed for much less in India today?

PART VI

Owning Up to Injustice and Grave Wrongdoing

56

Against False Moral Equivalence

When people speak of social injustice or misrecognition, they usually have in mind the persistent suffering of large marginalised groups such as Dalits, Adivasis, minorities or women. Such oppression of large groups is not the topic of this essay. Rather, I have in mind smaller, less dramatic, more everyday forms of injustices and misrecognitions suffered by individuals. I speak in particular of one wrong which I call false moral equivalence that individuals in our society appear to face increasingly in everyday life.

Everyday Forms of Injustices

Consider several people applying for two academic positions in a university. Only two can get them and they do. One has excellent qualifications, performs brilliantly in the selection interview and does nothing illegitimate to get the job. The other has reasonable qualifications, gives an average interview but more than makes up for these inadequacies by 'fixing' the selection process. He pulls every conceivable string. Despite this stark difference, the wider academic community fails to distinguish the two cases and brands them both as 'fixers'.

Another example: consider two government officials charged by their seniors with financial corruption. One, in fact, is squeaky clean but a victim of much envy and jealousy within the system or framed because he refuses to toe the line of powerful politicians. The other is a run-of-the-mill corrupt officer who has reached where he has by selling his soul at every stage of promotion. Both cases are brought to the notice of the wider public that being ill-informed, indifferent or lazy places both officers on the same moral footing by presuming both to be equally corrupt.

What wrong, when branded corrupt, has the clean officer suffered? What wrong has been done to the deserving candidate when he is clubbed with the real 'fixer'? My one-line answer is that both have suffered from false moral equivalence. What does this involve? An equally short answer: injustice through misrecognition.

One ancient principle of justice requires that those equal in some relevant respect be treated equally and unequal, unequally. It follows that when equals get an unequal share of a material or psychological good (say, income or reputation) or when unequal persons receive equal shares, then distributive justice is violated. This principle can be embedded in two different forms of life, however. In one, people are viewed as intrinsically unequal. Those born superior to others in all respects must never be treated in the same way as their inferiors. This hierarchical or aristocratic interpretation must be rejected. In the other, where moral equality of all humans and equality of opportunity is guaranteed, the principle reads differently: those equal in need, condition or ability must be treated equally and those not equal, unequally. To return to our example: the most qualified person who goes through a fair process of selection must get the job and also be recognised as truly worthy of it. Others found 'unequal in the relevant respect' are not worthy of it even when they get the position. When both are treated as fixers, the deserving candidate gets a reputation he does not deserve. The same is true for the person who is viewed as financially corrupt when, in fact, he is not. By treating 'unequals' as equals and falsely equating the two (the morally relevant quality of integrity is not present to the same degree in two persons), an injustice is inflicted on the 'clean' or deserving person.

Injustice by Misrecognition

The relevant injustice in such cases arises from misrecognition. Each of us has a certain understanding of what we are as well as an estimation of our worth. And yet, what we are is partly shaped by how others recognise us. If they get us wrong or attribute to us features we do not have, in short, misrecognise us, it can cause us real damage. If our society mirrors back to us a distorting, severely mistaken picture of who we are, it might leave us with lowered self-respect. Misrecognition is a somewhat intangible but real harm. It can make us feel small and humiliated. And when thrown back by everyone around us, we might, unless we are strong and secure, even begin to change our self-perception. Good feminist and Dalit scholars have made us realise the lasting damage caused by a denigrating self-image. But this feeling can be experienced by any individual in her everyday life; its ordinariness and individual quality do not detract from the crippling psychological damage it causes. To falsely attribute a bad quality to a person when, in fact, he does not possess it is to misrecognise him, and such misrecognition can leave a permanent scar.

False moral equivalence then involves unfairness by misrecognition. It is a potent instrument of psychological harm—a form of mistreatment. When good, meritorious people are ill-treated, they go through social and, eventually, self-estrangement. Everyday injustices and misrecognitions add up. Good people begin to lose not only their bearing, self-confidence and self-respect but also their souls. As everyone loses a sense of discrimination between right and wrong and adopts an attitude of 'anything goes' (*chalta hai*) or when everyone is equally guilty or innocent, we are well on our way to turning a community into a directionless mob in which virtually anyone can be arbitrarily targeted. The pernicious social habit of false moral equivalence shows not only our coarseness, that we could not care less, but also that we are trapped in an immoral abyss from which there may be no escape. And for anyone still left with a modicum of moral integrity, this is insufferable.

57

The Ignominy of Statelessness

It is frightfully disturbing to learn that forty lakh people living in Assam (in 2018) find no place in the draft of the National Register of Citizens. They could be deprived of their Indian citizenship and become stateless. Can those of us who are secure in our nationality ever put ourselves in the shoes of such disenfranchised people? What is it like to be deprived of citizenship or to experience the horror of statelessness?

Citizenship and Belonging

Citizenship is frequently associated with political rights, but it is linked, first and foremost, to belonging. To be a citizen is to belong to a particular politically organised community—the state, in the widest sense. True, it is not the only form of belonging. One can belong to a village or a language-, religion- or occupation-based community. But, particularly, under modern conditions, belonging to a politically organised community has become more important than other belongings. Our identity as citizens is more basic than other identities. Why?

This is because everything we need or desire and any reasonable goal we pursue depends today on our membership of a state. We may have moral rights as human beings but they are ineffective or meaningless without social–political recognition within a legal regime supported by the state. Thus, our life, family, basic liberties, employment, education, mobility and even everyday security depend on the overall protection and support of the state. If we do not belong to a state and carry no proof of it (ration card, driving license, Aadhaar card or passport), we have nothing. These passive citizenship rights cannot exist without authoritative, juridical backing, nor can active citizenship rights that enable us to participate in the making and remaking of our political community. In short, it is only as a member of a particular state (India, Bangladesh, the US, etc.) that we are able to live well, indeed to live at all.

It follows that to *not* be a citizen—to be stateless—is to experience the worst imaginable nightmare, even worse than long-term confinement in jail, a politically alienated life or living as an oppressed minority. In fact, the right to vote or to be political is far from the mind of those threatened with statelessness because such people are not covered by any law. They can be detained merely on the ground that they are stateless. They can be separated from their family. If their possessions are taken away, they can't report the matter to anyone. If they have no job, there's no one to appeal to. If they are hungry, no public distribution system can help them. They can be denied access to basic health services, even as they suffer from life-threatening diseases. They are homeless outsiders who can be deported any time with no one having an idea where they must go. Their whole social and political existence is illegal. Socially and politically dead, they barely exist; a deep existential insecurity is bred by statelessness.

Statelessness invariably begets an irreversible dehumanisation: criminalisation is common among stateless people, as are involvement in abusive relationships and 'survival sex'; invisiblisation is also common among them—every act must remain hidden from the state and the public. Stateless persons live in perpetual disguise, submerged in complete anonymity. They are truly the wretched of the earth.

Worse still, statelessness often paves the way for genocidal violence. Can one forget the fate of German Jews after the revocation of their citizenship? Divested of political belonging and social identity, they became subhuman. Wanted nowhere, they were rounded up and despatched to extermination camps.

This atrocious state of statelessness usually occurs when political persecution, declaration of war on certain ethnic groups or economic destitution forces people out of their homeland but the state where asylum is sought or where they have managed to temporarily find work doesn't eventually recognise them as citizens. Statelessness can also occur when new ethnically based borders are born. The creation of Bangladesh rendered thousands of Urdu-speaking Bihari Muslims stateless in their homeland. Bangladesh stripped them of their citizenship but Pakistan refused to accept them. Living on either side of the border without the requisite ethnicities, suddenly, for no fault of theirs, they found themselves stateless. This has also been the fate of pastoral groups, who have no real idea of settled existence or permanent home and who once travelled freely in a region but are now confronted with borders they can't easily cross. And because they thought of the entire region as their own and never belonged anywhere in particular, new borders liquidated their multiple belongings, rendering them stateless.

Nowhere to Go

Imagine what might have happened to Ugandans of Indian origin if, after expulsion by the brutal regime of Idi Amin, they were denied entry into the UK despite holding British passports? The much maligned but truly hapless Rohingya, with neither passport nor identity card, are denied effective citizenship in their homeland and subjected to various forms of extortion, land confiscation, eviction, marriage restrictions and forced labour on roads and military camps. Yet, they have nowhere else to go. Many, therefore, experience the nightmare of statelessness.

Statelessness is not a natural disaster but a man-made malaise, a consequence of newly formed nation-states obsessed with borders. True, this is an international humanitarian issue, but do contiguous states (Myanmar, Bangladesh and India) have no obligation to groups who not long ago lived as one people in a borderless territory? Can a newly erected virtual barrier completely erase centuries-old practice of habitation and mobility?

58

The Oldest Surviving Conservative Ideology

In early 2019, a chilling report appeared in *Deccan Herald* stating that in 2017, 210 cases of atrocities against Dalits occurred in the urban districts of Bengaluru and 106 in its rural districts. Likewise, Kerala reported 883 cases of such crimes between June 2016 and April 2017. Other reports said that there has been a 66 per cent decadal growth in crime against Dalits between 2007 and 2017.

The horror of these statistics is made vivid when one examines concrete events. On 12 April 2019, 200 people attacked a small group of Dalits for swimming in the Bhadra river in Karnataka[7]. Even as they thrashed these people, the perpetrators screamed that the river belongs exclusively to the upper castes. Evidently, Article 15 of our Constitution is not worth the paper it is printed on; it remains toothless, impotent and ineffective.

What kind of thinking underlies this brutal social violence in which innocent folk are targeted merely because they belong to a particular caste? Since most atrocities revolve around basic issues of land, wages and entitlements, poverty and powerlessness are frequently viewed as the cause of such violence. But such explanations do not go deep enough because they leave out the prime mover behind such atrocities—a deeply conservative, casteist ideology also known in some circles as Brahmanism. This precisely was B.R. Ambedkar's contention; he argued that without a robust movement against Brahmanism, Dalit emancipation is impossible. But then, we must ask what exactly is being opposed? What are the core features of Brahmanism?

Not 'Anti-Brahmin'

For a start, opposing 'Brahmanism' does not entail being 'anti-Brahmin'. To do so would imply that all Brahmins are responsible for these atrocities. This is as preposterous as ascribing blame to all

---

[7] Sumedha Pal, 'Two Days Before 128th Ambedkar Jayanti, Dalits Attacked for Swimming in Bhadra River,' Forward Press, 18 April 2019, https://www.forwardpress.in/2019/04/two-days-before-128th-ambedkar-jayanti-dalits-attacked-for-swimming-in-bhadra-river/

Muslims for any wrong committed in, say, the reign of Alauddin Khilji or to all British people for the Jallianwala Bagh massacre or, for that matter, to all Hindus for the lynching of an innocent Muslim. We should not fall prey to this crude notion of collective responsibility. In a society that is riven by caste, a person may belong to the Brahmin caste but not adhere to the core ethic of Brahmanism. He may even have morally disassociated himself from it. The resolution to burn the *Manusmriti* and thereby oppose Brahmanism was taken by Ambedkar jointly with G.S. Sahasrabuddhe, a Chitpavan Brahmin.

Indeed, Ambedkar went even further. In a speech at the G.I.P. Railways Depressed Caste Workers' Conference in 1938, he claimed that 'when I say that Brahmanism is an enemy that must be dealt with, I do not mean the power, privilege or interests of Brahmins as a community'. On the face of it, this seems odd. For what else could Brahmanism be except a defence of the power, privilege and interests of Brahmins as a community?

In fact, this statement is not that perplexing. Take an instance from our own history. The Rig Vedic society of 1,500 BCE had a community of ritual specialists that transmitted its ritual-related know-how from one generation to another. Others, the political rulers or ordinary householders, did not possess it. This group of Brahmins was granted some privilege on account of the knowledge it possessed. For satisfying the 'religious' needs of members of other communities, the group was even accorded respect not owed to others.

This produced inequality but the resulting hierarchy was fluid, contingent and reversible. This contingently generated superiority of Brahmins was not systemic or integral to the structure of society and therefore not necessarily demeaning to others. This sacrifice-centred Vedic Brahmanism is not to be conflated with the Brahmanism Ambedkar despised and wished to destroy. One should refuse to conflate the privilege of such ritual-performing Brahmins with Brahmanism.

A Deeply Conservative Ideology

What then is Ambedkar's Brahmanism? It is a sociopolitical ideology found in the Dharmashastras that encodes a memory of an ideal past and a vision of society in the future, one in which Brahmins occupy the highest place not only as exclusive guardians of a higher, spiritual realm but also as sole providers of wisdom on virtually every practical issue of this world. They possess superior knowledge of what a well-ordered society is and how a good state must be run. More importantly, their superior position in society and their superior knowledge stem from birth. This makes them naturally, intrinsically superior to all other humans, so superior that they form a separate species (jati) altogether. Nothing can challenge or alter this fact. No one becomes a Brahmin but is born so.

A person's acts may determine the position he occupies in the next life but not in this one. This is true not only of Brahmins but of every other jati. The position of each jati is unalterably fixed at birth. The Atishudra, the 'untouchable', is born into and therefore must occupy the lowest, most inferior rank; no action of his can alter this fact. This sociopolitical ideology makes hierarchy necessary, rigid and irreversible.

The hierarchical social order, it follows, corresponds to the natural order of things. No one can exchange his position with that of another or move up or down. Any attempt to do so is morally wrong. Dalits, according to this view, must remain in 'their place', and if they try to move up, they must be put down.

Brahmanism, or more strictly Dharamshastric Brahmanism, is then the most perfect form of conservatism, a status quoist ideology par excellence entirely suitable to elites who wish to perpetuate their social status, power and privilege. Paradoxically, this is the reason why it spread everywhere in India and beyond and why it endures: regardless of your religio-philosphical world view, if you are a privileged elite, you would find this ideology irresistible.

But there can be Brahmanical Buddhists or Jains as well. Those who convert to, say, Islam or Christianity may still continue to embrace this sociopolitical ideology. Many Muslims and Christians, for all practical purposes, are Brahmins or Thakurs who continue to inferiorise Muslim or Christian Dalits.

Dharamshastric Brahmanism naturalises existing power, privilege and higher status. The kings love it and wealthy merchants and landlords are happy with it. Indeed, because it gives them power over Atishudras, even the high-placed Shudras in this system of graded inequality are willing to acquiesce to it. In short, everyone at the top finds it appealing because everyone below is required to carry out the task as dictated by his current social position and not ask for more. Anyone who consents to, endorses or justifies this hierarchical order, regardless of his caste, creed or gender, is then a 'Brahmanist'.

Because this ideology is fundamentally against any kind of social mobility, it restricts individual freedom; because it is totally enamoured of hierarchy, it is ineluctably inegalitarian; and because it separates one group of human beings from another, it is deeply incompatible with any idea of fraternity. No wonder Ambedkar defined Brahmanism as the negation of the spirit of liberty, equality and fraternity. This makes Dharamshastric Brahmanism and the Constitution fundamentally opposed to one another.

59

The Anatomy of Racism

Racism has raised its ugly head in full public view once again. It was revolting to see an adult gasping for breath, writhing in pain, as the knee of the White policeman crushed his neck, and, within minutes, dying—the umpteenth time that a Black life has been barbarically taken away by police brutality in America. Despite the civil war over slavery and the civil rights movement for dignity and equality, systemic discrimination and violence against Blacks persists. Racism continues unabated.

My sole focus here is to come to grips with what racism is. In a nut shell—and with slight, only slight oversimplification—it is this: one can tell everything important about a group, its past, present and future, by noting the skin-colour of any one of its members.

Of course, noticing the physical characteristics of a person, say the colour of her skin, is not itself racist. Good writers are expected to provide a vivid description of a character's physical features, including skin colour. This need not imply the idea of race, leave alone racism. For instance, Indian epics describe Krishna as having *shyam varna* (dark skin). This description has no evaluative connotation. Being conscious of the colour of a person, your own or that of the other may be pretty innocent.

However, when specific bodily features (skin colour or shape of nose, eye, lips) are permanently clumped together and human beings are classified in terms of these distinct biological clusters, and if, further, it is believed that these shared features are inter-generationally transmitted, then we possess the idea of race, identifying a group with a common biological descent. Every single human being is not only seen then to be assigned to separate biologically determined groups but also as born with traits directly inherited from their biological ancestors. Each race is then believed to be fundamentally and permanently different from others—differences that are innate and indelible, for one can neither cease to have what one has inherited nor acquire characteristics that one does not already have.

The idea of race is deeply problematic. Despite many attempts, particularly in the thirties, to demonstrate its scientific basis, race or racial classifications have virtually no scientific foundation. If anything, the only conclusion from available evidence is that the whole of humanity has the same lineage, that there are no races within humans but only one single human 'race'. Yet, while scientifically speaking, race is a fiction, a large number of people believe in the existence of races. Race is very much a cultural and social reality.

The classification of humans into different races is a necessary but far from sufficient ingredient of racism, which depends on two additional, deeply troublesome features. First, a given set of biological characteristics is believed to be necessarily related to certain dispositions, traits of character and behaviour. Biological descent fixes a person's culture and ethics. Our capacity for reasoning—for 'civilisation'—and our propensities towards sexual lasciviousness or ability to make money can all be read off by examining our face and body. Second, these racial cultures and ethical systems are hierarchically arranged. Those on top are intrinsically superior to those at the bottom.

Racism, then, is a systematic ideology, a complex set of beliefs and practices that, on the presumed basis of biology, divides humanity into the higher 'us' and a lower 'them'. It not only sustains a permanent group hierarchy but also deeply stigmatises those designated as inferior. This sense of hierarchy provides a motive for, say, Whites to treat Blacks in ways that would be viewed as cruel or unjust if applied to members of their own group. For instance, contact with them is often regarded as contaminating or polluting. It should, therefore, be avoided or kept to a minimum. To prevent sexual contamination through intermarriage, the southern states of America had the severest laws sanctioning public lynching. How else could the 'colour line' be scrupulously maintained? This explains something important. Though colour consciousness should not be problematic in theory, in reality, an acute awareness of colour is almost always a symptom of racism lurking somewhere unnoticed.

Racism distinguishes even inferior races into two kinds. One inferior race is considered so much beyond the pale that it can't be lived with and must be exterminated. This is infamously illustrated by the virulent anti-Semitism in Nazi Germany that led to the final solution, the holocaust. The second type of race is fit only to be controlled, subordinated and enslaved. Anti-Black racism, our main concern here, is an obvious example. Closer home, some varna-related ideologies in the post-first–century Dharmashastras that stigmatised the Pratiloma castes, particularly the Chandalas, function as virtual equivalents of racism as do the now somewhat scarce Christian anti-Judaism or contemporary Islamophobia.

Racism naturalises a person's belief, character and culture. For example, being uneducated is seen not as socio-economic deprivation but a sign of inherited low IQ. Blacks are predatory beasts who lust after White women; they are also seen to have an innate streak of savagery, which unless kept down by brute force from time to time, might explode and destroy civilisation. It is this ideology of anti-Black racism that was brazenly on show in the nine-minute video clip of the merciless life-extinguishing force used by the police on George Floyd.

Some Americans notice and seem shell-shocked by racism only when such violence occurs. Hasn't the civil rights movement been successful in damaging racism, they ask? Is it not difficult now to justify any act by explicit reference to race? Is this not good reason to believe that racism will disappear from America by good laws, education and rational argument? Alas, the very success of the movement helped develop a motivated blindness to how open discrimination of Blacks has been displaced by another system of hidden discrimination. A systematic constraint on avenues for improving the quality of life forces their descent into pretty crime, incarceration, stigma attached to imprisonment and the severe discrimination and exclusion that follows the charge of felony. All these, as scholars such as Jane Hill have shown, have made the criminal system produce results as vicious as generated by colour-based slavery and racial segregation. For example, in a number of southern states in America, once declared a felon, a person is disqualified from voting. So once the criminal justice system labels people of colour as 'criminals', Whites have the sanction to engage in all the practices of subordination that they had apparently abandoned. The United States now has the highest rate of incarceration in the world, surpassing even highly repressive regimes such as China and Iran. The figures about Blacks are shocking. They are ten times more likely to go to prison than Whites; one in twenty over the age of eighteen is in jail; Black defendants convicted of killing Whites have been sentenced to death fifteen times more often than White defendants convicted of killing Blacks. (For a quick overview, see the Netflix film *13th*).

It is amply clear that the feel-good anti-racism of some Americans who view racism as an aggregate of mistaken beliefs held by individuals that can be dissipated by education and rational argument simply does not work. True, good education helps in dismantling racism, but the fact remains that much of it lies hidden within the social structure—in habits, practices and institutions. Vulnerabilities amassed over centuries of anti-Black racism leave Afro-Americans facing multiple intersecting hurdles to a good life. As mentioned, the current criminal system that awards unfair advantage and privilege to Whites while inflicting unmerited and unjust disadvantages on Blacks exemplifies this invisible monster. Only a peaceful movement to end institutionalised racism, with both Black and White participants, quite like the protests after Floyd's murder, can break the back of this evil. But can such a movement be sustained? Will it be allowed to?

60

The Immorality of Deep Humiliation

Everyone has experienced humiliation. In fact, to have a sense of self and to interact with other selves is to be exposed to the possibility of humiliation. Who has not experienced a damaging slur, a demeaning look or a hurtful posture sometime in their life—an affront to dignity and self-respect, a lowering of self-worth? But, if the act and experience of humiliation is so pervasive, why worry excessively about it? Just as physical injuries are an unfortunate part of life, and, in fact, necessary for the cultivation of certain virtues such as courage, why not treat mental injuries in the same way and take them in one's stride? Is there something intolerably wrong then about humiliation?

There is. At least certain kinds of humiliation are so grave that they have no place in a decent and civilised society. To help explain, allow me to give some examples.

Maltreating Dalits and Blacks

The scholar Gopal Guru has given us a horrifying picture of humiliation in eighteenth-century Maharashtra where Dalits were mostly confined to mahars (internment camps) and allowed to walk on the main street of the village only when servicing the upper castes. In the short span when they were permitted to do so, they had to clean these streets with brooms tied to their waist in order to erase their 'polluting' footprints. Even worse, they were compelled to walk the streets only at noon when their shadows were the shortest and therefore had the least chance of falling on and 'polluting' upper caste men who were also out in public. Guru poignantly points out that 'the beautiful mornings and cool evenings' were never available to the 'untouchables'.

The African American experience in the US was hardly different. It was common for Blacks to step off the sidewalk when a White man passed him. Could there have been anything more humiliating than to know that because you are Black you have to walk half a mile further than Whites just to urinate, to receive your food through a window at the back of a restaurant or to sit in a garbage-littered yard to eat?

Occasional offence, insult or disrespect lowers one's dignity but are tolerable—indeed, sometimes even productive. One's ability to restore one's dignity here is still intact. Humiliation constitutes grave wrongdoing when one's self-worth is irretrievably lowered. When that happens, people experience what might be called deep humiliation. Here, people begin to view themselves and are viewed as if they have no subjectivity—no thoughts, no viewpoint, no emotions or no sense of self. They are stripped of their humanity, as if falling outside the fold of human species. Of course, the mere fact of not being treated as a human is not humiliating. One may fear and appreciate the power and grace of tigers or admire the beauty of, say, flowers. Deep humiliation is experienced when one is seen not only as non-human but lower in rank than humans—when one is inferiorised. To deeply humiliate is to contemptuously see and treat people as subhuman.

And, this is why humiliation is a special form of maltreatment different from a mere denial of justice, freedom or fraternity. Forms of inequality, unfreedom and social alienation exist that do not involve humiliation. Constraints on freedom need not always entail a denial of dignity, for instance, when a person found guilty of murder is incarcerated but still treated humanely or when workers, though formally exploited by factory owners, are still accorded basic respect and granted welfare rights. But some instances of injustice or unfreedom are accompanied by inhuman, debasing treatment. Such forms of speech, gestures or actions carry a message to express an attitude towards those unequal or unfree that they do not matter at all, that they are entirely worthless, falling outside the ambit of humanity.

Structural Humiliation

What Dalits and African Americans as a group suffered in the past and what many continue to undergo even now is a systematic denial of self-respect and dignity, a continual rejection and a perverted pattern of ill-treatment. They experience a particular form of deep humiliation that is not episodic but structural, a feature of the social order. Here, humiliation is so normalised that neither the humiliator nor the humiliated need even feel that some grave wrongdoing is afoot. Cruelty is so routine—so recurrent—that people do not even notice it.

Another instance that is not quite the same, though comes close to it, is the belief widespread among conservative Hindus and Jews, perhaps also among people in other communities, in the 'polluting nature' of the menstrual cycle in women. Though not permanent, it occurs every month for a long time in their life and results in such a recurrent exclusion from the life of the community that it must count as part of the same family of maltreatment. And this is what is wrong with disallowing menstruating women from entering the Sabarimala temple, regardless of whatever religion- or tradition-related justification that might be offered for it.

Wilful Humiliation

This is not the only form of deep humiliation, however. Consider this: a person deliberately throws an object on the street and then demands that it be picked up; the father of an honest police officer is asked to publicly behave like an obedient dog. This is wilful humiliation. The philosopher Avishai Margalit writes of Jews being put to purposeless work in concentration camps only to be subjected to the pointless whim of the subjugator. This work had no tangible benefit for either the Jews or the Nazis. It performed no social function. Yet, for some time, it became a severe form of punishment meted out to a person just for being born a Jew. Not built into the social life of early twentieth-century Germany, it could not be called structural.

Such acts are designed solely to express the will of the perpetrator; the victim, having abjectly surrendered, has no will. Who can forget the haunting footage of the helpless Tabrez Ansari being mercilessly beaten to death by a mob merely because he was Muslim? Or consider rape incidents such as the case of Nirbhaya—many of them brutal acts of disempowerment so gratuitous and superfluous that they do not even serve the purpose of accomplishing the sexual act and end up humiliating not just the victim but all women in general.

In such cases, humiliation is meant not only to disempower people but to ensure that the humiliating act is stamped forever on their minds and to render the resulting debasement vivid to them with the sole purpose of satisfying the humiliator. In short, the pain arising in the humiliated gives the humiliator direct and unadulterated pleasure in the suffering of others. This makes it malicious.

Take another example. The expulsion of Kashmiri Pandits from the Valley was grossly unjust. Ways must be found to bring them back to the Valley and reconcile the communities. But should Jammu and Kashmir be dismembered as a state to restore justice to Kashmiri Pandits? Now, there is nothing humiliating per se in the rearrangement of a state into different administrative units. But when accompanied by gloating and triumphalism, does it not border on wilful humiliation?

There are many groups around the world that face a conjunction of structural, wilful and malicious humiliation. Can we call ourselves decent or civilised if we allow such deep humiliation in any form?

61

Empathising with Victims of Sexual Assault

In recent years, several women have come out publicly to speak about their suffering at the hands of sexual predators in our society. But do we—those of us who saw or heard them—really understand the full psychological impact of sexual assault they have experienced? Do we grasp the therapeutic value and empowering nature of this very public act of remembrance of past injustice?

Always Reliving the Trauma

For a start, these victims must have long endured unbearable stress and anxiety common among all victims of force and violence. They must have found it hard to focus on anything, suffered panic attacks, dreaded being alone and perhaps been consumed by thoughts of death or suicide. They must have relived that horrific moment several times, been startled when touched unexpectedly, jumped at unfamiliar sounds or felt the obsessive need to make themselves secure in their own home. In short, their bodies must have been traumatised.

As they tried to make sense of their suffering, they probably ended up blaming themselves for what had happened. To overcome guilt, they may have plunged into denial. And the longer the period of denial and repression, the deeper and more severe the trauma. Suppression of painful memory results in benumbing and disconnection from the world—a withdrawal from real human contact. Thus, they must have had feelings of profound social estrangement. Compounding all of this is a sense of complete helplessness generated by the failure to do anything to avenge the wrongdoing. This must induce a strong sense of shame. So the victims that we saw, heard or read must have endured deep insecurity, estrangement, shame, guilt and loss of agency.

But suffering does not stop at this. When persons are wronged, they not only suffer physically or psychologically but also are morally scarred, the most injurious of which is the damage to their sense of self-respect. No one likes to be told that they are inferior creatures or that they count for nothing. But this precisely is what the wrongdoer conveys. When persons are abused, they receive a message of their irrelevance. Intentional wrongdoing attempts to degrade us. Since self-esteem hinges upon critical opinion of the other, the message sent by the wrongdoer significantly lowers the self-esteem of the wronged. In such circumstances, the insult and degradation inflicted on assaulted women must surely have caused deeper moral injury.

Imagine, in the midst of this experience, being confronted by colleagues, friends and even family who are privately sympathetic to the trauma but advise you to remain silent in public, to keep the story to yourself and to move on. Imagine being told that public expression of your ordeal will only bring reprisals, harassment, more shame and dishonour. Asking victims to forget their tormented past is to treat them as if no great harm has been done—as if they have nothing to feel resentful about. Calls to let bygones be bygones, to wipe the slate clean or start afresh only reinforce loss of self-esteem in the victim. Besides, this works unabashedly in favour of the perpetrators, who believe that they have gotten away with their crime and grow in confidence that such injuries can be inflicted without resistance even in future. Therefore, rather than prevent, calls to forget end up facilitating wrong acts. If so, is it difficult to conclude that proper public remembrance alone restores dignity and self-respect to the victim?

Victims need to tell stories of their victimisation, relate their version of events, express retributive emotions of resentment or moral hatred, point to the aggressor and amplify his aggression. It is crucial that grave injustice done to them is publicly acknowledged by everyone *as* grave injustice and that the perpetrators own up full responsibility for their reprehensible acts. Only then can the victims move from a passive state of disengagement to active engagement with the world, learn to live their life again and rebuild relations with friends, family and members of the wider community. Because physical injury also leaves them mentally scarred and without any self-respect, this is the only route to reclaiming self-esteem.

Shattering the Silence

Breaking the dreadful miasma of silence that implicates everyone—victims, perpetrators and witnesses—is not easy. Perpetrators want silence because they want to shroud their guilt over their act or, even worse, extract an even greater sense of their own power and self-esteem by keeping the mouths of their victims shut. Victims are silent out of shame and fear; without conditions that bolster confidence and reduce apprehension and, in extreme cases, treat traumatic emotional disorders, they are usually reticent about entering the public domain. It is well known that only a minuscule proportion of rape victims acknowledge it, leave alone file cases. Finally, witnesses don't speak out because of indifference, callousness, selfishness or a misjudgement of what social norms require.

But there is no good alternative to public recall of such crimes. It brings them out into the open, challenges their denial or concealment by perpetrators and contests versions that, by sanitising events, distort their true character. The purpose behind public remembrance is to get the perpetrators or complicitous beneficiaries to admit to the knowledge of the crime and to own up responsibility for it. This is important because behind the mediatised drama of public acknowledgement lie painful stories of mutilated lives, broken families and personal betrayals. Public acknowledgement is the crucial first step towards proper healing and repairing of impaired moral agency. It is also crucial for restoring social trust. Erasing injustice without collective recall, acknowledgement and eventual reparation can hardly serve as a sound foundation for a sane society.

62

The Reparative Power of an Apology

It is likely that the word 'apology' has been mentioned several times in public recounting of sexual harassment that has gripped urban India. I myself heard it at least twice. A friend who had suffered sexual harassment several years ago admitted that she mustered enough courage to go public only after the #MeToo campaign started but wouldn't have done so if the offender had written a private letter of apology. Public naming and shaming wasn't easy, she said. Morally confused for days, she was deeply conflicted before she finally decided to act. Another victim was more categorical to the media: if the sexual assaulter had offered a public apology, she would have forgiven him and not pressed legal charges.

Hearing these accounts, I was reminded of a news story about an Algerian Muslim pilot who was falsely accused of training the 9/11 hijackers and spent nearly five months in a prison in London before the court exonerated him. The pilot asked for a public apology not only for the falsity of the charge but also for the emotional turmoil that it caused him and his family. But an apology was never given and he was forced to resort to legal action. To restore his own dignity and the self-respect of his family, he was left with no option but to sue the FBI and the US Department of Justice.

Repairing Relationships

Plainly, an apology is not a meaningless ritual. Our everyday life is replete with apologies. This is not surprising. Humans derive comfort from relationships. Our own sense of self-esteem depends on how others assess us. And that, in turn, depends on how we treat them. And yet, our daily interactions with family, friends, colleagues, 'subordinates' and even the wider community in which we live are beset with blunders. No relationship is free of at least temporary disfigurement. We behave insensitively by failing to respond to the needs of others, by ignoring rather than recognising them, by wrongly holding others responsible for things they haven't done, by treating them unfairly and by inferiorising, humiliating and degrading them. This causes immense distress and damages interpersonal relationships. Sometimes these wounds fester and grudges congeal, deepening an already spiralling estrangement. In other more–self-reflective moments, we acknowledge the wrong we have done, apologise for it and thereby arrest further deterioration in relationships. Indeed, it is hard to imagine a person's private life without apologies. But arguably, an apology has an important role to play even in more formal, public interactions. Apologies are immensely worthwhile in social practices of restorative justice. And if properly introduced in our criminal justice system, they may even improve it and transform its current cold and heartless character. Would it not make a real difference to the victim and, more generally, to our damaged social life if, apart from accepting legal punishment for the wrong done, the perpetrator apologises to the victim?

Shallow versus Genuine Apologies

How then does an apology work? From where does it draw its power? For a start, it is best to clarify that shallow, insincere and fake apologies are morally useless and socially ineffective. Far from repairing fractured relationships, they only cause further damage. They betray the sickness of the wrong doer because he continues to treat his victim as an object to be manipulated and an instrument with which to expunge his own sense of guilt. Such flawed rituals of apology are failed attempts at self-appeasement, a kind of window dressing. They do absolutely no good to the already wronged.

The structure of a genuine apology is pretty simple: the offender must properly acknowledge responsibility for the wrong done and show remorse for his act. Mostly expressed in words, it can also be effectively conveyed non-verbally. I learnt this when my wife and I visited her father's former home in Lahore. When its current owner learnt of our connection to the house, he invited us in, gave us a cup of tea, begged us to stay there for the rest of the visit and, as we left, wrapped his hand around mine with such a mysterious warmth that I felt a whole people were apologising for the displacement of my wife's family. It was as if he was saying that he wished this must never happen to anyone again. That, to me, is the crux of the matter. An effective apology comes with a commitment that the offence will never be repeated. An apology can never undo the wrong, but instead of asking the victim to forget and move on, it conveys that without acknowledgement and regret there is no forward movement.

Imagine the opposite: where the offender refuses to admit that he did something wrong. Surely, in doing so, he reinforces that he is not part of the moral world of those he has violated and that he does not abide by their rules. This remorseless outsider has neither shame nor sorrow and is likely to repeat the offence and become a serial offender. How then can the victim feel safe in this uncertain moral universe? How can she stop feeling insecure and threatened? On the other hand, by apologising, the offender demonstrates that despite his past acts, he partakes in a shared moral world. This rebuilds trust in the offender. Assured that she is safe from any further harm, the victim copes better with past suffering. Genuine apologies help repair broken relationships. They help restore a common moral world and, thereby, give us hope that life can begin afresh.

63

Justice, Forgiveness and the Call to Forget

Since Partition, India has witnessed innumerable acts of collective violence of which three clearly stand out as the most barbaric: the Nellie massacre in Assam in 1983, the horrific slaughter of Sikhs in Delhi in 1984 and the diabolical pogrom in Gujarat in 2002.

Need for Retributive Justice

No society that calls itself civilised allows such mass atrocities, and if, as an aberration, such ghastly events do occur, its criminal justice system ensures swift punishment to those found guilty. But India repeatedly permits these catastrophic transgressions. And when the process of retributive justice begins, it is reluctant, painfully slow and susceptible to political manipulation. Yet, whenever retributive justice has worked, as in the 2018 Sajjan Kumar verdict, it has brought some *sukoon* (peace) to survivors. It is unbelievable that justice delayed is still seen as justice affirmed.

The reception of the December 2018 judgement, coming thirty-four years after the Sikh massacre, once again demonstrates that victims of one-sided collective violence desperately need retributive justice; they must not be deviously nudged to move on without it, to let bygones be bygones and to forget and forgive. Not surprisingly, it is the perpetrators of violence or insensitive bystanders who say this. Forgetting is neither possible nor desirable. Traumatised survivors may be forced into silence, but they can't forget their loss or suffering. For a start, forgetting can't be brought about intentionally; no one can wilfully strive to achieve amnesia. The more one goads oneself to forget, the more one remembers the brutality of the act and the loss of loved ones. More importantly, such a demand can't be morally justified. Imagine that someone close to you was lynched in front of your very own eyes. Wouldn't you be haunted by images of this gruesome act forever? Can the intensity of the initial trauma diminish with the passage of time if, for instance, you lost your only child to this collective insanity? Can the wound ever be healed? How preposterous it is to be asked to move on. Even when friends and family urge you to stop grieving and to try loosen the grip of this nightmare, they don't expect you to forget the trauma but to find ways to rebuild your life. To my mind, an appropriate form of remembrance is the only partial remedy for this lifelong ailment.

Resentment and Self-respect

Forgiveness is more complex. To forgive is to forswear resentment towards the person who has caused you grievous harm. Now, no one can seriously argue that renunciation of resentment is always morally appropriate and that one must always forgive. To begin with, one can hardly fault people for resenting those who have seriously harmed them because resentment is interwoven with self-respect. Only those without an iota of self-respect, completely self-estranged or benumbed will fail to experience resentment towards the offender. So the relevant question is not whether or not to forgive but rather under what condition is forgiveness appropriate. And the answer is this: only when it restores the self-respect of victims. And when can that happen? Only when the perpetrators publicly acknowledge their wrongdoing, distance themselves from the wrongful act and join victims in condemning their own past actions.

All this is mighty difficult because it can come about only with a profound moral and spiritual transformation in a perpetrator's personality. The experiential process of owning up responsibility begins with the gradual realisation that the wrongful act sprung from the deepest recesses of one's being—that there is something deeply wrong with what one is. This requires a genuine confrontation with one's self, not just in the mind but also at the level of gut and feeling. Such honest moral self-appraisal is gut-wrenching. As one undergoes this long-drawn-out and painful process, one punishes one's deepest self or, as some might say, one's *antaratma,* or soul. Only such punishment of the soul generates a profound transformation in one's identity. No perpetrator is ready to seek forgiveness without it. And no victim can be ready to forgive unless this transformation is personally witnessed. Genuine repentance may pave the way for forgiveness. The victim can then say, 'He has suffered enough; let him go'. This call to forgive has to come from within. It follows that no one can forgive under compulsion or on behalf of the victim.

Understanding Forgiveness

It is sometimes claimed that forgiveness has the effect of erasing wrongdoing—that it is an invitation to reconcile with evil rather than conquering it. But this is mistaken because appropriate forgiveness follows an honest acknowledgement of the wrongful act by the wrongdoer and repentance before his victim. To forgive then is neither to convert a wrong into a right nor is it identical to excusing a wrong—as when one excuses a child for causing harm—on the ground that he cannot really be held responsible for it. Since a wrong is not simply whitewashed, to forgive is not a compromise with evil.

Forgiveness must not be confused with mercy. Out of mercy, punishment may be reduced without forgiving the wrongdoer.

Conversely, a victim may forgive a wrongdoer but she will not be entitled to free him of legal accountability or seek a reduction in punishment. Indeed, sometimes it is the legal progress or outcome that triggers 'a punishment of the soul'. When it does, it may be morally appropriate to forgive, should the victim choose to do so. Forgiveness indicates an alteration in the victim's attitude towards the offender not a change in the legal course of action.

Victims or survivors can't forget the wrongs done to them. Justice is necessary to address the wrongs and alleviate suffering. But forgiveness too can play a reparative role, provided it is seen as complementary to justice and not a substitute for it.

PART VII

Have We Lost Our Way?

64

Have We Lost Our Way?

It is becoming hazardous to read Indian newspapers. The health minister of Assam says that the the sufferings of cancer patients are divine justice for past sins[8]; an elected member of legislative assembly demands, chillingly, the beheading of an actor; Muslim clerics beaten mercilessly for no reason and, to top it all, the soul-destroying incident of a four-year-old—yes, a toddler—sexually assaulting his class mate.[9] Have we lost our way as a country, a society and a civilisation?

Please don't think that I am about to pounce on the party in power, although politics undeniably has some role to play in this. I worry about a long-developing trend of profound social and cultural malaise that afflicts all of us and the damage such incidents inflict on our collective psyche.

Internal and External Goods

To give a comprehensive picture of all the causes for this cultural and moral mess is beyond my capacity. I mention just two that come immediately to mind in the hope that this opens a space for further discussion. Both depend on a distinction made by the Scottish philosopher Alasdair MacIntyre between external and internal goods of a social practice. First, an overwhelming focus on external goods takes attention away from the internal goods of social practices. Second, unpleasant human attributes that accompany the relentless pursuit of external goods severely diminish those ethical and moral qualities without which human life is poor, nasty and brutish even if not exactly short or entirely solitary. I take each in turn.

[8] PTI, 'People Have Cancer Because of Their Sins, This Is Divine Justice: Says Assam Minister,' *The Economic Times*, 23 November 2017, https://economictimes.indiatimes.com/news/politics-and-nation/people-have-cancer-because-of-their-sins-this-is-divine-justice-says-assam-minister/articleshow/61760849.cms?from=mdr

[9] TNN, '4-Year-Old Sexually Abused in School by "Classmate",' *The Times of India*, 24 November 2017, https://timesofindia.indiatimes.com/city/delhi/4-year-old-sexually-abusedin-school-by-classmate/articleshow/61760133.cms

Every practice is driven by an internal good. Take fiction writing, for example. One of its many internal goods is to imaginatively give us a vivid sense of the dilemmas and moral complexity of human life and to tighten our grasp over human predicaments; the internal good of legal practice is to deliver justice; of medical practice, to cure, heal and help people live a healthy life; of democratic politics, to enhance the collective good to benefit every single citizen; and, of ordinary morality, to never harm, if not always do good to others. Internal goods are intrinsic to every social practice, give it its point and partly define what it is. These internal goods cannot be realised if standards of excellence appropriate to each practice are not followed. Plenty of hard work goes into perfecting them. Furthermore, when achieved, internal goods extend the powers of the entire community—indeed, enrich everyone.

Take an example from cricket: when Ranjitsinhji invented the leg glance or Tendulkar perfected the upper cut or Pakistani bowlers developed the reverse swing, they not only enhanced the quality of their own game but benefitted the entire cricketing community. Here, healthy competition over excellence enhances everyone's game. The more innovations there are in cricket, the more these shared goods are collectively enjoyed. I believe this is virtually true of all excellence-driven human practices—farming, cooking, shoemaking, carpentry, writing, dancing, playing football, architecture, law, democratic politics and so on. Whatever they generate can be possessed or enjoyed by everyone. One can either excel at them or not, there is always room for improvement and they can never be practised enough. Indeed, if you don't put these skills to use, pick up bad habits on the way and go astray, you will lose them altogether. And their loss is collective too.

This precisely is where external goods come into the picture. All these practices can also bring with them goods that are external to these practices—money, fame and power. They are external because they can be achieved even outside each practice. Diseases can rarely be cured outside medical practice, but to earn money, one need not be a medical doctor. Also, specific standards of excellence are not necessary for securing external goods. Indeed, they are frequently achieved by neglecting them. Not all famous or rich lawyers or doctors are good as their reputations suggest. However, if these external goods are achieved as a by-product of the pursuit of excellence, one need not shun them. The point is that if one follows a career in cricket, law or politics with the primary aim of making money, exercising power or gaining fame, the internal goods of these practices will never be achieved. And when that happens, the entire humanity loses. To single-mindedly pursue external goods at the expense of internal goods is bad enough, but to lose the very distinction between the two does irreparable damage to everyone. It is this trend of fudging the crucial distinction between the two goods that is deeply troublesome.

Negative Emotions

The pure pursuit of external goods has another terrible consequence. An obsession with them undermines our capacity for self-reflection and cultivation, strangles our imagination and induces thoughtlessness, narrow-mindedness and prejudice. Moreover, these goods are individual possessions, and because one has them at the expense of others, they promote self-seeking. The more power, money or fame one has, the less they are available for others to possess. This promotes negative emotions such as jealousy, envy and malice and considerably diminishes our capacity for empathy, care and compassion. They corrode the moral and ethical fabric of society and, in the end, brutalise us and our children.

I see inscribed in these incidents a chilling brutalisation, and in the naked pursuit of power, money and two minutes of fame, the triumph of external over internal goods. They reflect an inexorable march towards a fall from the deepest values of humanity.

65

Is India Still a Minimally Decent Society?

A few years ago, I met a deeply troubled elderly person on a flight to Vijayawada. 'I still can't get over the fact that a child was raped in a temple in Jammu. Not long ago, thousands of people came out on the streets in Delhi appalled by what had happened to Nirbhaya; but in the horrific temple incident, it seemed it was business as usual soon enough,' he said. 'The health of a society is not all that different from the physical health of individuals.'

He continued:

> Neglect the early signs, ignore the symptoms of a serious disease and it will surreptitiously take root and spread its tentacles. One day you appear to be fine and before you know it, you are incurably sick. We are fast losing our sense of outrage and civility. Before we realise, we will lose all sense of even minimal decency. Barbarity is always lurking around the corner in every society. Do you think we too are becoming barbaric?

I pondered for a while and said, 'We are a fundamentally decent people but zones of barbarity appear to be sprouting everywhere.' Why else would we tolerate the savagery in Unnao, the merciless killing of a family in Murshidabad and the lynching of a man in Jharkhand? Societies with people living economically degraded lives have often bordered on the indecent. But now it seems that even societies with economically aspiring lives are getting there, falling well short of minimal decency. 'Unless we put ourselves on moral red alert, we are sunk,' I added.

Basic Procedural Justice

The phrase 'minimally decent' implies that the best available ethical standards in a society remain unrealised even according to its own lights. A minimally decent society is not free of exploitation or injustice. It need not embody political equality. Yet, it possesses one singular virtue: it prevents excessive wrongdoing with the help of effective injunctions against killing, maiming or ill-treating others. It also has a system of what the English philosopher Stuart Hampshire called 'basic procedural justice'. This is an elementary form of justice that involves fair procedures of negotiation and arbitration that permit the recognition of untidy, temporary compromises between people who differ vastly. Basic procedural justice enables different conceptions of the good life to coexist 'without any substantial reconciliation' and 'without search for the common ground'.

This coexistence is possible by virtue of a restraint on 'unmeasured ambition, on limitless self-assertion and on the obsessive desire for an ever-larger slice of the cake'. This enables almost every voice to be heard, ensures some visibility for everyone in the political domain and guarantees that even the most marginalised and exploited remain a part of the negotiation, howsoever unequal the conditions under which it takes place. In short, a system of basic procedural justice keeps conversation and negotiation going among all members in society. People involved in even the fiercest of disputes are 'prepared to recognise the need to balance argument against argument [and] concession against concession'. Basic procedural justice 'makes possible a minimally decent life, which has a value independent of any wider conception of the good'.

Flattened Moral Landscape

By contrast, a society where minimally moral constraints are thrown to the wind is barbaric. This happens under degrading economic conditions, but shockingly, minimally moral rules are also abandoned by groups in pursuit of greatness or, simply, economic or political success. (For them, dharma must not come in the way of the vastly more important artha or moksha). Once moral constraints on action—for instance, notions of basic fairness and procedural justice—are eliminated from public life and the minds of people and a 'bombed and flattened moral landscape' is created, nothing is forbidden or off limits and the way is fully open to violence and domination. One now witnesses evil: 'A force not only contrary to all that is praiseworthy, admirable and desirable in human lives but which is actively working against all that is praiseworthy and admirable,' said Hampshire. In a barbaric society, where basic procedural justice is dismembered, conversation is replaced by oppressive silence and the entire mechanism of negotiation and arbitration vanishes. Hampshire was compelled to draw this conclusion in the midst of the Second World War and, in particular, the face of the horror of the Nazi regime. 'I learnt how easy it had been to organize the vast enterprises of torture and of murder, and to enroll willing workers in this field, once all moral barriers were removed by the authorities,' he wrote. Force, inducement of fear or prolonged conflict often create pliant, demoralised masses fit for domination, thereby destroying morality in public life.

Amoral Private Life

When morality is destroyed in public life, it does not leave the rest of the social world unaffected. Evil spills from the public to the private domain and pervades intimate realms. Friends, lovers, members of the family can all be complicit in dubious actions. Indeed, the very distinction between friend and enemy is blurred. The sociologist Veena Das, reporting on victims of the massacre of Sikhs in Delhi in 1984, talks of how the traumatic violence of the crowd suddenly revealed to one of its victims the fragility of her kinship universe. Shanti, the victim, disclosed that 'it was my own mama (mother's brother) who first advised my husband to hide and then revealed the hiding place to the leaders of the mob. He bartered their lives for his own protection.' Pulitzer Prize–winner Tina Rosenberg gives a moving account of a wife–husband duo Vera and Knud Wollenberger, dissident members of the peace circle in communist East Germany, who risked their jobs and freedom and were constantly spied upon by the state security police (Stasi). After the fall of the Berlin Wall, Vera joined the East German Parliament and campaigned for Stasi victims to access their personal files. When she eventually succeeded in accessing her own file, it was full of reports from a Stasi informer code-named 'Donald'; it contained information that could have been known only to one other person. Donald was her own husband! The horror of this monstrous universe can hardly be overstated. The misfortune of distrust amid general friendlessness and lovelessness is the greatest evil that has befell human beings.

I wish I could, with greater confidence, assure my elderly friend that we are a minimally decent society and more. But as I witness more precincts of indecency grow around me, I am myself troubled, filled with fear and anxiety that we might be regressing. As societies lose minimal decency, it is hard to pull them back on the road to freedom, equality, justice or emancipation. All these substantial ideals, which not long ago propelled large-scale collective action, are suddenly rendered vacuous as people scramble to put together conditions of bare life. Yet, precisely in such uncertain times, rather than reach out for higher, near-perfect ethical standards, it is crucial to remain grounded if grave wrongdoing is to be avoided. Gandhi remains our moral compass on such issues. Though aimed primarily at deeper self-transformation, his fasts were also practical instruments to cement the fragile social agreement that brutality must be eschewed at any cost.

66

The Moral Coarseness of Our Public Culture

If some wrong is done to people close to us—our family or friends—we respond with utter horror, as we must. Why then do we react feebly or, worse, not at all, when people beyond our little community are treated cruelly? More specifically, why has there not been greater collective outrage at mob lynching of a poor Muslim or the horrendous brutality regularly faced by Dalits?

Why is it that instead of a chorus of straightforward condemnation, we confront moral indifference or troublesome public statements that we must first or also condemn other instances of brutality in the past? Imagine Nirbhaya's mother being told in the aftermath of the dastardly incident that any denunciation of what happened is conditional: we must in the same breath also condemn all brutal rapes in the past. The moral coarseness of this response simply jumps to the eye.

Our Public Culture

Has the savagery around us numbed our sensibilities to the suffering of others? Has the 'dirty' politics around these incidents put off 'decent' men and women, compelling them to withdraw into their shell and fall silent? I don't know. I admit to having no direct explanation of this phenomenon. But I draw attention to two aspects of our public culture that contribute to our shared moral coarseness.

First, many of us, the metropolitan middle and upper classes, have begun to believe that moral values are individual preferences, a matter of subjective taste, something each individual can choose, so that what is valuable for one person need not be valuable or good for another. Moral values, it is claimed, vary from individual to individual. There is no objective morality—call it moral subjectivism. Two lessons are usually drawn from this: that (a) we can never arrive at a common understanding or agreement on moral values, and since there is no shared morality, (b) no one should pass moral judgement on others. One step further and we arrive at the calamitous consequence of presuming an absence of common moral judgement even on issues where agreement can easily exist, such as, it is wrong to be cruel to other human beings. This too is mere subjective opinion.

The second, equally serious, is the other side of the moral subjectivist coin. This is the widespread belief that while no common judgement is possible in value-laden human affairs, in the non-human domain—in the world of nature and things, where no moral values reside—a unique common judgement—one right answer—is always available. Get rid of subjectively moral values from the world, free it of moral or human understanding and shared judgement and objective knowledge—objectivism—will follow. Furthermore, wherever humans can be viewed as objects or things, as in purely scientific treatment of human affairs, mainstream Western medical regimes or in the economic domain, a unique value-neutral answer exists, valid not just for one but for all.

Where both subjectivism and objectivism converge is that they make common human understanding either impossible or redundant. In the moral domain, subjectivism tells us that there is no common human understanding. And the objectivism of the scientific world view tells us that a common understanding is possible only in a world free of moral values.

But an urgently needed moral response to all kinds of social situations, including lynching or bombing of innocents, depends precisely on human-to-human or common understanding, the ability of one human to actually or imaginatively share a situation with others and to understand his pain, suffering or predicament. Moral judgement and moral outrage depend on empathetic understanding and compassion.

But we are not born with these capacities; they are learnt. Understanding the perspectives of others by their own lights and imagining their sufferings and predicaments is an acquired skill; we are taught to rise above one's own provincialities, to respect difference and plurality, to value the social uses of reason that help explore new forms and levels of agreements or to experiment with reasonable disagreements, to critically examine received knowledge, to make sound judgement in the face of complex dilemmas and to achieve greater self-understanding.

All these capacities depend upon thought and imagination that are cultivated. And for all this we need not physics, chemistry and mathematics but philosophy, literature and narratives embedded in different religious traditions. We need to read and think with the *Panchatantra*, the *Jataka*s and the Mahabharata; with Plato, Buddha and

Confucius; with Al-Ghazali and Rumi; with Annamacharya and thinkers of the Varkari tradition. In short, we need education in the humanities.

Not Just Employability

Our complex moral sensibilities are cultivated less within the family and more through systematic teaching in the humanities. An education system that neglects the humanities is slowly moving towards a moral disaster. But it is just this—a technocratic, humanities-free education system that devalues common human understanding—that many of us from the middle and upper classes wish to have for our children. By viewing education solely in terms of its employability quotient and how it helps us secure jobs—as instruments of greater material prosperity for individuals and tools for multiplying objectively measurable national assets (GDP, bigger profits and greater power)—we unwittingly invite moral coarseness upon ourselves.

When it comes to our family and close friends, our raw moral intuitions suffice. These intuitions are so strong that they overwhelm the moral vacuum encouraged by our humanities-devaluing education system. But when it comes to all other humans, our raw intuitions are too feeble. We desperately need a humanities-sensitive education to cultivate a sophisticated moral sensibility for moral enlargement beyond our kith and kin.

Alas, what we are receiving instead is further moral restriction. A culture that once treated all its elders with generosity and respect shows increasing sign of moral callousness towards even old parents. I fear this development may not be unrelated to the brutishness with which we treat those outside our fold.

67

The Pernicious Idea of Exclusive Belonging

The idea that each human being belongs to only one religious or linguistic community, a single culture or a unique civilization appears to be ubiquitous. Many have begun to believe that our identity is defined by membership to only mutually exclusive groups. If we are Bengali, we cannot be Odia or Assamese; if Hindu, then not Muslim or Christian.

This idea of exclusive belonging is relatively recent. Indeed, even today, a substantial number of humans appear not to have it. Or if they do, only very faintly. Multiple belonging is common because we imbibe from other cultures when we go to them. And because ideas and values, energetic and nimble-footed, come to us as they seek uncharted territories. This fluidity in understanding who we are is ineradicable and infinitely better than a condition in which we are confined to a fixed, categorical idea of identity.

Identity Is Multilayered

That we belong exclusively to one culture, religion or language is undesirable and unfeasible. It is not feasible because our overall identity is far more complex and multi-layered than what we articulate or others believe of us. To take the manifest part of ourselves as our only identity is to accept a truncated, impoverished self. It is undesirable because it forces us to rely exclusively on one tradition when, in fact, we can be nourished by many. We live much better when we are open to multiple influences and enriched by varied currents of thought and value.

Intersecting Cultures

Take any one of us living in Delhi. We are heirs to myriad streams of Hindi, Urdu and Punjabi. Local dialects apart, these are shaped by old Sanskrit and old Persian, close cousins in an ancient family of languages (consider words such as 'asura' and 'ahura' or 'yajna' and 'yasna'). Those who speak them do not realise that several words in their tongue are of Arabic origin (aadmi, maalik, etc.). Since languages are not simply a means of communication but constitute multiple worlds, the criss-crossing and overlapping worlds they inhabit are infinitely more complex and expansive than is recognised. Monuments and public spaces that surround us (Humayun's Tomb, Ramlila Maidan, the Parliament building) and the varied cuisines that shape our taste and sensibility are also creations of intersecting cultures. So are the identities they shape.

The same is true of moral frameworks that ground our commitments and convictions—structures of values that have developed over 5,000 years. I doubt if there is any Indian who has not been shaped by multiple ancient strands that compose Hinduism, the precepts of Buddha and Mahavir, the partly homegrown Islamic and Christian traditions and the teachings of Nanak and Kabir, not to forget the enormous impact that Western values have had since Vasco Da Gama stepped ashore and all the way to the globalised world we now inhabit. The idea of exclusive allegiance to any one of these flies in the face of evidence and is based on ignorance or deliberate denial. Why should we, instead of embracing all of them, insist on exclusive belonging and loyalty to just one?

A Serious Objection

At this point, it might be objected that a person's identity is defined not by everything that has influenced her but by those elements she has evaluated to be of greater importance. Someone can say that her fundamental commitments flow from a single framework—and this alone defines her identity. Identity is defined by what is publicly affirmed because of judgement of its real significance. It announces where we truly belong—to what we owe our overriding allegiance.

A person's identity, the argument goes, is defined by his orientation to an incomparably higher good. It underlines the quest to be a certain kind of person—to give oneself a direction. Does this often not require removing all 'alien or bad features'? Is not this movement towards something higher often a battle between good and the evil within? Why cannot this be seen as a certain kind of purification? A shuddhikaran for a Hindu or, for that matter, a jihad for a Muslim. If so, does it not follow that one is a Hindu because of one's aspiration to realise what is most valuable in Hinduism rather than in any other ethical tradition? To tell such a person that there is a Muslim ingredient in his self is irrelevant because the whole point of his existence is to become a good Hindu and remove extraneous, non- or anti-Hindu elements. This seems like a forceful rebuttal. But it overlooks two stronger challenges.

First, the encounter between two different ethical traditions results in mutual transformation of what is truly worthwhile in these traditions. Arguably, the ethics of Vedic people originally comprised three ends of life: kama, artha and dharma. It needed the teachings of the Buddha to add a fourth value—moksha. Similarly, the Arya Samaj challenged idol worship as a perverse substitution of the original Vedic fire rituals; but can one deny that it was also influenced by the Islamic conception of a formless god? Religions have frequently shaped one another's conception of the ultimate good even as they conceal or stigmatise the source.

Second and equally important challenge is that most of us are powered by multiple moral sources. We acknowledge within us the presence of different, even incompatible, normative orientations. Consider the French philosopher Paul Ricoeur's disclosure that the private reading of the Bible was central to the pietistic Protestant milieu in which he was born. This part of his upbringing—leaning on prayer and the undogmatic examination of conscience—had little intellectual content about it. But Ricouer was equally impacted by another milieu wherein critical thinking and public standards of rationality were essential. He says, 'I always moved back and forth between these two poles: a biblical pole and a rational, critical pole. A duality that has lasted through my entire life. I remained faithful to this double allegiance.' I believe this self-description captures the life of many intellectuals. Many scientists take their Hindu outlook seriously; many philosophers are at home in their Jewish, Islamic or Catholic spiritualities. Loyal to both, they feel that something terribly important would be lost if either was snatched away from them.

Multiple Allegiances

Indeed, I will not be surprised if there are many Muslims today who are inspired by both the Ramayana and the Koran. This was something commonplace till the mid-twentieth century in large parts of Haryana's Meo community. It is still common to find some of our greatest singers, musicians and poets moved equally and simultaneously by Hindu and Muslim mysticism. I saw a film on Bismillah Khan in which he tells the viewers how blessed he was to live in Benares (now Varanasi): 'I can step down the ghats, bathe in the Ganga, walk up to the masjid for namaz and then head straight to the Balaji temple for riyaz.' The fact is that large numbers of people in the past embraced not just dual but multiple allegiances, and this is unlikely to disappear in future. The demand for a single, exclusive allegiance makes for a sorry, desiccated self.

The idea of exclusive belonging or allegiance is a pernicious intrusion into world cultures. Equally dangerous is a political project that foists a singularity or homogeneity and calls for the obliteration of multiplicity and fluidity so that we become purely one or the other. The demand to 'purify' and rid ourselves of anything 'foreign' that contaminates is not only hard to meet but—if we are to lead a better, richer life—also not worth complying.

68

The New Face of Ideological Violence

In 1598, a group of Vaishnava clergy sought the king's permission to install an idol of Vishnu at Chidambaram, the site probably of the most sacred of Shiva temples in the subcontinent. Horrified Shaiva priests responded by a threat to commit mass suicide to protest this. Indeed, twenty of them jumped to their death from the gopuram (a temple's entrance tower). This telling detail from a relatively new book on pluralism by a young American scholar Elaine Fischer vividly illustrates the nature of religious violence in early modern India. Worshippers would rather give up their own life than take the life of others with different beliefs and practices. Killing someone from another sect was simply inconceivable.

In the light of this, what is happening today is cataclysmic. India has had many faults but eliminating people for holding different beliefs was certainly not one of them. For more than two millennia, India has had vibrant traditions of atheism and rationalism—the Jains, Buddhists, followers of Mimansa and Samkhya. They were vigorously opposed by worshippers of gods and goddesses and ritualists of all hue but were never viewed as an existential threat. Claims of superiority were frequently made in public alongside scathing satire and black humour. There was vitriol too, but physical violence was rare. Ashoka's inscriptions as early as the third century exhort different religio-philosophical groups to refrain from insulting and humiliating hate speech. Ashoka did not even consider it worth mentioning that people must abjure injuring, leave alone killing, each other. He took it for granted that this did not happen in his kingdom. This is not to say that ancient societies were entirely peaceful. They were also rocked by political and everyday violence integral to all hierarchical societies. However, what India did not witness until the advent of colonial modernity is what may be called ideological violence.

Forms of Violence

Violence comes in many forms. One kind that springs from greed, anger and fear has been around forever—call this plain violence. Then, of course, there is political violence, that is, violence to conquer territory to acquire and maintain state power. Yet another—a third—form of violence, which might be called ritual violence, has existed in archaic societies, where occasionally humans but far more frequently animals were slaughtered and sacrificed to procure this-worldly goods as well as to maintain cosmic order. In India, some of this ritual violence also ensued from the distinction between pure and impure, present in caste and gender-realted violence.

Ideological violence is different from all these forms of violence; it stems from the dogma that one's own beliefs and practices are so precious and unique that they alone must be publicly visible. Since these are inherently indisputable and have a monopoly over truth, any challenge to them is wasteful or pernicious and, therefore, must be silenced or erased. It is accompanied by the idea that those with identical beliefs share a special bond of brotherhood, which must not be severed by slightest deviations from within; therefore, internal dissenters must not be tolerated. On the other hand, those who hold different beliefs are outsiders to be fought, expelled and even exterminated.

Ideological violence was once linked to the development of a certain conception of religion. It can, therefore, also be called religious violence. But in the last two centuries, it has permeated a cluster of non-religious ideologies such as Stalinism, Fascism and xenophobic nationalism. Perhaps that is why it is best not to call it religious but ideological violence.

The horrifying spate of murders—Narendra Dabholkar, Govind Pansare, M.M. Kalburgi and Gauri Lankesh—by what appears to be the same kind of killers has shown us a new face of this very ideological violence. To be sure, shades of ideological violence are found in inter-sectarian warfare in West Bengal; Kerala too is beset with ideologically motivated intergroup violence. But what is unique about these killings is that violence is directed by assassination squads run by hate groups against hapless individuals for merely holding and expressing their (different) views in public. This pernicious squad-violence against ordinary middle-class professionals is unique in recent Indian history.

A New Fear

One other feature of these serial assassinations is deeply troubling: unless quickly contained, they generate a new kind of fear and a new set of fearful people. It is true that some or the other group of people have always lived in fear in our society. For instance, Dalits in villages perpetually live on the brink of upper-caste violence; women who can, never fearlessly venture out at night; journalists in small towns routinely face the wrath of the powerful; minorities suffer public backlash during and in the aftermath of riots and even middle- and upper-class families live in fear in gated communities in cities such as Delhi. But what is new and shocking about these recent murders is an attempt to silence assertive, public-spirited, outspoken citizens in metropolitan towns—an effect also sought to be achieved by legal intimidation of intellectuals and activists.

Are we so uprooted now from our traditions that we can't bear to see public articulations of alternative viewpoints? Is there an effort here to forge one monolithic ideology in the public domain? Hatred and violence squads are strategically located and activated to disrupt debate and conversation on issues of common concern, which foster civic alienation and political fragmentation. If, indeed, a nation is a people in conversation with one another, cyberbullying and physical aggression against fellow citizens are conversation-stoppers. An attack on this conversation is an attack on the nation.

69

Are We Ravaged by Egoism?

Several years ago, driving on the then wide and spacious Ring Road in Delhi, I was nearly hit by a car that dashed out from a side lane. I brought my car to a screaming halt, sprang agitatedly towards the offender and asked him if he knew that the driver on the main road has the right of way. Completely unruffled, he replied, '*Jo jis road par chalta hai, wahi road uske liye main road hoti hai*' (Whichever road one is on becomes their main road). I used that incident as an example to teach my students the meaning of relativism. But it can as easily be used as an example of how people brazenly put their own self-interest before the interest of others. Already a symptom of a developing social disease then, today the malaise has deepened. There is a free reign in our society of unspeakable moral insensitivity. In short, a very worrying aspect of contemporary India is a rampaging egoism engulfing us all.

Let me immediately allay the fears of those who suspect that the target of my attack is self-interest. It is not. Indeed, it is extremely important that self-interest be distinguished from egoism. It is the galloping growth of egoism that alarms me, not the legitimate pursuit of self-interest.

Self-interest

Self-interest is the awakened attention of one's self towards its own desires or good. This awakened attention to one's own good may lead one to desire it when it is absent, to actively pursue it in order to attain it and to have positive feelings when it is achieved. There is clearly nothing wrong in this. Indeed, we want people to recognise their interests and pursue them with care and concentration. We reprimand a diabetic parent who eats sweets on the sly, a child who does not wash his hands before dining or a student who does not study before an important exam. Not knowing one's interests or failing to pursue them appropriately is hardly a virtue.

Indeed, we not only need to pay heed to our self-interest but also keep enriching it. We need to discriminate between what is good for us and what we desire and attend to our real self-interest and recognise, for instance, that it is unhealthy to regularly consume fast food—even inappropriate to even want it—and to switch instead to a home-cooked balanced diet.

But what if my self-interest, rich or poor, conflicts with the interests of others? Isn't egoism just this: the pursuit of self-interest at the expense of others? Is this the problem of rampaging egoism—that all of us are pursuing our own interests disregarding the interests of others? Not quite. Why?

Egoism

Egoism is a pathological by-product of modern reason, a rationally evaluated perspective for which the only entity in the world that matters is one's own self. All other persons are entirely worthless. Essentially, it comes in two forms. If the self coincides with one person, we obtain individual egoism. If it extends to a group encompassing several persons, then we have communitarian egoism. Such egoism may focus on the family, the caste or a linguistic, religious or national community. For communitarian egoism, only my community has value; other communities are entirely worthless.

This should immediately clarify that a person pursuing self-interest even when disregarding others is not necessarily an egoist. An egoist's disregard for the interests of others is different from the non-egoist's. The difference is this: egoism emerges only when an act that disregards others is propelled by the deeper belief that others have no value at all. The self-interest of two persons who recognise each other's value may conflict, but such conflicts can be resolved or reconciled because deep down they share a moral framework. But the egoist is numb to others; he altogether lacks a moral dimension.

In fact, the pursuit of self-interest can even serve justice. Let me offer some examples to illustrate my point. An apple is placed before Viren and Neel. Viren already possesses six apples and wants the seventh. Neel has none. Both Viren, who is clearly greedy, and the needy Neel want the apple. But Neel, disregarding the current interests of Viren, takes it. Though Neel has successfully pursued his self-interest at Viren's expense, he is not an egoist. Take another example. Ram and Ravi are travelling in a compartment of a fast-moving train. Neither can leave the compartment. Ravi lights a cigarette. Since Ram suffers from asthma, he requests Ravi to stop smoking but to no avail. Ram snatches the cigarette from Ravi and throws it out of the window. He has acted to protect his interest, disregarding the interest of Ravi, but he is not an egoist. These are not fanciful examples of philosophers. The poor who suffered in, say, the Odisha cyclone and looted food reserves of local baniyas because of the complete breakdown of the public distribution system can hardly be called egoists.

So, what is worrying about our current sociocultural malaise is this: there are lots of people amid us who are acting against others to not only realise their self-interest but also to brutally convey a message to others that they are altogether worthless. What else is conveyed by the callous indifference to children dying out of neglect in hospitals, by an eighty-year-old Swami Agnivesh being kicked and abused, by the savagery of the rape of little girls and by the lynching of innocents by feral mobs?

70

The Deep and Disturbing Thought behind Lynching

On 3 December 2018, Station House Officer Subodh Singh was assaulted and then shot dead by a mob in Syana area of Bulandshahr after a protest by right-wing groups against alleged cow slaughter turned violent.[10] The lynching of the police officer and a youth was not a spontaneous moral reaction by a hastily assembled crowd. Group violence unleashed upon an alleged transgressor is always spurred by a complex interplay of interest, prejudice and power.

Let me selectively offer one such explanation for this frightening incident—one that emphasises power. Extreme aggression creates fear in one's opponents as well as in those who refuse to take sides. The Bulandshahr lynching were intended not only to terrorise a minority—the alleged cow slaughterers—but also those keen on impartially implementing the law. The killing was meant to instil fear in officers within the state machinery itself. This is a plausible account. But I want to go beyond it and examine the ideological underpinnings of lynching. Since mob lynching is not restricted to any one ideology, I wish to go beneath the surface of ideologies to identify the elementary structure of thought present invariably at their core. What is it? Here is my tentative answer: marked differences between 'us' and 'them'. But even this, stated so simplistically, is an insufficient explanation for lynching. Why?

---

[10] Piyush Rai, 'Cop Among Two Killed in Mob Riots Over "Cow Slaughter" in Bulandshahr,' *The Times of India*, 4 December 2018, https://timesofindia.indiatimes.com/city/meerut/mob-violence-in-bulandshahr-over-cow-slaughter-cop-among-two-killed/articleshow/66920578.cms

Living with Differences

Consider the following: suppose that you and I are different in one respect, say religion, but not in others. This difference usually implies that you participate in a practice different from mine—I go to a temple and you to a church. But it does not follow that you and I, despite our religious differences, cannot come together in other respects. After all, those who go to the church or to the temple also speak a language, are citizens of a polity, are part of a family, live in a neighbourhood, have jobs and hobbies, and relate to people around on many other issues. In short, our membership to a religious community is only one among many memberships to several different communities. Invariably, a person has multiple networks or solidarities. So if Christians are asked whether it is important for Hindus in their midst to go to church, they can easily respond saying, 'No, that is exclusive to us and not required for them. They go to the temple.' Clearly, this 'us' and 'them' discourse is quite harmless. The distinction in this form cannot be the ideological cause of violence against others.

But now, let us imagine that this religious dimension begins to colour all other dimensions of life. Religion then becomes our dominant or defining feature. Let us say everyone believes that despite their common activities they are primarily defined by their religion. Such people will draw sharp boundaries between their own communities and that of others. They will view themselves as utterly different from each other. Such differences might even lead to conflict. Can such people live together? I believe they can because despite conflicts they will invariably find some commonality. Life needs social cooperation; it would come to a standstill if people focussed only on radical differences rather than on what brings them together. Besides, conflicts need not turn violent. Therefore, on its own, even a sharp boundary between 'us' and 'them' (sharpened religious differences) does not cause violence, including lynching.

Deep and Radical Otherness

So, what else is required? The missing component in this way of thinking is not just the simple idea of 'them' and 'us' but also a more complex belief with two components. First, that only our group matters: only *we* are worthy, good, right or true and all others are unworthy, evil, wrong or false; *they* are wholly insignificant or hold views that are completely false. Second, while those who are like us are our brothers or intimate friends, those not like us are so inferior, wrong and such a menace that they can't stay with us. It is impossible to converse or have a dialogue with them or reach out to them if an agreement or consensus has broken down. They are enemies, constituting a permanent existential threat, to be expelled or exterminated. It is this strong sense of one's own intrinsic superiority and the others' unmitigated inferiority, accompanied by the view that these others can't be lived with, that lies at the root of such exclusionary violence. If a group or any section thereof partakes in this way of thinking, the entire society is clearly heading for disaster.

The consequences of this deep and radical otherness are not only catastrophic for the targeted community but eventually for the community of violent offenders itself. This is because those who see others as enemies invariably get sucked into a vortex of suspicion towards members of their own community. It is not long before they start looking for the enemy within their own intimate community who are seen to deviate from the true or virtuous path set by powerful ideologues in the community. Anyone who sympathises with others is seen as a betrayer, as deviant and abnormal, and one who tries to be neutral or impartial, as no longer 'one of us' but a traitor. All such transgressors must be quickly brought in line. And since modes of persuasion disappear from such exclusivist communities, the deviant within who strays from doctrinal truth or has the temerity to refuse complete loyalty or allegiance must also be violently excluded.

Behind lynching then lies the vicious idea that moral truth or goodness is possessed by one group alone, and all others who do not have it or stray from it are enemies to be fought, conquered or decimated.

71

India's Culture of Toxic Masculinity

Three images of social violence haunted me in 2019. The first was that of a teenager beaten mercilessly by a village elder. Her crime? She dared to elope with her young lover. Second, after the acquittal of all six men accused of lynching Pehlu Khan, television channels replayed the visuals in which a crowd of men participated gleefully in the atrocity. The third was of three Dalits being thrashed over allegation of theft. The barbarity of this violence can hardly escape anyone, but equally striking is the absence of any woman among the perpetrators. This theatre of cruelty has an all-male cast.

Of course, women perpetrate violence too: they can be aggressive and brutal, particularly to other women. But undoubtedly, the culture that stokes such violence smacks of machismo. Though not solely responsible for such violence, this culture plays a central role in its recurrence, justification and glorification.

Scholars have drawn attention to the fact that ideas of masculinity are tied less to the body and more to sociocultural ideologies and practices. Manhood is not naturally given but a goal to be achieved. To be born a boy is a privilege but one that can be lost if one is not properly initiated into the masculine practices. Besides, male adults must maintain this privilege by regular performance. They must demonstrate that they are real men—manly—rather than womanly men. And what better way to do so than by giving someone a good, solid walloping? If one ceases to perform these masculine acts or gives up the beliefs that constitute them, one slips out of manhood and becomes effeminate.

Model of Manhood

What are the core features of this model of manhood? First, aggression is natural and desirable in men. A 'real' man is eager to pick up a fight. If he does not, he is told to wear bangles on his wrists. Even the slightest intrusion in his physical, mental or social space is unacceptable.

Second, men must be tough—muscular and unemotional; they must not grieve or cry and be easily perturbed. I am reminded of a Latin American friend who told me that he loved the drama and action in Hindi films but was perplexed when confronted with the hero's androgynous features: 'Why do they cry so easily?' Relatedly, it is uncharacteristic of men to adopt the point of view of others and show empathy, understanding, gentleness and compassion. Part of what it means to be tough is to suppress empathy for others and be embarrassed by fear or any other vulnerability.

Third, men must be ambitious and ruthless. Once they set a goal, it must be achieved regardless of consequences to others. Since winning is all-important, other men striving to achieve the same goal are rivals to be eliminated. Extreme competitiveness, in this model, is a classical male characteristic.

Fourth, it does not behove men to consult others, negotiate with the weak or settle for anything less than what they want. They take independent decisions that brook no questioning, as famously put by Amitabh Bachchan in one of his films: '*Bas keh diya na*' (Enough, I have said so). Once a man speaks, it is final and an order to be obeyed blindly. Men are sovereign, free and autonomous; they are in control of the world they inhabit, the women they rule over and the children they beget. In short, part of their freedom lies in having dominion over others, particularly women and 'servants'.

All these must be contrasted with features that inhere in women: being irrational, bereft of self-restraint, emotional, empathetic but lack judgement and impartiality and cry easily. Women are physically and mentally weak, and therefore must be dependent on and protected by their male superiors. It follows that when men display such traits, they become weak, soft and wimpish. Acting like a woman is a betrayal of manhood. Cold-blooded violence shows the opposite: that manliness is fully alive and kicking.

Masculinity against Freedom

Another key feature exhibited through images of social violence and integral to a culture of masculinity is the belief that 'real men' are directly responsible for sustaining a moral order. Being its guardians, they must restore that order when it is disturbed. Since the teenage girl had violated the honour of the community, she deserved the severe punishment meted out publicly and directly by an older, wiser man of the same community. How else can her subjection within the social order be conserved? Likewise, Dalits and cultural aliens (Muslims) must know their designated place in society. Any attempt to become equal must be put down. How dare a Dalit sport a moustache or dream of riding a horse? He must be shown his place. To men with such ideas of masculinity, the argument that they must not take law in their own hands falls on deaf ears. This is unsurprising because from their own perspective the law must be broken if it breaches the more-fundamental moral order.

It is hard for me to assess the extent to which Indians are outraged by masculine violence. Are we unable to prevent this violence? Can't we be bothered to stop it? Or do we secretly endorse it? The very best in traditional and modern India, in their own distinctive ways, avoided the pernicious binary at the heart of this male-centric world. For the Buddha, compassion was not a feminine virtue but a key moral value for all humans. Mahavira tried to inculcate the ethical significance of ahimsa not merely towards all humans but every living species. Ashoka realised the futility of social and political violence and advocated harmonious coexistence among different religio-philosophical groups. The early Dharmasutras proposed that knowledge is not the exclusive preserve of professionally learned men (Brahmins); much can be learnt from women and those falling low in status hierarchy. In our times, Mahatma Gandhi showed how peaceful resistance against the oppressor can be more effective than violent confrontation. But in the world of violent masculinities, these are unmanly attributes fit only for women and the weak.

Real freedom for all is the heartbeat of the order envisaged by those who sought independence from colonial rule. But the central feature in the culture of toxic masculinity is domination, which is deeply incompatible with a freedom-sensitive, egalitarian ethic. Why then does an archaic, conservative and masculine moral order, which is sustained largely by aggressive and violent men, persist and continue to find support among aspiring sections of our society?

It is perplexing too that social violence is continually reproduced in a democracy. Democracies are meant to encourage the not-so-masculine values of consultation, negotiation, discussion and compromise; they enjoin us to accept that we might not get all that we want—that it is one thing to show strength, firmness and courage but quite another to be self-obsessed and obstinate, to posture belligerently and to bully the vulnerable. In peaceful, functional democracies, people have the quiet confidence that they will defend themselves against aggression, but they know equally well that there is nothing particularly heroic about violence. The greatest Indians have defied male stereotypes and refused to be trapped by the male–female binary. Will today's Indians follow them, reduce violence and secure freedom for all?

72

The Demolition of Reason

It has always been an exaggeration to claim that man is a rational animal, distinguished from others by his capacity to take rational decisions. But it is no hyperbole to say that all humans can learn to reason with beneficial consequences. Reason has many functions—to help arrive at a common understanding and consensual decision; discern what is and is not relevant; express our deepest thoughts and lend them coherence; differentiate right from wrong, good from bad and the significant or the urgent from the trivial. We are not purely rational and indeed should never be. But not to use reason when it is badly required is plainly foolish or outright devious.

Reason in Its Most Debased Form

Seen widely in our world and amplified in the electronic media, however, is the collapse of reason. Or rather, the deliberate, wicked surrender of virtually every form of reason and the adoption, instead, of various strategies of evasion, obfuscation, deflection and denial. Conversations are stalled, discussions disrupted and facts manipulated and distorted. Reason now appears to serve, as never before, only self-interest and power. Though reason may not have disappeared completely, it is certainly reduced to its most debased form—one that is cynical and instrumental.

When reason is so sullied, words become vacuous—mere sounds without meaning. Intellectual differences are reduced to a cockfight or mere shadowboxing. Witnessing a group of British journalists picking holes in the argument of the far-right UKIP leader Nigel Farage, exposing obvious inconsistencies and throwing widely known facts at him to show that he was a liar, the Turkish writer Ece Temelkuran likened this effort to playing chess with a pigeon who knocks over the pieces and shits on the chess board. 'The pigeon departs, proudly claiming victory, and leaving behind a mess for you to clean up,' she said. How does one engage and find common ground with those who make disruption and ignorance their primary values and are guided by them? Temelkuran describes the impossibility of having a proper political discussion with Turkish President Recep Tayyip Erdogan's supporters. Talking to them is 'like making a milkshake without the lid on,' she said. Reason is utterly helpless when people choose to defy it.

Rounds of Whataboutery

One of the most troubling features of current debates on television is that every substantive discussion of an important public issue is instantly replaced by an avoidable and unreasonable slanging match between the BJP and the Congress, as if all Indians are supporters of either the BJP or the Congress. More importantly, attention is diverted to real or imagined wrongs committed in the past by the Congress, which helps evade fixing responsibility and accountability for wrongs committed in the present. For example, the horrific killings in Delhi cannot be discussed because 'how dare those responsible for the 1984 pogrom against the Sikhs bring up Delhi 2020'? Likewise, a complaint about the muzzling of the press or about the fear experienced by ordinary citizens to speak out against the current regime simply has to be upstaged by a passionate denunciation of Indira Gandhi's Emergency. But why does the failure of one party to give us some good (say, freedom) erase the failure of another party to do the same? Why can't people complain against both?

Consider this: forty years ago, a man was caught red-handed while stealing and was punished. Today, he himself is robbed and goes to the police to report the crime. But the police ask, 'Aren't you the same man who committed a theft in 1980? You have no right to lodge a complaint.' This is absurd. Does a man forfeit his right to complain or protest merely because he once committed a wrong? What kind of an argument is this? Admittedly, some arguments have relevance and validity in the immediate aftermath of a crime. But they lose force as time passes and circumstances change. It might be valid to speak in the forties of the responsibility of Nazi Germany for the mayhem it caused by starting the Second World War but farcical to keep carping about it in the twenty-first century. The crime has long been acknowledged, punishment has been meted out and Germans, even those who had morally disassociated from it much earlier, have apologised in word and deed. They have even institutionalised the remembrance of wrongdoing in memorials. This renders redundant any further reprimand of the Germans. What use is it bringing it up now, especially by those who are destroying liberty today?

The Emergency was a horrific event, a permanent blot on Indian democracy, and so we must remember it continuously to ensure that it does not recur. But it would be ludicrous to ask the Congress, the leading Opposition party, to shut up if it protested against the imposition of Emergency-like measures and crazy to order ordinary citizens, who first suffered in the seventies and might suffer again, to stop being 'selective' when protesting against an assault on free speech, the suspension of habeas corpus or the mauling of an independent judiciary. To compel anyone to speak about every single past violation of rights in the same breath as current violations is a devious way to bully everyone into silence.

Let us return to the present. We know that slogans such as '*Goli maron saalon ko*' raised by some political leaders were an unambiguous incitement to violence. They were caught on video, reported to the election commission and suspended from campaigning. This is an incontrovertible fact. Soon enough, horrific violence engulfed the national capital where the slogan was first raised. When a public interest litigation was brought to the court, pleading that an FIR be registered against the culprits, the defence pleaded that unless all such hate speeches are examined nothing should happen. As if this was not perplexing enough, another ridiculous feature entered the discourse. The speech of a Congress leader, which was not found to be inflammatory earlier, was pushed into the media and played out as a war cry by those who know its legal insignificance. Why then did they do so? To confuse and mislead people and to vitiate discourse. Is it not excellent ammunition for a new round of whataboutery?

Evaluating Political Actions

Not long ago, I got talking with a taxi driver about the National Register of Citizens in Assam. I said that I was sorry to hear about the fate of the officer in charge of the survey whose professional integrity was redoubtable earlier but who now has five FIRs registered against him. His crime? He had discovered large numbers of Hindus without documents to prove their citizenship and now declared illegal immigrants. Unfazed, he said, 'But Sir, such a man would have been shot dead in Pakistan,' implying that India is tolerant compared with Pakistan. After all, India only paralyses people with false cases, whereas in Pakistan, the same conduct is rewarded with death penalty. This is whataboutery gone mad. Political actions in India today are evaluated by two standards. First, the worst practices of the Congress, and second, the repressive acts, real or imaginary, of a rogue state across the border. The political class and all those mesmerised by it have simply sidestepped constitutional principles and political morality.

73

The Loss of Intellectual Autonomy

No person in today's world likes to be told what to do or think. The young are particularly keen to have the freedom to decide which beliefs to form. Intellectual autonomy is widely considered to be an important value. This was probably not true in the past when large numbers of people were illiterate, knowledge was produced and stored by a few and there was wider social legitimacy for submission to those with power and authority.

However, even then, poets and philosophers routinely felt that intellectual autonomy is smothered by temptations of power. Asked by his pupils on how to relate to rulers, the medieval philosopher-saint Al Ghazali said, 'It would be disastrous to go to a ruler to offer unsolicited advice. It is acceptable to offer your opinion if the ruler sought you. But it is best if he goes his way and you go yours.'

Intellectual Autonomy Undermined

Since the end of the eighteenth century, as technologies of knowledge production became increasingly available to larger sections of society, intellectual autonomy has been threatened not only by state power but also in other insidious ways. Colonialism is a case in point. The British strategy of intellectual control was implemented by crafting a system of education rather than brute coercion. Although the best of our thinkers outmanoeuvred this system—after all, the most original Indian thinker of this period, Gandhi, was a product of this very education system—it created acute anxiety among self-reflexive thinkers. For example, Sri Aurobindo lamented the 'increasing impoverishment of the Indian intellect' in the face of new knowledge imposed by European contact. 'Nothing is our own, nothing native to our intelligence, all is derived,' he complained. 'As little have we understood the new knowledge; we have only understood what the Europeans want us to think about themselves and their modern civilisation. Our English culture—if culture it can be called—has increased tenfold the evil of our dependence instead of remedying it.'

A more catastrophic malady resulting from this 'well-meaning bondage' was the loss of intellectual autonomy. The watchword of Indians, he argued, has become 'authority', blind acceptance of ideas coming either from outside—Europe—as was the case of the then English-educated Indians, or from inside—the fossilised traditions—as was the case of traditional pundits. It was as if the only choice before Indian intellectual elites was a hyper-Westernised modernism or ultra-traditionalism. Some elites would have every detail of their life determined exclusively by Western ideas. Others would have them fixed only by shastra, custom and scripture. Each wanted to reform the other, which was nothing but a call to substitute the authority of Guru Sayana with the authority of Max Mueller or the dogmatism of European scientists and scholars with the dogmatism of Brahmin pandits. The absence of real choice was a symptom of an undermined capacity to think on one's own, which is the power of humans to accept or reject nothing without proper questioning.

Much the same conclusion was reached a decade later by the Indian philosopher K.C. Bhattacharya. In his 1928 talk 'Swaraj in Ideas', Bhattacharya feared that Indians might suffer from a subtler form of domination 'when one's traditional cast of ideas and sentiments is superseded without comparison or competition by a new cast representing an alien culture which possesses one like a ghost.' To be sure, when two cultures come into sustained contact with one another, there is bound to be give and take. One culture might even give to the other more than it takes from it. However, all creative assimilation involves a real conflict of ideas, and elements of an alien culture can be accepted only after 'full and open-eyed struggle has been allowed to develop' between the two encountering cultures.

Two Alien Ideas in India Today

I am afraid we have allowed two deeply problematic alien notions to penetrate our collective consciousness without thorough questioning or proper comparison with ideas emanating from our intellectual traditions. One is the idea of religion, and the second, a particular conception of the nation. Religion, as a demarcated system of practices, beliefs and doctrines, is largely an early modern European invention and begins its existence in and through the theological disputes of the sixteenth and seventeenth centuries.

Under the impact of colonialism, this category came to India and obliged Indians to think of themselves as members of one exclusive religious community, not just different from but opposed to others. It is true that gods and goddesses, ethical norms and prescriptions and rituals and practices did exist in some form in the past. But these were not thought to be part of one single entity called Hinduism, so that those who owed allegiance to any one of these sets of practices did not think of themselves as belonging to a single system of belief and doctrine in competition with and opposition to all others. Indeed, mobility across communities and multiple allegiances were common. As a result, most people refused to be slotted into rigid, compartmentalised entities. They were religious but did not belong to a religion. This has virtually ceased to be the case.

Second, religious belief or practice, or adherence to a doctrine, was never viewed as a condition for membership in a wider national community. One's religious or linguistic identity made little difference to one's belonging to the nation. Alas, for many inhabitants of our territory now, a nation cannot but be defined in a single religious or linguistic term. An exclusivist conception of the ethnic nation—entirely against the spirit of local Indian religions or conceptions of nationhood—which was first devised in Spain in 1492, developed further during the European wars of religion and perfected in the eighteenth or nineteenth century has seized the Indian mind. Thanks to narrow-minded educational institutions and now the electronic media, the idea was first disseminated and then unquestioningly accepted by Indians as if it were a long-held indigenous Indian idea. In accepting alien ideas of religion and nation without proper comparison or competition with Indian ideas of faith and community, we have sacrificed intellectual autonomy and gone down the road to hell from which Europe has itself yet to recover.

To define one's identity or community in terms of a single, exclusive religion—Hindu, Muslim or any other—is a perverse European notion, a mark of our cultural subjugation and a symptom of the loss of our intellectual autonomy. To have done so is to have uncritically abandoned our own collective genius for something ill-suited to our conditions. Can this be reversed? Is it too late to heed Sri Aurobindo's warning or follow Gandhi's example? Can we recover our collective intellectual autonomy?

74

The Perilous State of Academic Freedom

To express opinions is the fundamental right of every Indian, so also is to claim that these are true. But whether in fact they are true isn't in the hands of the person who expresses them. Their truth, validity and even plausibility are determined through contestation and scrutiny by others.

More importantly, some types of scrutiny are more scrupulous, thorough and rigorous than others. They uncover indefensible, baseless or unsustainable opinions. They demonstrate that other opinions are less biased, withstand the test of time and have a greater openness in accepting their fallibility. In doing so, these inquiries produce a better, clearer understanding of the world, providing a deeper insight into the complexities of the human condition. Therefore, they are of a different qualitative worth than others, more deserving of being called 'knowledge'. Knowledge production begins with opinions but does not end with them.

Academic freedom protects such spaces of contestation and scrutiny through which knowledge is produced. It refers to the freedom of scholars to conduct critical enquiry and the freedom of teachers and students to collectively deliberate on any idea without fear of sanction, censure or illegitimate interference. To sift knowledge from mere opinion requires a sound training in research and an awareness of professional standards of scholarship, norms of peer engagement and time-tested, disciplined ways of knowing (methodologies). This is true of all practices involving standards of excellence. For instance, it is not my subjective opinion that Viv Richards was a great batsman. This fact is established by the collective judgement of the greats of international cricket.

Patiently Acquired Skills

In short, academic freedom protects patiently acquired skills and practices of all such knowledge-producing and knowledge-transmitting agents (teachers, researchers and students). Since academic practices are sustained within institutions, academic freedom includes the autonomy of institutions where teaching and scholarly research is conducted.

My intellectual interest in academic freedom was provoked in 1999 when I was asked to contribute a short essay on the state of academic freedom in India to *Academe*, a journal of the American Association of University Professors. In that article, I claimed that the freedom of scholars and the autonomy of academic institutions is usually threatened by internal as well as external factors.

Internal threats appear when academic institutions are weakened from within, as when academics themselves lose sight of the standards of excellence internal to the practice of research and teaching. External threats develop, on the other hand, when academic institutions are undermined by oppressive communities, the coercive apparatus of the state or unbridled market forces. I had then argued that Indian academia was severely threatened by oppressive communities and self-imposed impediments by academics and less so by the market or the state.

I took my own community to task for having succumbed to what I called the over-ideologisation of the mind. Many academics, in a hurry to bridge the gap between theory and practice, seemed to me to have replaced patient, open-ended deliberation with dogma and prefabricated, lazy solutions. Other internal threats to academic freedom flowed from wider societal malaise. For instance, merit-based institutions were being converted to little fiefdoms run by academic tin gods doling out petty patronage to loyal supporters and creating suffocating tyrannies for others. In such contexts, ideas were applauded or condemned not for their intrinsic worth but with an eye on who articulated them—one of 'us' or one of 'them'. A person's caste, creed or political proclivity mattered more than the evidence or argument provided. Such habits of the mind were hardly conducive to the growth of a tradition of scholarly work.

A more serious danger to academic freedom in India came, I believed, from illiberal communities. I illustrated my point by pointing to the fate of the late historian Mushirul Hasan, who was victimised by extremist fellow-Muslims for a rather innocuous remark on the ban on Rushdie's *Satanic Verses*.

Interestingly, barring the brief period of Emergency, academic freedom in post-Independence India, I claimed, was not throttled by the state. I did not remember instances of seminars being monitored, academic books being banned or the imprisonment of academics for their views. However, covert and overt pressures on academic institutions by democratically elected governments were commonplace. As it began to lose its dominance, an edgy and insecure Congress party had started becoming increasingly unprincipled and randomly interventionist. In West Bengal and Kerala, even communist governments could not resist illegitimately interfering in college and university appointments. Much the same is said to be true of BJP governments that, by allegedly packing the governing bodies with its members or supporters, have undermined the integrity of prestigious academic institutions.

What is the state of academic freedom today, twenty years after that article was written? I fear that more and more academics in positions of power appear to be not just over-ideologised but politically indoctrinated. A deepening societal intolerance has only intensified attacks on academic freedom. The exclusion of several important books from university syllabi, entirely on non-academic grounds, exemplifies this.[11] State interference has increased, sacrificing critical pedagogical practices in the name of the government's idea of national interest. The continuing victimisation of Jawaharlal Nehru University (JNU), New Delhi, one of the premier academic institutions of the country, by the current government's own reckoning illustrates this.[12]

Knowledge a 'Commodity'

Alarmingly, new threats to academic freedom have emerged. One comes from the corporatisation of academia, by which I mean the modelling of universities on business corporations. This has naturalised the viewing of administration as management, faculty as paid personnel and students as consumers who have a right to demand what should be taught, as if knowledge can be purchased as a commodity according to one's taste. When corporate power exercises control over faculty and curricula, vice chancellors and

---

[11] Aranya Shankar, 'Dalit Authors, Mahasweta Devi Removed from English Syllabus, DU Comes Under Fire,' *The Indian Express*, 26 August 2021, https://indianexpress.com/article/cities/delhi/du-committee-mahasweta-devi-two-dalit-authors-english-syllabus-faces-flak-7470324/

[12] Shalini Ojha, 'What Happened at JNU Last Night? All Your Questions Answered,' NewsBytes, 6 January 2020, https://www.newsbytesapp.com/news/india/everything-that-happened-inside-jnu-last-night/story and 'International Statement from Academics Regarding Attacks on JNU, *The Caravan*, 9 January 2020, https://caravanmagazine.in/noticeboard/statement-academics-attack-jnu-vc-resign;

college principals can hire, fire and change faculty assignments with as much whim as any corporate CEO.

But the most serious threat to the world of knowledge comes from 'anti-intellectualism' that finds the very idea of thought reprehensible. Thinking, reasoning, questioning and critique are deemed dangerous and must be treated with utter disdain. The distinction between knowledge and opinion is entirely blurred; ideas of informed authority, professional academic standards and academic expertise are ridiculed. The very idea that the task of education is to transform students into critical agents who actively question the common sense of a society is severely undermined.

If these trends continue, the university as a site of autonomous scholarship, independent thought and uncorrupted inquiry will be disassembled. Our best young minds will emigrate and the very future of our country imperilled by another 'brain drain'. India may not easily recover from this blow.

75

Squash the Vicious Syndrome between Communities

The invisibilisation of Muslims from public life must concern every Indian. So must the disturbing habit of some fellow citizens who do everything in their power to alienate them. What must Muslims feel when the most blatant acts of wrongdoing against them are publicly justified? And while a historical understanding of the current state of Hindu–Muslim relations is necessary, the continual rationalisation by reference to what happened in the past—say, in pre-Independence India—is quite another matter.

Ambedkar on Hindus and Muslims

Undeniably, relations between Hindu and Muslim elites had soured by the forties. Every major Indian thinker living in the first half of the twentieth century wrote about it, but perhaps no one matches Ambedkar's cold-blooded observations. In the forties, while Gandhi tirelessly advocated Hindu–Muslim unity, Ambedkar wrote,

> It is no exaggeration to say that it is a record of 20 years of civil war between Hindus and Muslims. The acts of barbarism against women, committed without remorse, show the depth of antagonism between the two communities .... The tempers on both sides are like tempers of two warring nations .... What is astonishing is that these cold and deliberate acts of rank cruelty were not regarded atrocities to be condemned but treated as legitimate acts of warfare for which no apology was necessary.[13]

Chillingly resonant with some brutal events in our own times, isn't it?

Ambedkar alludes here to what I have called the majority–minority syndrome—a diseased network of relations so poisoned, accompanied by an assortment of negative emotions (envy, malice and hatred) so extreme, that it propels groups to vengeful savagery. This sends them on a downward spiral of deeper and deeper estrangement. In such syndromes, mutual animosity circulates freely, adding layer upon layer of grievances. Chronic mutual paranoia develops over time and intergroup relations are perverted. Ambedkar appears to have entered the mindset of extremists on both sides—of those who act with the sole purpose of humiliating and hurting each other. Hostility to the other is their defining feature.

The growth of the syndrome prevented a reasonable and accommodating solution to problems between Hindus and Muslims. It also halted reforms within communities. Ambedkar very quickly understood that any freedom-enhancing or equality-inducing changes are put on the back-burner when this syndrome grips a society. When groups regard each other as a menace, they expend all their energy preparing to meet 'the menace', he said. The exigency of a common front against the other generates 'a conspiracy of silence over social evils'. Neither party attends to them 'even though they are running sores requiring immediate attention ... for the simple reason that they view every measure of social reform as a source of

---

[13] B.R. Ambedkar, *Writings and Speeches: Pakistan or the Partition of India*, Volume 8, (Bombay: Education Department, Government of Maharashtra, 1990), 184–186, 236.

dissension, internal division that weakens the ranks when they ought to be closed to meet the menace.' This ensures social stagnation. A spirit of mindless conservatism begins to dominate the thoughts and actions of both sides.

Why the Syndrome Persists

Ambedkar had written these sentences a couple of years before Independence. Seventy years later, the context has changed radically. The majority of Hindus and Muslims, concerned more with their material well-being, do not wish to get sucked into this syndrome. Muslims, though still a large minority but far less powerful now, know the havoc the syndrome causes. Barring a small reckless section, they do not wish to be drawn into it. The withdrawal by either group should, in principle, derail the syndrome. But in India, it persists. Why? One, it has a psychological existence. Though it still festers in the psyche of a tiny section of both communities, it has grown exponentially in the last two decades in the minds of Hindu extremists. Second, it also has a social existence, relentlessly being manufactured in Indian politics. Sadly, even the virtual presence of the syndrome appears to bring electoral advantage. Naive citizens fall for it and give strength to what is by now an illusory syndrome. But its social consequences are particularly horrendous for the Akhlaqs of our country.

Not long ago, in the opinion pages of the *Indian Express*, a controversy raged on the plight of Muslims in India. Some interesting explanations were offered but none was clear-sighted enough to grasp the simple point made by Ambedkar that besieged communities inevitably stagnate. Instead of attending to problems within their community, they spend their energy battling hostile aggressors. The prospect of inter-religious domination boosts intra-religious domination. And the heaviest price for the disappearance of internal reform, Ambedkar reminded us, is paid by the most vulnerable sections of that community—women, children, the aged and the poor. Muslim orthodoxy thrives on Hindu extremism. The burqa cannot come off the body of Muslim women until hostility from Hindu extremists is off their back.

Extremism gnaws at basic decency. Every act of violence against the other sows the seed of a barbaric society that will spare no one. An uncivil society is the last thing we need or wish to bequeath to our children. Each time we allow something nasty to happen, we dig our own grave. Surely, it was this realisation that prompted academics and former government officials to write strong letters urging the prime minister to check extremism. And make no mistake, hostility to Muslims damages Hindus too. Hindu extremism stifles Hindu minds and strengthens conservatism within it. In a very profound sense, the mindset behind the rape of the Muslim girl in Kathua is intimately connected to the rape of the Hindu woman in Unnao.

76

The Marginalisation of Justice in Public Discourse

Two ideas appear to dominate our public discourse today. One, somewhat implicitly, self-interest. The second, far more explicitly, national glory. How the pursuit of material or cultural self-interest affects others does not seem to bother us. There is little acknowledgement that the pursuit of greed and narrow self-interest leads to severe inequalities—an unequal division of social benefits.

Also missing is the thought that the burden of realising national goals such as development must be shared equally by all. True, nothing of importance is achieved without sacrifice. But why should some people sacrifice virtually everything they have and others benefit without forgoing anything at all? Given the compulsion to advance our self-interest, this burden is easily passed on to those among us who are powerless to desist it. Isn't it wrong that the least paid workers and peasants in our society are expected to offer the greatest sacrifices for building the nation? Why this grossly unfair division of social labour? Yet, concern for a fair distribution of benefits and burdens—the core issue of justice—is rare in mainstream public discourse.

Sharing Benefits and Burdens

What is distributive justice and why does it matter? Almost two decades ago, my younger daughter startled me by asking 'What is justice, Baba?' I saw a bottle of water before me, so I began explaining to her something like this: 'There are many things I can do with this bottle. I can grab it even if I am not thirsty, keeping it solely for myself. Or, out of love, I can give it to you even if I am thirsty. Finally, I can give it to some other person not because I love her but because I can see that she needs it most. This is justice.' A few days later, as we stopped our car at the traffic lights, a 'beggar' came expectantly towards us and we gave him a packet of biscuits. My daughter immediately said, 'That's justice, no? We gave something away to him even though we don't love him.' My daughter hadn't grasped the concept of justice just yet, but she was on the right track. At the very least, justice requires us not to be greedy and grab things; instead, we share them with those we don't know or love. Simply put, a sense of justice is born when we begin sharing things with strangers.

In fact, the idea of distributive justice presupposes not only a social condition marked by an absence of love or familiarity but also other things that the Scottish philosopher David Hume termed 'the circumstances of justice'. For instance, a society where everything is abundantly available would not need justice. Each of us will have as much of everything we want. Without the necessity of sharing, justice becomes redundant. Equally, in a society with massive scarcity, justice is impossible. In order to survive, each person is compelled to grab whatever happens to be available. Justice, therefore, is possible and necessary in societies with moderate scarcity.

Justice also presupposes that people are neither totally alone nor organically united with others. If one were Robinson Crusoe on an uninhabited island, there would be no one to share the loot with. And, if one was totally fused with others, with no distinction between self and the other, then also, sharing will be unnecessary. Surely, one cannot share anything with oneself! To sum up, justice acquires value in societies with moderate scarcity and where people are forced to deal with those who they don't necessarily love. It presupposes a moral psychology in which humans are neither wholly selfish nor entirely benevolent. Since most societies share these conditions, we may safely conclude that justice is a necessary social virtue and has great moral value.

Giving Persons Their Due

But what is justice? The basic idea of justice is that each person gets what is properly due to him or her, that the benefits and burdens of society are distributed in a manner that gives each person his or her due. But this begs the question 'What is meant by a person's due?' Here, a distinction must be made between hierarchical and egalitarian notions of justice. In hierarchical notions, what is due to a person is established by her or his place within a hierarchical system, for instance, by rank determined at birth. Certain groups are born privileged. Therefore, their members are entitled to a disproportionately large share of benefits and a disproportionately small share of burdens. On this conception, justice requires that the benefits and burdens be unequally shared or distributed. To take just one example, in a society ridden with caste hierarchies, those born into 'high castes' are entitled to a much greater share of wealth, power, cultural status and knowledge. Conversely, those born into 'low castes' get whatever is their proper due—very little and sometimes nothing.

This conception of justice has rarely remained unchallenged. Innumerable examples can be cited from Indian history where aspects of this hierarchical notion had been temporarily opposed—in the early teachings of the Buddha, passages in Indian epics, Bhakti poetry and protest movements such as Veerashaivism. In our own times, however, this challenge has become robust, explicit and sustained. This is so because of the prevalence of the idea that each person, regardless of caste, class, colour, creed or gender, has equal moral worth. All have an equal, originary capacity of endowing the world with meaning and value because of which they possess moral worth or dignity. If so, we need a different conception of justice, of sharing or distribution and of giving people their due that is consistent with equal dignity. In societies still infested with live hierarchies, people must first struggle for recognition as equals—for what might be called basic social justice. Then, they must decide how to share all social benefits and burdens among equal persons, which is the essence of egalitarian distributive justice.

Needs and Desert

Two main contenders exist for interpreting what is due to persons of equal moral worth. The first is a need-based principle, according to which what is due to a person is what she really needs—whatever is necessary for general human well-being. Since our basic needs are identical, justice requires their fulfilment in every single person. Beyond this basic threshold, our needs usually vary; therefore, justice further requires the fulfilment of different needs, for instance, the specific needs of a scholar as well as a mountaineer.

The second is the principle of desert, according to which what is due to a person is what he or she deserves, which is determined not by birth or tradition but by a person's own qualities, for instance, 'natural' talent or productive effort. In short, though we start as equals, those who are talented or work hard should be rewarded with more benefits and be less burdened. Conversely, those contributing unequally to the creation of wealth or cultural assets, don't deserve the same benefits as the first lot. This underpins the idea of equal opportunity to all, albeit with justified inequalities of outcome.

Break the Deafening Silence

Most reasonable egalitarian conceptions of justice try to find a balance between 'need' and 'desert'. They try to ensure a distribution of goods and abilities (benefits) that satisfies everyone's needs and a fair distribution of social burdens or sacrifices required for fulfilling them. After this, rewards are permissible to those who deserve more by virtue of natural gift, social learning and personal effort.

Our society is afflicted by deep material, cultural and knowledge-related inequalities. Worse, these inequalities are growing by the day. Sometimes they are accompanied by blatant assertions of unequal moral worth; though today, a deafening silence on social and distributive justice is more common. It is, therefore, imperative to ask where we stand in relation to different forms of egalitarian justice mentioned in the preamble of our Constitution. Alas, we are falling way short of the standards of social and distributive justice. When will this trend be reversed? Putting justice back into public discourse should be our priority. Or else, the dreams of our nation will never turn into reality.

77

Nationalism and the Crisis of Federalism

Several chief ministers have complained about the growing crisis of Indian federalism. The Central government backing out of its legal commitment to compensate the states for Goods and Services

Tax shortfall is one ground for this complaint and just the tip of a dangerous iceberg. A deeper problem lies in a flawed understanding of nationalism and the government's disregard for democratic principles. Federalism can function only in the hands of those with a grasp of India's democratic nationalism. Both are indispensable and neither works properly without the other.

Three Nationalisms

Two broad conceptions of nationalism developed in the subcontinent before India achieved Independence. The first, the idea that a community with a strongly unified culture must have a single state of its own bifurcated India into two nationalisms. One defined culture in ethno-religious terms and was articulated by the curiously similar Hindu Mahasabha and the Muslim League. Hindus and Muslims were separate nations and needed their own states. For the Hindu Mahasabha, Indian nationalism simply had to be Hindu nationalism. This primacy of Hindu identity potentially had adverse consequences not only for religious but also linguistic minorities, including those Hindus who viewed their mother tongue as important as their religion. For Hindu nationalists, a Hindu identity permanently outweighed being Tamil or Punjabi.

The second manifestation of the same conception was articulated by sections of the Congress party, which too saw the nation as defined by a common culture whose adherents must have a state of their own. But this common culture was not ethno-religious. It was defined instead by shared historical experience, the struggle against British colonial rule and developed through an interpenetration of ideas emanating from different cultural sources. For want of a better term, call this second nationalism civic. More inclusive than any ethno-religious nationalism, its secular, composite content is qualitatively different from Hindu or Muslim nationalisms. However, surprisingly, its basic form is not unlike Hindu nationalism. It too conceives common culture in terms of a strong idea of unity that marginalises or excludes other particular identities. A civic Indian identity, shaped at best by a thin composite culture, trumps other public identities, including linguistic ones.

A third nationalism accepts that communities nourished by distinct, territorially concentrated regional cultures have the capacity to design their own states as also educational, legal, economic and other institutions. They possess self-governing rights. Yet, they eschew independent national aspirations, seeing themselves as constituents of a larger, equally significant common culture with another state that belongs to everyone. Indeed, they build on this shared culture and come together to consolidate the nation. Occasional conflicts between the common culture of the central State and distinct cultures of constituent states are admitted but mechanisms to prevent them are also created. This may be called a coalescent nationalism consistent with a fairly strong linguistic federalism; The central State associated with it is not multinational. At best, it is a multinational State without labels, one that does not call itself so—a self-effacing multinational State.

Being Linguistically Federal

In the thirties, all three conceptions of nationalism circulated among political elites in India. By the forties, however, coalescent nationalism was submerged by the other two. After Partition, India rejected ethno-religious nationalism, but its ruling elites, obsessed about the dangers of further fragmentation, began to view with suspicion the political expression of even linguistic identities. No one was more uneasy with this than Jawaharlal Nehru himself, who wondered if a federation structured along ethno-linguistic lines might tempt politicians to mobilise permanently on the basis of language and divert attention from issues of material well-being. Second, like religious identities, it was feared that ethno-linguistic nationalism might 'freeze' linguistic identities and increase the likelihood of inter-ethnic violence, encourage separatism and eventually lead to India's break up.

Thus, when the Constitution came into force in 1950, India adopted unitary, civic nationalism as its official ideology. Though a federal arrangement was accepted, the second tier of government was justified in functional terms and not on ethical grounds of the recognition of group cultures. The security and unity of India were cited as the primary reason. A unitary mindset shaped by the experience of a centralised colonial State was resurrected, and it seemed that the idea of a coalescent nationalism with multicultural federation was lost forever. A special commission to examine this issue concluded that language-based provinces were 'not in the larger interests of the Indian nation'. Yet another committee that included Nehru considered the recommendations of the commission and felt that while 'the present is not an opportune moment for the formation of new provinces, if public sentiment is insistent and overwhelming, we, as democrats must submit to it'.

Before long, the unitary arrangement and the conception that underpinned it proved inadequate. The third nationalism, which had been back-burned, came right back into the game as India shifted its allegiance slowly to a system of states that rejected the wholesale absorption of ethnic identities into a larger civic identity. This happened when the fledgling Indian democratic state was forced to encounter mass politics. Demands for autonomy and for sharing political power were immediately made by regional leaders. The issue of linguistic states became the focus of popular agitation, forcing the creation, in 1953, of the state of Andhra Pradesh for Telugu-speaking people. Soon after, the States Reorganisation Commission was set up to reorganise states on linguistic basis.

The commission argued that justice requires the creation of partially self-governing states that recognise all major linguistic groups. Besides, their creation improves administrative efficiency, deepens democracy and alleviates anxieties of regional minorities induced by fear of linguistic domination. Since domination eventually invites resistance and conflict, which undermine the nation-state, only federalism can block language-based majoritarianism, contain conflicts and strengthen Indian nationalism. Only coalescent nationalism creatively combines claims of unity with claims of recognition of diverse cultures. A robust democratic arena allows the play of complementary multiple identities, and through dialogue, discussion and negotiation, helps resolve disputes.

Following the commission's recommendations, states were reorganised in 1956. Soon, mass agitation forced the division of the province of Bombay into Maharashtra and Gujarat. In 1966, Haryana was separated from Punjab to become an independent state. Much later, states such as Arunachal Pradesh, Mizoram, Jharkhand, Chhattisgarh and Uttarakhand were carved out. India slowly became a coalescent nation-state, moving from the 'holding together' variety to what is called the 'coming together' form of (linguistic) federalism. This meant that regional parties were stronger than earlier in their own regions and at the Centre. This sowed the seed of a more durable centre because it was grounded on the consent and participation of regional groups that at another level were also self-governing. Indian federalism also attempted to remove its rigidities by incorporating asymmetries in the relation between the Centre and different states; treating all states as equals required the acknowledgement of their specific needs and according them differential treatment.

States as Equals

This coalescent nationalism has served India well and benefitted several groups in India. True, it has not worked as well in India's border areas such as the Northeast and Kashmir. But their problems can only be resolved by deepening not abandoning coalescent nationalism. Indeed, the Indian experience shows that whenever the Centre has been non-manipulative, treating politicians and people of regional states with respect, the entire polity works smoothly. On the other hand, whenever regions are treated disrespectfully and norms of democratic functioning abandoned, powerful, even violent, forces have been unleashed, leading to grave instability.

The contemporary crisis of federalism is due to the attack on coalescent, democratic Indian nationalism by a conceptually limited and morally weak idea of Hindu nationalism. Unless this offensive is curbed and these trends reversed, I fear we might begin to see major cracks in our distinctive nationalist project. That would be nothing short of disastrous for the Indian republic.

78

Three Takes from the *Padmaavat* Saga

What did the long, painful saga of the film *Padmaavat* tell us about ourselves and the social and political life in contemporary India? At least three messages were conveyed. First, that freedom of expression is important, not only to those who publicly affirm its value but paradoxically even to those who show scant respect for it.

Why do I say this? All groups baying for a ban of the film know that they could not have moved even an inch towards their goal if their freedom to express themselves was restricted and the fullest possible range of media tools—print, electronic and digital—was not at their disposal. If they had been prohibited from using the media, they would not have been able to build public opinion or put pressure on the government. Just imagine if state power had been in the hands of a group with zero tolerance for the very idea of jauhar or with people who were so incensed by even the slightest hint of its appreciation that they feel the need to slap a gag order on its proponents. Would this issue then ever come in the public eye? Has not the constitutionally guaranteed right to free expression enabled these groups to nurture their views in the past or to articulate them today?

The Need for Free Expression

And this, indeed, is how it should be because human beings are fundamentally expressive creatures. Expressing themselves is as important to them as eating or sleeping. Conveying their beliefs, desires and feelings through bodily performance and speech, oral and written, in some public medium is quite simply a human necessity. We take this so much for granted that its centrality is recognised only when we are deprived of it. Since, in contemporary democracies, the opinion of each person matters and can be included in the decision-making process only when publicly expressed, this wider human need to express freely has acquired a greater salience than ever before. Those who think that freedom of expression is a luxury only for English-educated liberals, a preference of a small Westernised elite, are deeply mistaken. Equally off-target are those who think that the poor have no need for free expression because their sole aim in life is to make two ends meet. It is now widely recognised that man-made disasters affecting the poor have been averted only because of the presence of a free press. As Amartya Sen pointed out, famines began to disappear when committed journalists were able to publicly highlight the distress of those affected by droughts. Indeed, free public expression by the powerless and the vulnerable is a condition for every popular struggle against injustice and oppression. For instance, our anti-colonial struggle against British imperialism depended fundamentally on the free exercise of speech. The less controls there were on popular expression of grievances, the more the struggle for independence grew.

Reassertion of Hierarchy and Dominance

So if virtually everyone recognises the importance of freedom of expression, what's the current fuss about? Alas, the second message transmitted through the *Padmaavat* episode is that the right to free expression of some groups is more important than that of others. The underlying belief of groups such as Karni Sena is that freedom of speech should not be content neutral but tied to their own preferred content. So only those people who toe our line and who have only positive things to say about us are free to say something; any speech that sheds a different light on our views or even mildly questions our favoured narrative should be stamped out. Virtually anything deemed disagreeable hurts our sentiment, and what hurts communal sentiment has no place in public life.

The *Padmaavat* affair demonstrated that any group that musters power and rustles up a mob has the freedom to communicate to others that relative to their own right, the rights of others have little or no value, no matter how reasonable or sensible the latter's approach or even when done in the fictional domain of the arts. In short, what we witnessed as the saga unfolded was the reassertion of hierarchy: freedom of expression is a right that can be exercised only by those with a particular mindset or ideology; others can go fly a kite. And for groups with such a mindset, everything is permitted, even violent threats, which are routinely regulated in civilised societies.

A third message alarmingly conveyed to us was even worse than the bland denial of the equality of free expression. At issue, it seems, was no longer freedom of expression but the rude assertion of domination. The very significant value of free expression of most was sacrificed to install domination by a few. If representatives of a particular group can get tacit support from the party in power, every other group and institution, including the Supreme Court, the guardian of our constitutional values, must bend to its will. As if calls to behead a *Padmaavat* actor were not enough, a respected and senior lawyer of the Supreme Court who defended the public screening of *the movie* and the head of the censor board that passed the film were both threatened. The film industry, a national treasure and one of India's greatest exports, was humiliated by and made to grovel before the so-called fringe elements. In short, on display was the bizarre spectacle of a small group holding the entire nation to ransom. And frankly, I feared for the state governments that pandered to this group. Have we not, so often, seen a Frankenstein devour its own creator?

79

Statues as Deeply Contested Heritage

Across the globe, people in large numbers have been seen toppling statues that stood as icons of their past oppression and continuing humiliation. Not long ago, we witnessed the tearing down in Bristol, UK, of the statue of Edward Colston, a slave owner. Consequently, statues of imperial rulers were removed in India too. Once considered heritage, symbols of a past to be celebrated, they are now viewed as anachronistic, best erased from public memory.

This is not surprising because heritage is almost always contested. It is not naturally given but what humans imagine and construct. What we call 'heritage' is not everything we happen to inherit from our ancestors. It necessarily involves a selection of what we presently consider significant in this inheritance. Every society decides what is and isn't heritage. Since every collective decision involves politics, the construction of heritage too is deeply political, a field of power not among ruling elites alone but also among all the people whose concern it is.

The Past in the Present

Why care for heritage? Because it contributes to and enhances our collective self-understanding. Our heritage affirms our collective identity and is a source of pride. It is important also because it is that part of history which is continuously brought to life by artefacts and integrated with our lived collective experience. It is that part of the past that we live and with which we live. And because it directly touches identity, it evokes strong feelings.

Heritage construction involves ethics too. It is the valued past of societies—both intangible, preserved in narratives, music, performances etc., and tangible, materially embodied in monuments and statues. Not a value-neutral term, 'heritage' is saturated with ethical evaluation, a judgement of what is worth remembering and preserving. Conversely, it pushes some features of our history into the background—fit for forgetting or, at best, dispassionate historical reflection. Integral to the construction of heritage then is an assessment of what must be remembered and forgotten, what calls for respect and celebration and what may be termed a 'stain', an object of recurring regret, mourned publicly and remembered only so that it could be prevented in future. Raj Ghat is not only a place where we remember Gandhi but also where we mourn his assassination by one of his own countrymen.

Heritage is a way of addressing and rectifying past wrongs. The Holocaust memorial in Berlin and Washington's Vietnam memorial are both gestures towards reparation—monuments of public apology.

Reactions in Diverse Societies

In complex, stratified and diverse societies, the part of history that is self-affirming to some can be a source of self-denial to others. A thing that provides recognition and pride to some may ignite misrecognition and shame in others—it can be offensive, hurtful and disrespectful. Even when it does no such thing, it may simply not speak to them. Public display of the heritage of only a few is a source of profound estrangement and exclusion for others. Heritage is often linked to cultural domination and therefore invites resistance. It follows that heritage is that which brings comfort or unease and to which people are either attracted or repulsed. Wherever symbolic power is unevenly distributed, artefacts that manifest this accumulated power provoke passionate disputation. Is it surprising then that a statue of a slave owner or member of the imperial ruling elite provokes indignation among those who were formerly enslaved or colonised? Likewise, in societies where caste hierarchies abound, the continual denial of public recognition to Dalit symbols leads to demands for greater inclusion of their heritage. And after much struggle for recognition, when Ambedkar's statues finally make their way into public spaces, why would they, or indeed we, not be outraged if it is vandalised?

Inescapably Public

For the rest of this essay, I confine myself, inescapably, to public statues—not hidden away or installed in special parks and museums with restricted access but installed in public squares and at crossroads, unavoidably open for all to see. Who then decides what will be on such public display and why? Because differences are inevitable, as indeed are attempts to influence and pressurise key decision-makers, how should such collective judgement be reached? How must differences be prevented from turning into interminable disputes or even violence? To see statues of oppressors being torn down is understandable, but why reach that tipping point? Why not decide what to do with them after collective deliberation among all stakeholders? Why leave heritage, a matter of long-lasting importance, solely to elected governments that come and go? While politics around heritage is unavoidable, is it not best to have dialogue, consultation and deliberation among people at large, including with artists, philosophers, historians, architects and alert guardians of cultural memory? Didn't public discussion yield a fine decision in the sixties to remove the statue of George V from under the imperial canopy near India Gate but leave it empty as a gentle reminder that monarchs and dictators have no place in our republic?

The Mahatma and Mohandas

Take the example of Gandhi's statues on account of their obvious global significance, complexity and, since they are surrounded by controversy, their current relevance. Some strongly feel that the Mahatma must be off the pedestal because of his alleged collusion with the empire, or more so for his racism. Assume the worst. Shall we then allow the violent removal of his statues? Now, Gandhi was neither born a mahatma nor became one overnight. He began life as an ordinary man and as a child of his social milieu with straightforward middle-class aspirations. It is easy to imagine him inheriting caste prejudices in his childhood and, after arrival in London to study law, imbibing the prejudices of his colonial masters and to see himself as close to educated British elites than to Indian peasants or the 'untouchables' and, when in Johannesburg, to the oppressed black community.

The real question worth addressing is whether he continued living this way, consolidating his racist and casteist views, or struggled to jettison these prejudices instead, not just superficially but by confronting the repugnant part of his deepest self, the kind of bad person he had been, and then transforming that self into something altogether different. By all accounts, Gandhi struggled with his demons all his life and eventually became the Mahatma that he was—a global figure of immense ethical significance admired by his adversaries and inspiring great men such as Martin Luther King and Nelson Mandela. The statues erected globally honour and celebrate the struggle embodied by this self-reflective Mahatma and not Mohandas Karamchand Gandhi, the parochial, upper caste Gujarati or the barrister loyal to the British Empire. Those who want to demolish his statues are simply going by an early fragment of his life that he himself disowned with great effort. There can be nothing more absurd or tragic. Imagine the fate of statues of all great men of the past on the sole ground that they fail the 'patriarchy test'. Who in the past would pass it? Not Marx, the revolutionary, or Ambedkar, our greatest Dalit leader, or Mandela or Martin Luther King, icons of Black struggles, or even, I am afraid, all the male gods worshipped by many. The general lesson to be drawn is this: a decision to preserve or remove statues cannot be based on current stereotypes of historical figures or narrow standards of political correctness that highlight a general flaw characteristic of an entire era but must instead rely on the complex, collective judgement of a person's overall contribution to the social, political and intellectual life of his or her time. Gandhi, in my view, passes this test. Colston or Cecil Rhodes do not. We must carefully avoid anachronism in our judgements of the past.

Bring Some Statues Up

At a time when statues are being brought down, why not talk of bringing some up? I am puzzled by our persistent obsession with political power, even when used for good purpose. Why is there no movement to erect statues of M.S. Subbulakshmi, Kumar Gandharva or Begum Akhtar for their massive contribution to our cultural heritage? Won't it be most appropriate to have a statue of Mohammad Rafi or Kishore Kumar in busy public squares near metro stations or bus terminals?

80

A Hunger for War but No Appetite for Peace

The news has just beamed on television screens that Putin has called off the war, expressed remorse at what he has done and deeply regretted the horror he unleashed. He also publicly apologised for mass murders and for the suffering he caused to the survivors. This has a tremendous impact on other modern warrior politicians.

George Bush and Tony Blair both apologise for the devastation they caused in Iraq. Suddenly, we, humans, are on the verge of a dramatic and revolutionary change in our perspective on the world and the way we think about ourselves. This is a genuine step towards a peaceful world, one in which wars have no place and violent conquests are a thing of the past.

I have allowed my utopian imagination to take flight despite an ongoing war that impacts the entire world, hardly a good time for moral self-indulgence. But something like this has occurred at least once, around 260 BCE, when Ashoka famously renounced war and conquest. Ordinary people have bemoaned war ever since. Massive popular protests against wars have been witnessed in our own times. But there is no other instance, to my knowledge, when a conqueror denounces his own actions and takes humankind in a new moral direction.

Hyper-masculine Culture

It took a cataclysmic act to transform Ashoka. For until then he was himself a follower of the warrior ethic. In pre-Ashokan elite culture, hyper masculine virtues were eulogized. In the Rig Veda, Indra, the god of sky, rain and thunder, being strong and violent, is also the god of war. Blessed with a muscular physique and terrifying demeanour, he, through sheer brawn, is able to push the world apart into two halves (Heaven and Earth), release primordial waters and split open the cosmic mountain so as to free imprisoned sunlight and cattle. With his *ojas*, a Sanskrit word signifying both physical strength and the power to dominate, Indra pulverises his rivals. To politically subjugate the enemy, he happily destroys, crushes, splits apart, slays and breaks an enemy's rage. 'Real' men take Indra, the most important Vedic god, as their role model and are called *śū́ra* (big or strong men; champions). They are skilled in horse and chariot combat. They flex muscles in cattle raiding expeditions and glorify warfare. Here, violence and conquest are a way of life. Invasion and occupation of someone else's territory are considered entirely legitimate.

Moral Consciousness against War

Ashoka himself followed this ethic until the conquest of Kalinga, when the scale of wanton destruction—the displacement of 150,000 people and the death of at least 100,000—left him distraught and changed his perspective.

> On conquering Kalinga the Beloved of the Gods (Asoka) felt remorse, for when an independent country is conquered, the slaughter, death, and deportation of the people is extremely grievous … all survivors … suffer violence, murder, and separation from their loved ones. Even those who are fortunate to have escaped its direct impact suffer from the misfortunes of their friends, acquaintances, colleagues, and relatives.[14]

Thus, the war had tragic consequences for practically every resident of Kalinga. He goes on to say, 'Even if a thousandth of that many were to be slaughtered or deported today, it would have weighed heavily on his mind.'

Romila Thapar rightly notes that 'the regret and remorse at the suffering in Kalinga is not the regret of a man moved by a passing emotion, but the meaningful contrition of a man who was consciously aware of the sorrow he had caused.'[15] Henceforth, Ashoka publicly denounced the glorification of conquest and dismissed the idea that fame and glory are goods in themselves. The only kind of fame and glory he wished for was one achieved by obeying and following dhamma and morality, both public and political.

From here on, central to the king's dhamma was *sarvajana, sarvaloka hita* (welfare of all living beings in this world and hereafter). War and conquest upset the physical security of humans as well as the valid pursuit of these goods. Therefore, these must be eschewed. True glory lies in elevating life-sustaining goods of ordinary persons above power and conquest. Thus, by formulating dhamma, Ashoka attempted to reshape the Brahmana–Kshatriya masculine culture in its entirety. By rejecting the warrior ethic, he launched a radically new vision of kingship in which violence became a contingent rather than a necessary, constitutive feature.

In Ashoka's ethic, wars or organised violence between or against groups bring chaos and devastation. They do not spring from human nature nor are they intrinsic to the human condition. They stem from insatiable greed and gargantuan ambition. Although it is hard to imagine a world without anger and aggression or conflict-free human condition, multiple ways exist to manage and contain them. Large-scale violence and war are avoidable.

[14] Ashokan Rock Edict XIII

[15] Romila Thapar, *Asoka and the Decline of the Mauryas* (India: OUP, 2012).

Humanity's Refusal to Learn

Yet, the human species refuses to learn. Alternatives to organised violence stare us in the face but powerful rulers carry on regardless. Worse, they invariably justify their cruelty, offer puerile rationalisations and incessantly reinforce the belief that war is a part of human nature and violence ingrained in our DNA. A subtler justification of war points to the good results it begets. Didn't the position of women improve after the Second World War? Did war not get Europe its welfare state? Did it not improve longevity by improvements in education, technology and medicine? These arguments are absurd. Of course, bad things have unintended consequences that may be good for us. But that is not reason enough to aim to bring about the bad. We must seek out the best peaceful alternatives to secure the good. In any case, we can't forget that wars are instigated by strong, ambitious men to intimidate the weak into giving up something generally valuable. Wars bring devastation to many in order to bring enormous material gains to a few. It is, therefore, painful to see our elected governments pay vacuous lip service to peace. At international fora, we condemn acts of war and pontificate on their futility. But in the same breath, we ridicule peacemakers as effeminate. Our public discourse is replete with the glorification of machismo.

No Respite from Wars

Ironically, human awareness against the inevitability of war has grown at a time when the frequency and scale of war has increased exponentially. The twentieth century can be aptly described as the age of wars, with the first quarter of the twenty-first century already an extension of the twentieth. I won't be surprised if not a single day has passed in the last hundred-odd years without large-scale violence and destruction in one or the other part of the world and not a single year since the 'long peace' in which the most powerful countries in the world have not bombed one or the other perceived enemy. Ordinary people in some or the other regions of the world have suffered its brutal consequences long after the formal war were over. It is now more than two thousand years since we developed a well-articulated moral consciousness against war. But humanity is nowhere near walking the talk.

PART VIII

Essays on the Pandemic

81

Vividly Imagining the Plight of Migrant Workers

The current pandemic has forced us to think about the plight of workers in our country. While the virus has demonstrated the enormous value of health workers, it has also enhanced public awareness of the pivotal role of migrant workers in our economy. We have been compelled to realise that between 100 million to 125 million people leave their villages, families and homes and travel to faraway towns and cities to find work; their invisible hands harvest crops and feed us, clean streets, run factories, build roads and construct our houses.

The Trek Back Home

Living away from home is never easy. A home is not made of brick and mortar, certainly not tin or planks of wood. It is where one finds comfort, nurtures relationships and raises a family. It gives sanctuary from daily struggles. An extension of one's identity, it provides us a sense of belonging. A place of tranquillity and serenity, it is where one longs to be when not there. This can only be where one's family, friends and community reside, not an inhospitable, overcrowded room with strangers. Not surprisingly, hungry migrant workers were determined to trudge hundreds of kilometres to reach 'home' in their villages. I believe many would have preferred to do so even if they were fed by their employers or the State, which clearly they were not. Surely, they were entirely justified in asking why Indians stranded abroad were flown back in special planes or middle-class students brought back to their hometowns from coaching centres in Kota, Rajasthan, but no such arrangements were made for them? Why this differential treatment? Are they not citizens of the same country? Are they any less Indian?

Their Condition in 'Normal' Times

The plight of migrant workers during the lockdown should become an occasion to reflect on their abysmal condition in 'normal' times. Many 'contractual labourers' rarely see a written contract. A minimum, regular wage per month is legally required but seldom paid. Many do not receive wages for months, and at the end of the season when they are finally paid, it is often less than what was agreed. There is a lack of transparency in accounting—excessive, arbitrary and unexpected deductions from final payments are common.

Lack of regular wages means that workers either borrow from employers or from local moneylenders. This renders them even more financially vulnerable because of indebtedness. Quite often they work long hours, between ten and thirteen hours a day, and live in tents or makeshift shanties without access to potable water, toilets and electricity. I doubt if they are ever fully protected from the elements. Many of them do not have a kitchen and are forced to eat from local street vendors who live in similar conditions. Working and living under dire circumstances, is it a surprise that they wished to return to their original homes when sudden lockdown was announced?

The prime minister spoke of the need for empathy and compassion during pandemics. These are admirable moral virtues, which are always necessary, not just in emergencies. But ultimately, individual virtues are insufficient to deal with social malaise because what matters is not the feelings of individuals but the enduring collective sentiment that is crystallised around a stable course of action by public agencies. Effective public policies are indispensable. Gurudwaras and non-governmental organisations may complement its efforts to feed the hungry, but it remains the prime duty of the state to do so.

Work, Home and Dignity

In short, a regime of social policy pivotal for a minimal welfare state must be installed to address the basic needs of all Indian citizens to meet any contingency. This must be done not only during pandemics but for all times. Socioeconomic rights, including the right to work, have long been part of our Directive Principles of State Policy. By enacting the Mahatma Gandhi National Rural Employment Guarantee Act in 2005, the Indian Parliament set in motion a process that makes a specific and significant welfare provision constitutive of the very idea of citizenship. To be a citizen of a polity is to be entitled to an opportunity to work. Now, manual work in extremely hot conditions on parched terrain is an energy-draining, back-breaking chore, not quite a source of self-realisation central to the emancipatory vision of Gandhi, Hegel or Marx. And yet, even such paid manual labour is a far cry from receiving charity. Under the democratic norms of equality, living on charity is demeaning and lowers self-esteem. There is a sense in which any voluntary work, no matter how arduous, quietly uplifts and enhances one's dignity and basic self-respect, a point gracefully underscored by a group of 'painters' (migrant labour) in Palsana, Rajasthan, who chose to give a fresh coat of paint to an entire school building in return for the shelter provided to them during the lockdown.

Work is one among many sources of satisfaction and self-respect. The directive principles focus on other things such as proper housing. It is time the state took these seriously. While no state can build a home—which needs personal care and must be our own handiwork—the right to housing can certainly be guaranteed because it is implicit in the article enjoining the state to provide a decent standard of living.

Multiple Deprivations

However, such social policies will not be forthcoming unless we, who make these policies, stopped viewing the poor as subhuman. This is a controversial statement and requires some explanation. I believe the best of us carry the image of the poor as labouring creatures with basic material needs who beget children. They suffer when deprived of these material needs. Our humanity lies in empathetically acknowledging this suffering. This, however, is not an image that we have of ourselves. We have more complex social, cultural, political and even spiritual needs. We need quality time with our children and leisure for ourselves; companionship and friendship to sustain a flourishing social life; music, literature, art and poetry for intellectual growth; and time to fulfil our obligations in the public domain. We also need our privacy, hours of solitude and space for self-reflection. Our suffering too is different. We have anxieties, phobias, inner turmoil and loss of a sense of self.

These profound differences exist between 'them' and 'us', but it does not cross our minds that the poor have multiple deprivations—not only material but social, cultural, familial and spiritual. When did a policymaker ever worry about the quality of family or spiritual life among the poor? Or whether they have time for their children or for leisure? Or how impoverished they might be because of their inability to adequately self-reflect.

I do not wish to make the absurd demand that our state policies be designed to care for all these non-material needs. My point is that unless policymakers have the same conception of the poor as they have of themselves—persons with rich, varied and complex needs—they will not realise the grave consequences of the material deprivations endured by the poor or show the urgency to remove them. In short, policymakers need to realise that they are dealing with complete human beings. Unless they are able to vividly imagine the poor as fully human, they will never design proper policies to address even their material needs. Alas, this will not happen unless policymakers feel their pain—literature and cinema can help here—and there is real, continuing contact between the two.

82

Halting the March of Rumours

In 1984, just as Delhi was convulsed by a pogrom against the Sikhs, the city was rife with rumour that the entire water supply had been poisoned. Such rumours are not new. For centuries, European Jews were falsely accused of poisoning wells during wars, epidemics or civic unrest. Paris in the late eighteenth century, deeply polarised along class lines, was replete with rumour that the rich distributed lethal, contaminated flour to the poor.

It is no surprise then that during the COVID-19 pandemic, the rumour mill has Muslims deliberately throwing infected 2,000-rupee notes on the road or Muslim street-vendors spitting on vegetables and fruits. Periods of social stress or natural disasters are fertile ground for rumours, which not only spread like wild fire but have grave consequences—scapegoating, social boycott, violence and arson or even lynching and murder.

The Anatomy of Rumour

Where do rumours spring from? Why and how do they spread so fast? Why do they thrive in a crisis? Not all rumours are pernicious.

Some are potentially harmful but, like meteors in the sky, disappear without much impact. But the ones that concern us here are toxic, occur with cataclysmic events and have devastating results. How must such rumours be checked?

For a start, a rumour is an untested piece of information, opinion, report or story. Therefore, its veracity is doubtful. This unverified, ambiguous status is at the heart of a rumour, making it largely what it is. The moment an account is publicly demonstrated and accepted to be true or false, it ceases to be a rumour. In a sense then, a rumour's truth or falsity is irrelevant to its efficacy or impact. Yet, every unconfirmed account is not a rumour. To become one, it must have other features. First, it must have a ring of truth. Something in it must make it contextually plausible for the listener or the reader. If an account is obviously bizarre—the sun will freeze overnight—or instantly falsifiable—Sachin scored a thousand runs in an ODI—it cannot become a rumour. Second, it short-circuits reason. Laced with passion, it works by seizing the collective psyche of the victims. Suddenly, many start to believe it. This also lends it a third important feature—it circulates rapidly. Fourth, it manifests itself through an event. It is a passing gust—sometimes it is a tornado that leaves devastation in its wake, but is ephemeral. Fifth, even when deliberately planted by only a few, it derives authority largely from the mob. Indeed, expert-authority is helpless against its seductive power. So, a rumour is a useful half-truth with strong emotional overtones that spreads fast, gripping individual minds to create a common consciousness and agency, often with grave social consequences.

Rumours are efficacious in societies already prepared to receive them. What then are the conditions that beget them? First, a context where there is either an information void or an information overload. Unable to satisfactorily make sense of their world in these uncertain contexts, humans become cognitively unstable and anxious. To meet their cognitive needs, they are forced to rely on bits and pieces of available knowledge, a patchwork of half-truths and a ragbag of allusions that together provide a fragile, uncorroborated framework for interpreting events. Rumours feed on this mythic framework. Add emotional anxiety to this cognitive framework and one has a ready-made arena for rumours to flourish. An overheated mind burns all evidence that comes its way and surrenders to rumours, often in the service of emotional needs. Recall how during demonetisation, the poor, although desperate and anxious about losing their own money, still found emotional satisfaction in the rumour that crores of rupees secretly stored in cash by the rich were rendered worthless.

Why They Circulate

Jamuna Prasad, a psychologist at Ranchi and Patna Universities, was among the first to establish a link between high levels of anxiety and the easy spread of rumours. Typically unrecognised when he was alive but posthumously celebrated as a pioneer in the social psychology of rumours, Prasad established the link by studying the social impact of the deadly Bihar–Nepal earthquake of 1934. Others have shown that in times of acute crisis people lean on knee-jerk speculation and prejudice. A group of 'outsiders', already distrusted and disliked, becomes an easy target, ready to be blamed for the current mess. Rumours succeed in societies ridden with an us–them syndrome—ones that are already polarised. Indeed, by binding people, creating temporary solidarities against a perceived enemy, rumours deepen existing polarisation. No wonder they come in handy to those who benefit from such divisions.

With uncertainty, fear and the radical other already firmly in place, the last piece in the jigsaw puzzle is provided by a vivid story of grave wrongdoing by an 'enemy' who has allegedly unleashed the calamity. A rumour *is* that story. And the more horrifying, outrageous and disgusting the story, the greater its emotional resonance and the quicker its spread. But as has been mentioned, to get kickstarted, it must already be believable. Some factual detail needs to be added to the fiction to give it plausibility that it otherwise lacks.

The 1984 carnage compelled Sikhs to go to gurudwaras in large numbers. This kindled the rumour that they were stockpiling arms and planning to attack and plunder the city's posh colonies. The truth, altogether different, is that they went there seeking refuge. So in the entire narrative, only one element was factually correct—and this little truth alone made a giant lie plausible. Likewise, it is a fact that many Muslims have experienced arbitrary violence, stigma and ostracisation in contemporary India. Given this threat, panic-stricken Muslims in Indore unjustifiably beat up a team of doctors who had come to test them for COVID-19. They easily succumbed to the rumour that it was not medical quarantine but needless, malicious separation from their families that motivated the visit.

In polarised societies, fear and vulnerability make rumour-mongering easy. But there are other reasons why they get widely entrenched. Three of them stand out. First, the desire to conform gets the better of a questioning mind. Rather than face sanction and ostracisation for sticking out, people find it safer to emulate members of their group. Second, ironically, a belief gets entrenched after like-minded people discuss it among themselves. Discussion has a cascading effect; the more one talks about it, the more a biased rumour grows. Third, a denial by a mistrusted outsider, no matter how great her expertise, only ends up solidifying rumours. Group dynamics in polarised societies works with a logic all of its own. Every person is necessarily partisan. A neutral ground for impartial voices is simply unimaginable.

Reducing Their Efficacy

Briefly, here is the conundrum: Since societies can never be fully informed or secure, rumours are inevitable, and in times of acute crisis, they are a menace. Yet, providing rational rebuttal or furnishing relevant information is unable to stem the tide. Must rumours then be viewed like a tsunami before which we are helpless?

This fatalism is unwarranted. Transforming the conditions conducive to rumours can reduce their efficacy. Depolarising society, loosening the grip of prejudice and calmly addressing the collective anxieties and obsessions of a group are deterrents but, alas, only in the long run. In the short run, regulatory laws to check rumours are imperative, as also is the need to have critical insiders with authority deny injurious rumours, not least on the ground that eventually they harm even those who propagate, spread and exploit them. Community leaders and democratically elected office holders must play a crucial role in halting the march of dangerous rumours.

83

The Death of Fatalism

The pandemic, it seems, is an epoch-changing moment. Millions have fallen sick and hundreds of thousands have succumbed to the disease. We have been caught unawares and still do not know how to deal with it. Historic events such as this compel us to raise big questions usually submerged in the hustle and bustle of life: what is and what isn't in human control? How to make sense of collective helplessness in the face of abrupt changes? What is the place of contingency, fortune and misfortune in our life? Fatalism provides one answer: human agency is insignificant. We are permanent victims of inscrutable forces beyond our control.

With the arrival of the pandemic, the surge of fatalism seems inevitable in popular consciousness. What else can we expect in the land of karma—the idea that birth, status, marriage, occupation and all of life experiences including death is predetermined? Isn't our personal destiny inscribed on our forehead or in the lines of our palm? Are we not already allotted a share (*bhaga*) of fortune or misfortune at birth? Isn't Hinduism virtually synonymous with fatalism? Surely, we must then expect a lot of fatalistic gloom in these times.

The Near-Absence of Fatalism

Yet, there is scarce evidence for it. I don't see ordinary people resigned to their fate, an inscrutable, unpredictable force that acts on humans against their will, mocks their agency and humiliates them. Instead, they expect governments to take charge, doctors and nurses to save lives, scientists to deliver a cure and fellow citizens to behave responsibly. The poor do not seem to abjectly surrender to their fate either. They are willing to take huge risks and return home, not die of hunger when abandoned by governments. In short, Hindu fatalism seems to be a myth spun by Western orientalist imagination or perhaps sustained by the rich who imagine the poor to be victims of fate, which is not what the poor believe about themselves.

This near-absence of fatalism in India is not a gift of modernity. Historically, large segments of Indian thought are non-fatalistic and give an important place to human agency. The philosopher Sukumari Bhattacharji made a plausible case for the absence of fatalism in various ancient texts such as the Rig Veda, the Brahmanas, the Samhitas, the Upanishads, the Aranyakas and in Jaimini's *Purva Mimamsa*. The theory of karma found in the teachings of the Buddha and Mahavira is not just atheistic but also valorises human agency. Though the idea of fate exists, it is immanent, inscribed in and dependent upon human action spread over many births. Likewise, in Puranic literature, fate and human agency coexist. In the Mahabharata, there are two kinds of rishis. The Pravrtti sages (engaged in the world) draw upon the power of *tapas* (religious austerity) to dominate their surroundings; the Nivrtti sages (renunciates) actively acquire spiritual knowledge by which to escape their surroundings. Both reject the argument that humans are victims of forces beyond their control. In ancient India, perhaps only the atheistic Ajivikas embraced fatalism.

In Indian folk literature, one frequently finds a god or goddess coming to write the *bhagya* (share of fortune or fate) on the forehead of a new born. Several Indian languages have a term for it: *talaiyeluttu* and *talaiviti* in Tamil; *haneli barediddu* and *hanebareha* in Kannada; *phalalikhita* in Sanskrit, etc. In Hindustani too, phrases such as *'Hamari kismet mein yeh likha hai'* are common.

This is often taken as an affirmation of Indian fatalism. But then the same literature invites us to use our wit to overturn or at least modify *the bhagya* writ on our forehead. Fate can be thwarted by action, particularly by those prepared to take risks. It can also be challenged, especially among the underprivileged, by 'witchcraft' or worship of ancestors and local deities. Anthropologists such as Kathleen Gough record the derision with which Dalits in Tamil Nadu dismiss ideas of *bhagya, phalalikhita*, or inexorable fate. For upper castes, astrology appears to perform the same function, for it suggests appropriate strategies to manage *bhagya* or avert *durbhagya* (misfortune) rather than surrender to it.

In conditions of extreme and prolonged distress, entire world views may emerge that make human vulnerability permanent; make unexpected, unpredictable forces salient; and render human agency, order and reason insignificant. Consider the idea of the absurd that underscored the futility of the search for meaning—quite like fatalism that stresses the futility of human action—that emerged during the Second World War. But extreme action-negating world views such as fatalism must not be conflated with perspectives that give importance to fate. Fate is an integral, recurrent feature of the human condition. In every civilisation, such concepts emerge unbidden. All ancient world views had a term for it: *moira* in Greek, *ming* in Chinese and *bhagya* in Sanskrit. Modern world views too must incorporate fate.

Why? The human world can always be viewed as a great contest between human agency and nature, something currently beyond control. The more humans are able to control their destiny, the less room in their perspective they have for fate. The more the world is comprehended, the less inscrutable it is. But there are times when most human beings feel utterly helpless—say, in times of wars, natural calamities, social upheavals or personal misfortune. In such moments of extreme vulnerability and loss of control when things seem beyond rational comprehension, ordinary human beings with their practical consciousness rely on notions such as fate. They submit, surrender and resign themselves to and eventually accept their condition: 'so be it', 'such is my lot', etc.

Human Powers versus Chance

In short, an ongoing battle rages between what the Italian humanist Machiavelli called *virtù* (human powers) and *fortuna* (chance or fate). We need to constantly experience and evaluate which way the balance will tilt. Individuals, societies and, indeed, humanity must have a realistic view of what is given and the extent to which it can be altered. It is impossible to entirely give up a conception of something beyond us and equally to entirely reject a modicum of responsibility for one's actions. We are always in part responsible for what is happening to us, though this contracts or enlarges depending on circumstances. However, one element that perpetually evades control is the sheer fortuitousness in our lives—accidents, coincidences, disease, disasters, sudden bereavements, etc.—which defies human agency and thwarts the best of plans. It compels us to rely solely on the idea of fate. Indeed, more than good luck, fate is linked to misfortune and death. No wonder accidents that result in death are called fatal and human beings who perish in disasters are called fatalities.

In sum, while fatalism that over-valorises fate and nullifies human agency must disappear, views that introduce the dialectic of fate and human agency to account for contingency, misfortune and bad luck cannot be erased. However, even their relevance or efficacy can be reduced by better understanding, sounder explanations, with the wisdom to know what can and cannot be controlled and, indeed, by properly evaluating what should or should not be controlled.

84

The Heavy Burden of Social Suffering

It is a truism that suffering is part of life. No one, literally no one, is exempt from it.

A deep philosophical interpretation of this claim is provided by the great Buddha: the mere fact of human existence entails suffering because everything in the world is ephemeral. Its imminent disappearance is experienced as a loss, causing grief. This elemental imperfection in the world keeps us all in a near-permanent state of *dukkha*, or radical discontentment.

Inescapable Truth

There is a second extremely important sense in which all human beings are subject to suffering. We all undergo a deeply negative, unwanted experience when our daily routine is disrupted by disease, sickness, ageing, death, natural catastrophe, etc. During a life cycle, all humans are equally vulnerable to this experience. The Buddha spoke with great wisdom about it, as did the Indian epics. Indeed, most religions in the world attempt to address and make sense of this ubiquitous but inescapable human suffering that is both physical and mental (feelings of profound meaninglessness, anguish and despair). Paradoxically, our very capacity to reflect—to remember our past and imagine a future—intensifies this suffering.

The Buddha spoke not only about the deeply felt suffering caused by major disruptive episodes in life but also minor yet persistent daily suffering and disaffection caused within an individual—an effort gone waste, an unfulfilled aspiration or a missed opportunity—because of persistent irritations within social interactions. Indirectly, he differentiated suffering by its duration—short-term and episodic or long-term and continuous. The great Ashoka introduced another dimension, implicitly distinguishing suffering by its source—its cause lying within human agency or outside it. Owning up responsibility, he expressed remorse at the immense and continuing agony he caused the people of Kalinga. He acknowledged how the anguish caused by a war he waged began a chain reaction, creating an ever-widening circle of co-sufferers.

The dark and tragic Mahabharata also speaks of a relatively short eighteen-day war in which immense human suffering was inflicted by one group on another. Thus, we may distinguish forms of human suffering by their (a) source, (b) intensity and gravity and (c) duration. With these, we can home in on a third form of *dukkha* in which grave disruptions caused by humans become an enduring feature of daily life, as when humanity was continuously ravaged by the two world wars.

Traumatic Images

Such colossal misery inflicted by one group on another or by a ruler on the ruled might be called socio-political suffering. This reprehensible experience, a consequence of various acts of commission or omission by powerful people in society who go to war, impose harsh economic measures, deliberately sow social divisions or work for the benefit of a few with no regard for the welfare of the powerless, is entirely avoidable. Until recently in human history, this systemic violence and institutionalised oppression was barely recognised for what it really is: something not given to but made by humans.

It is this man-made suffering that in recent times has invaded our lives: lakhs of penniless, barefoot workers trudging hundreds of kilometres under the scorching sun; a pregnant woman carrying a load on her head or lying on a cart pushed by her husband; a mother delivering a baby on the pavement, and moments later, standing up to continue her journey, or another mother wheeling a broken suitcase with a four-year-old clinging to it; a 10-year-old collapsing on the roadside, exhausted by the heat; a rickshaw wallah from Delhi cycling all the way to Bihar with all his family and worldly goods; scores hiding in the entrails of a dumper to avoid the punitive gaze of the police; thousands spending endless nights on railway platforms waiting for the promised train to arrive and take them home; hundreds killed on railway tracks or roads by speeding trains or vehicles, their food, blood and chappals strewn everywhere. These were induced neither solely by COVID-19 nor by the decision to lockdown but largely by how the lockdown was handled, reminding us of Arthur Schopenhauer's comment that 'the world is Hell, and men are on the one hand the tormented souls and on the other the devils in it'.

These images that flashed past us were shattering, first because they displayed the sheer corporeality of suffering—pain and injury, unimaginable fatigue and exhaustion, exposure to excessive heat, stomachs aching with hunger, parched throats, nausea and dizziness—and second, because they exhibited unbearable mental distress—suppressed rage, anguish at the plight of old parents or little children, homesickness, fear, loss of dignity, humiliation, social rejection, betrayal and the incessant realisation that you live with others who treat you as disposable waste or garbage. They all combined to generate a comprehensive attack on one's personhood, accompanied by a feeling of overwhelming despair that one exists at all. We have been witnessing here a concentrated form of what millions of people undergo daily in some or another part of the world, starkly bringing into relief that large-scale disruptions such as the current pandemic constitutes structural suffering of millions and points to the horrendous ways in which many societies are currently organised.

Moral Indifference

There is something wrong with this world and—gravely and astonishingly—with our moral indifference to this daily denial of humanity to others. How is it that we, corporeal beings, equally vulnerable to pain and anguish, allow others to experience conditions that we will not ourselves accept for a minute? How can we accept a process of self-formation that simply fails to make us moral? How can a nation be built without *sahahridyata* (shared feelings or empathy)? How can a social structure exist that renders superfluous those very people who put their life and blood in maintaining it? Are we engaging in an archaic ritual of violence that is incomplete without the sacrifice of the most precious and indispensable among us?

Alas, this moral coarseness—the ability to shut off from discomfiting conditions, to not see or feel for them, or hear or think about them—is not just a defensive psychological strategy to keep sane but also an ingrained habit that constitutes what we are, which is a part of our training since childhood, a trait in our character. Perhaps, it is integral to our chosen, self-indulgent lifestyle, one sustained by social and economic processes that originate in the carefully hidden oppression of others. Surely, some of these practices have an old lineage, for instance, in the hierarchical caste system founded on mistreatment of indispensable others; others are very much a product of modern technology and organisation. Doesn't a common amoral thread run through the remote-control bombing of civilian populations, the organised machinery of genocidal violence, the calamitous destruction of the environment and the structural poverty of millions?

We are all culpable in this grave wrongdoing. Yet this shared responsibility is graded. Those with more power and wealth—those who run the state and big corporations—must bear greater responsibility for the collective suffering.

There may have been a time when most people oriented themselves to a world that was little more than what Schopenhauer called 'a penal colony', where life itself was viewed as punishment and in which nothing untoward or irregular was found in the torments of life. Natural calamities and man-made oppression were viewed as a part of the order of things. This seems to have changed everywhere, including in India, particularly by the experience of the anti-colonial struggle and the vibrancy of contemporary political democracy. Today, more and more people hold some others responsible for part of their suffering and expect governments that are run in their name to do something about it. Indeed, when appropriate, they directly and publicly blame governments too. So, fellow citizens and governments, beware!

85

Revisiting Scientific Temper

An unexpected benefit of COVID-19 is the growing awareness of how disease is transmitted and what might be done to prevent it. Virtually every television channel has insisted on washing hands with soap or alcohol-based sanitizer, sneezing into the crook of one's elbow or coughing into a handkerchief, besides keeping a safe distance from one another. These precautions presuppose an elementary understanding that COVID-19 spreads through the inhalation of droplets released by the infected person's cough or sneeze and by contact with infected surfaces. The existence of coronavirus that invades our bodies and causes the infection is also a part of this presupposition. In short, this indicates a tacit acceptance of elements of the empirical–causal world view. It was heartening to see even babas and yogis concede that if symptoms include respiratory disorder and high fever then contacting doctors trained in evidence-based medical systems is necessary. Baba Ramdev even admitted that there is no evidence that drinking cow urine can cure COVID-19, even though, he claimed, it could help in preventing it.

Towards Fact-based Reasoning

It does not follow from this that our society has imbibed this outlook on the world, for many astrologers were seen claiming that SARS-CoV-2 was caused by the conjunction of Rahu and Ketu. Some swamis are convinced that the cure lies in propitiating the virus by performing rituals accompanied by a cocktail of cow urine, dung and ghee. Even so, it is heartening that when push comes to shove, many Indians might be more willing to rely on evidence-based reasoning than on ineffective, false speculations or brazen misinformation. When what is at stake is life itself, people choose whatever they find is effective. Should we not assume that they do so because they, at least some of them, are convinced that performing rituals is unlikely to produce the desired outcome but regular washing hands likely will? That the Rahu–Ketu story is less plausible than the virus-infection story? This switch from speculative stories involving malignant spirits to stories involving non-subjective, material and observable entities occurs when people themselves experience what works and what does not.

Two generations or so earlier, curative pill-popping became part of the wider public culture. Although its misuse, dangers and excesses are well-documented, it can't be denied that careful intake of pills under expert supervision and in correct dosage can help cure infectious diseases. With our rather enlightened response to COVID-19, we appear to have reached a similar stage in the public culture of disease prevention. Equally important is scrupulous data gathering. Indian news channels continually gave figures on people infected by SARS-CoV-2; countries where the incidence of disease was high; what percentage was cured and what percentage died; of those who succumbed, how many already suffered from other fatal ailments; and whether or not a correlation exists between age, propensity to infection and fatality. There is greater public awareness about the role of data in disease management and prevention. These are small steps towards the wider acceptance of evidence-based reasoning and a tiny victory for the empirical-causal explanatory story of the world. Since these are crucial ingredients of the scientific outlook, one can even say that we have made some progress towards inculcating a scientific temper.

Observing, classifying and recognising patterns of regularity and identifying their causes are all integral features of science. Yet, not all of us do science. Nor do we need to. What has become increasingly vital for our survival today is that everyone grasps the broad features and uses of science—that we imbibe scientific temper. Science is important because science works, and we need scientific temper because in its absence the benefits of science won't reach everyone.

The Role of Science in Life

Bringing a rather outdated term 'scientific temper' back into circulation might raise some hackles, however. How can modern science be valorised after an awareness of the devastation it has caused? Nuclear destruction, industrial pollution, climate change and a technologically induced sedentary lifestyle are all undeniable facts. But science continues to play a limited but critical role in human life. In one sense, it always has. This is to do with our inescapable interaction with the natural world and our need to harness its powers. Pre-language science in which knowledge is embodied in skills, and which is neither consciously nor symbolically available but generated in practical interaction with the world, has been around for two million years. And scientifically oriented stories with an explicit, language-dependent understanding of nature developed some 40,000–50,000 years ago when—to explain, predict and control nature—we began telling each other how and why things happen. An idea then took hold that performing a particular ritual to appease the spirits delivers us from disease and death and could provide all the goods we need (magic, astrology, shamanism, etc). Our pre-modern stories attempted many things, including to explain, predict and control. Modern science is a radically improved version of this limited aspect of earlier stories. Besides, it has originated from and built upon them. Scientists readily acknowledge that myths, legends and stories continue to be the source of current scientific insights. In this sense, a science independent of myth and religion is woefully inadequate for living. The other big limitation of modern science is that it plays virtually no role in mutual or intercultural understanding or in our indispensable ethical projects of self-exploration, self-understanding or self-realisation. That role in providing collective and individual self-knowledge and ethical guidance is played by the humanities, interpretative social science and religions.

With these qualifications, we must readily acknowledge that scientific temper is useful in certain contexts and necessary for specific purposes. If so, what are the other preconditions for building it? First, a disposition to not accept any opinion or claim at face value or to reject in haste anything that conflicts with one's own settled views, for instance, to not immediately accept when told that eating a clove of garlic will reduce high BP or that the rate of economic growth in India is 7 per cent. A healthy scepticism towards these figures is crucial. Moreover, no claim or data can be accepted merely because it is supplied by those in majority, political power or a religious authority. Evidence-based claims are the enemy of prejudice and dogma. Second, good science recognises that truth is always elusive and all human endeavour, including scientific enquiry, is imperfect, corrigible and in constant need of critical scrutiny and revision. Third, in principle, science is anti-authoritarian. No matter how hierarchical scientific institutions or how powerful their leaders are, the fact remains that if a research assistant comes up with a result that challenges an established scientific claim, it must be examined, and if confirmed to be valid, it must be allowed to displace the view held by the established authority. So if scientific temper is important, what kind of public culture is needed to advance it? Who must be responsible to take it forward? And how can we nudge people into evidence-based reasoning without recourse to self-interest alone but also because of a commitment for the common good?

86

The Return of the Expert

The expert is back in public discourse. Dismissed until recently as an enemy—a self-indulgent blabber and an arrogant armchair intellectual—he returns now as a valuable adviser and an ally, as someone we cannot do without. The flamboyant display of ignorance has been suspended. Populist leaders who had openly berated experts and spoke of their tyranny are now singing their praise. Though forced by the coronavirus, this is an extremely welcome change. Why? Are experts blameless or exempt from criticism? Is the criticism of experts never justified? What is expertise anyway?

Who Is an Expert?

Humans realised quite early that individuals cannot lead a life doing everything by themselves. They must rely on others who occupy different social roles. But mere division of labour does not yield a society of experts. To have the competence or technique of doing something is not the same as having expertise in it. One may be able to ride a bicycle or play cricket but not do it well. Expertise comes with doing something extremely well, which, in turn, relies on developing more than technical skills. It comes when skills are nurtured patiently and honed constantly. Its acquisition is impossible without continuous, time-consuming practice, and its growth depends on making mistakes and learning from them as well as listening to constructive criticism from others. Thus, to become an expert, one must imbibe the broader culture surrounding good work.

This brings me to a preliminary specification of an expert: they are not just role occupants or bearers of mere technique but role models for others; they become an authority in their chosen fields by investing time on developing special skills, understanding the standards of excellence in their own fields, trying to measure up to them and hoping to raise the bar. They become someone who can teach others. A person may occupy the position of a gardener but becomes an expert only with experience, incessant learning, imaginative self-improvement and the ability to pass on her skills to others. In short, experts are people with special skills and virtues, with legitimate authority in their own fields and with the stature to advise and teach others. This distinguishes them from non-experts, competent fellow workers and novices.

Skills may be primarily learnt informally or formally. Those trained informally or working predominantly with their bodies, particularly their hands, include farmers, gardeners, cooks, carpenters, potters, mistris, vaidyas, traditional healers, musicians and dancers. However, the enormous complexity of contemporary social and economic life necessitates that everyone must be literate and have a bare minimum of formal schooling. This would have been sufficient in the past to make experts out of them, but today, it is merely one enabling condition of expertise. To become experts in some domains now, long years of formal training and education are required. The feature that distinguishes modern professionals—medical doctors, engineers, architects, lawyers, microbiologists, physicists, historians, economists, sociologists, etc.—from their informally trained counterparts is their prolonged formal education resulting in knowledge. In such domains, experience is necessary but not sufficient. Both informal skills and formal knowledge are of immense value today.

Denigrating Experts

If it is good to have experts in society, why have they been devalued in recent times in public discourse? Two long-standing reasons come to mind. First, not long ago, expertise in our society was firmly believed to be inherited. But while shastric knowledge was overvalued, the practical knowledge of the informally trained was denigrated. They were not recognised as experts. However, a contemporary scientist does not genetically transfer science to his child. Why then is shastric knowledge a birth-related privilege of a few Brahmins? And how many of us acknowledge the expertise of malis who tend beautiful gardens? Why are they less of an expert in their fields than a doctor is in his? Though some change in this mindset has occurred, it is not enough. For instance, vaidyas, nats and nartakis were once considered lowly and socially stigmatised, but today's medical doctors, actors and dancers are not.

In a sense then, an understandable disaffection with the expert is part of a continuing democratic revolt against the very idea of inherited shastric expertise. This revolt will not cease if inherited expertise is merely replaced by epistemic arrogance, a sense of superiority stemming from delusional infallibility. Indeed, unless experts cultivate the virtues of humility and corrigibility in an atmosphere of equality and solidarity, their relevance will remain under a cloud.

The second reason is the easy translation and transfer of authority from one field to another, enabling experts in a few fields to wield power and authority over others. The traditional Brahmin may have been a shastric expert, but how come this narrow expertise yielded a general social authority over others? Besides, experts jealously guarded their knowledge as a secret and refused transparency or accountability. A challenge to such translation and transfer of authority from one specific field to others is justified. So part of the blame for the gradual fall of the expert lies with the historically transmitted culture surrounding him. Expertise must be disentangled and rescued from this hierarchical culture.

Education and Expertise

However, the real roots of today's specific problems lie elsewhere—in the current mindset of the populace at large. The main trouble comes paradoxically from the very condition of general literacy and education in our society. All of us are encouraged by our generalised education to conflate expertise with competence and to believe that knowledge comes easy. In this age of speed, the very idea of patient learning is severely threatened. For quick fixers, skill acquisition is a waste of time. If everything can be swiftly self-taught, why bother with experts who slog. (Just consider the recent trend to self-medicate.)

The situation is worse in the social sciences and humanities. I am astounded by the gumption of super-confident, self-styled historians or pop statisticians who, without an iota of doubt, claim to know the past or the percentage of minorities in the overall Indian population. This is independence and equality gone berserk.

This problem is exacerbated by Wikipedia, Google and WhatsApp. The internet allows us to treat every information and opinion as equally true. People simply view evidence selectively and with prejudice, confirming whatever it is this they already believe in and disregarding all evidence or argument against it. Abused easily, the internet turns truth into falsehood and opinion into dogma. This is mobocracy in the world of the intellect. Everyone has a licence to kill objective or inter-subjectively validated knowledge. This climate is hardly conducive to the survival of experts who seek validation for their claims. Moreover, it helps the political and economic exploitation of their difference from non-experts. With the expert's scrutiny out of the way, the avaricious capitalist can easily sell his well-advertised goods and the wily politician, his false promises.

The arrival of COVID-19 has changed something, at least on television. The prime minister was seen imploring us to shun *andhvishwas* (blind faith or superstition), disregard rumours and continually fact-check. A good beginning! Doctors from the best medical colleges were seen providing scientific answers to questions from laypersons. The word 'evidence' was heard frequently. Statistical data was cited from Johns Hopkins University and Imperial College London. People seemed passionately interested in the research on vaccines by the best Indian institutes. Fake news was officially having a bad time! One Hindi channel even had a truth index called '*sacchai ka* sensex'. This 'sacchai', the source of facts and evidence, came from experts. One unintended benefit of the current pandemic—if one looks for a silver lining in our gloomy world—is the return of facts, truth and experts. One can only hope that the restoration of respect for expertise will not be confined to medical doctors and researchers but extend to historians, social scientists and socially grounded intellectuals, who were all badly needed to check the mayhem that followed the announcement of the lockdown and its dreadful impact on migrant workers.

PART IX

The Fragility of Life

87

Facts Matter Even More in the Post-truth Age

I've heard it said that facts are unimportant, that only public opinion matters, implying that political action or public policy must be guided not by facts but by the opinion of the people. An even more pernicious claim is also made that there are no facts in the world, only biased interpretations and subjective opinions.

Both these strange claims have alarming practical consequences. Imagine you've been robbed and went to the police station to register a complaint where the policeman horrifies you with the response, 'I don't think this is a fact; it's only your opinion.' Worse, imagine you went to a doctor complaining of chest pain and the doctor says, 'I don't consider this a fact; it's only your biased view.' If you are really having a heart attack, well then, good luck!

Indifference to or denial of facts is more common in public life. Governments refuse to face uncomfortable facts and deny them forcefully—high unemployment, the economy's downward spiral, violations of rights, scandals. Such refusal to acknowledge facts has terrible consequences too. Not addressing the problem of unemployment, for instance, can lead to social unrest, violence and even terrorism.

Simple and Complex Facts

How are facts accessed or established? Not all facts have the same form. Some are simple while others have an increasing degree of complexity. The more complex a fact, the harder it is to establish and the greater the room for ambiguity and multiple descriptions. Consider the following: John F. Kennedy (a) died and (b) was assassinated. It was easy to quickly establish that he died. But more information and time were required to establish his assassination by Oswald, which was corroborated by several witnesses, films and forensic evidence. But why did Oswald do it? It is claimed that he acted willingly or unwittingly at the behest of the CIA. But to establish this fact—the motive—is more difficult; it was never conclusively established. But even here there are better and worse arguments, and as in legal judgements, its facticity is grounded not in evidence alone but also in reasons. Facts here are whatever has the best argument on its side. But comparing and ascertaining the validity of all reasons take time, effort and skill. And we may still not come to a definitive conclusion. So the issue is not the existence of facts, but that where multiple agents are involved with complex collective motivations, it is hard even for educated persons to directly access facts. Perhaps, facts such as the bad state of the economy fall in this category.

Furthermore, when vested interests muddy the waters by planting misleading information, spreading lies and deliberately creating a fog around the event as the tobacco industry is once supposed to have done. Facts, then, become extremely elusive. Such a condition of opaqueness has penetrated so deep in societies in recent times that it has become our default position, a part of our second nature, to be sceptical about all factual claims. Living in a world of radical uncertainty—the era of 'post-truth'—we don't know who to trust to get facts. How then does one get out of this conundrum?

Age of Domain Expertise

We once lived in a society where knowledge in some domains was believed to be inherited not socially acquired (shastric knowledge), and knowledge in other domains, for instance, farming, weaving, singing, was so socially insignificant that it was considered no knowledge at all. In any case, a select group of experts acquired the sole authority to pronounce on what the truth is in all domains of knowledge. As this society disappears, we find ourselves in an exactly opposite condition where we make radical self-reliance our ideal, and the easy availability of information on the internet breeds the delusion that we can be experts in everything. Alas, when we are unable to achieve this, we plunge into a state of radical uncertainty, unreliability and mutual distrust. Mercifully, these are not the only options. I believe it's best to recognise that knowledge is evenly distributed in contemporary societies where a more complex cognitive division of labour exists, and that expertise now is more democratised than ever before. All of us are skilled at something and experts in some small, specialised domain. We acquire the ability through formal or informal training to recognise or establish facts in the many domains that make up our social world.

Economists might know more about the aggregate state of the agriculture sector but farmers know crops and the conditions under which they grow. In the social world, therefore, we must aspire to an appropriate mix of self-reliant and other-reliant knowledge and to provide alternating and reciprocal leadership in fact acquisition. Facts and social trust are related and crucial to the working of society.

What happens when experts themselves have conflicting views? Here, individual accomplishments count. Some within each of these expert domains are hardworking and sincere, avoid self-deception, recognise their failures and work to overcome their flaws. Such people with intellectual virtues and strength of ethical character usually accomplish more. Our best bet, therefore, is to rely on the more accomplished people in each domain. All teachers are not selling ideologies; some are better than others at providing an empathetic, wide-ranging perspective on an issue. Likewise, not all doctors are trying to make a quick buck. Some willingly tell you when you don't need any treatment, and when you do need it, and when you must get diagnostic tests done to determine the course of the treatment. This is also true of media persons, lawyers, bureaucrats, electricians, shopkeepers, businessmen and perhaps even politicians.

We all benefit when governments are guided by public opinion grounded in the best available facts provided partly by experts in each of the relevant domains. But the identification of facts is impossible without the mechanism to identify reliable experts and without social trust more generally. Conversely, cynicism about facts is symptomatic not only of a cognitive crisis but also of a wider moral malaise of societal distrust.

88

We First Need a Uniform Criminal Code

Four back-to-back incidents in 2016–2017 highlighted a major crisis in Indian society. First, the stunning defiance of a parliamentarian soon after thrashing an airline employee. Second, the hounding of young men and women by 'anti-Romeo police squads'. Third, the merciless killing of Pehlu Khan by an unruly mob. And finally, the brutal assault on a Nigerian student by a murderous crowd.

To be sure, such incidents have happened before, but these came together in such quick succession that one wondered if we were witnessing an attack on the entire legal system. This was not just random lawlessness or occasional appropriation of law in one's own hands but appeared to signal a breakdown of the rule of law.

What is this rule of law? To begin with, the mere existence of laws is not the rule of law. A society governed by laws enacted arbitrarily, merely on the caprice of a single individual or group and changing frequently on the whim of the political authority, is not based on the rule of law. A key feature of the rule of law then is that it excludes arbitrariness in the exercise of power. For example, a policeman must not question or detain me without identifying who he is or specifying the grounds for suspicion. If he fails to do so, I should resist him as I would any ordinary person who grabs me unlawfully. The so-called anti-Romeo police squads have frequently acted in clear violation of the rule of law when arbitrarily questioning ordinary citizens. The rule of law implies that even police, the most visible agents of the state, are not above the law.

Equality before the Law

Nor indeed are legislators or government executives. It is this legitimate expectation—that our criminal law is the same for everyone, be it a state official or an ordinary citizen—that belied the capitulation of the government before the Shiv Sena MP. The rule of law exists only if the law applies equally to all. Politicians and ministers must follow the law as all other citizens. There cannot be one law for one group and a different one for others. If heavy penalties are imposed on 'lower castes' for the same crime over which upper castes get off lightly or, as in some countries, the evidence of two or more women is required where the evidence of one man is deemed sufficient, a fundamental egalitarian principle—the equal worth of all individuals—is violated. Nothing can be more repulsive for followers of the rule of law; legal discrimination based on attributes such as racial, religious or linguistic identity is simply unacceptable. People cannot get away with murder just because they belong to a majority religion, are linguistically dominant or, worse still, have a certain racial profile. The crowd that assaulted the Nigerian must be dealt with exemplarily—so must the killers of Pehlu Khan. It was bad enough that cow vigilantes killed an innocent man, but if they are treated lightly because of their tacit claim that as cow protectors they had acted in Hindu interests and therefore must be treated differently than this marks the collapse of the rule of law.

It can hardly be overemphasised that a breakdown of the rule of law affects everyone. Today, a Muslim dairy farmer is targeted;

tomorrow, it can be a Hindu peasant or pastoralist who routinely transport cows and other animals from one place to another. Angry crowds or ill-motivated killers often fail to distinguish persons of one religion from another, as we discovered painfully from the ghastly murder in America of Sikhs mistaken for Muslims.

Rights and the Rule of Law

More importantly, in our country, a rule of law that meets formal criteria of non-arbitrariness and impartiality is not enough. Lots of carefully designed laws that apply equally to all permit the state to invade our privacy or society to discriminate against women, but they can be constitutionally challenged because substantive justice is part of the meaning of the rule of law. In India, as Justices Bhagwati and Chandrachud, among others, have pointed out, the rule of law means the rule of a rights-sensitive constitutional law. Laws must respect the rights of individuals and groups, both against each other and against the state. This has the further implication that both individuals and groups can demand of the courts to enforce their rights. It follows that a judiciary indifferent to the violation of rights by vigilante groups or government is failing the Constitution and the rule of law.

We desperately need to restore the rule of law. And while a common and just civil code would be a gratifying achievement indeed, can the Indian state please implement a common criminal code first?

89

Using Facts to Hide the Truth

The Hathras atrocity is weighing on the national conscience—or whatever is left of it.[16] People witnessed not just the most brutal face of social oppression but also a cynical and brazen use of the

[16] Reethu Ravi, 'From UP Police's Delay in Filing FIR to Forced-Cremation of Victim: Timeline of Hathras Horror,' The Logical Indian, 30 September 2020, https://thelogicalindian.com/humaninterest/from-up-polices-delay-in-filing-fir-to-forced-cremation-of-victim-timeline-of-hathras-horror-24091

state machinery to support the oppressors[17]. The inhuman assault of the teenage Dalit girl—I shall call her Bharati—that eventually killed her was followed by a hesitation by police to file the first information report, the callous and deferred medical examination, the neglect of the dying declaration, and, most alarmingly, the haste with which the police burned the body without appropriate rites or the presence of family members.

This wilful destruction of evidence was followed by political tyranny: family members were virtually put under house arrest, the entire village was barricaded by massive police force and Opposition leaders and media persons who tried to reach the victim's family were stopped and roughed up.[18] It was an appalling instance of dictatorial behaviour that made a mockery of our constitutional democracy.

Shaping the Discourse

I shall not, however, focus on any of these, attending instead to the slippery speech acts of the spokespersons of the ruling party as they tried to shape the discourse around the horrific incident. Using false arguments to deceive the listener is a common form of sophistry. But what happened here was the use of true statements to hide other more urgent and relevant truths. This is no ordinary fake news or misinformation but the clever use of seemingly appropriate words and phrases with the clear intention of deceiving the populace. Few better instances are available of how facts and truth are used to generate a false discourse.

I illustrate my point here with three examples. Take first the issue of misdescription. I heard it being said on a television channel that 'I was

---

[17] Anuja Jaiswal, 'Hathras DM Threatened Us, Allege Dalit Girl's Family,' *The Times of India*, 2 October 2020, https://timesofindia.indiatimes.com/city/agra/media-will-leave-well-be-here-dalit-girls-family-says-hathras-dm-threatened-them/articleshow/78434214.cms

[18] Aditi Murti, 'CBI Releases Long List of U.P. Police Failures in Hathras Gang Rape Case,' The Swaddle, 22 December 2020, https://theswaddle.com/cbi-releases-long-list-of-u-p-police-failures-in-hathras-gang-rape-case/; GC News Desk, 'Political Turmoil in UP, Section 144 Imposed in Hathras, Media-Politicians Banned Entry,' *Goa Chronicle*, 1 October 2020, https://goachronicle.com/political-turmoil-in-up-section-144-imposed-in-hathras-media-politicians-banned-entry/; Kriti Mehta, 'Opposition Leaders Claim "Facts Suppressed" as UP Police "Forcibly Cremate" Hathras Gang-rape Victim,' Times Now, 30 September 2020, https://www.timesnownews.com/india/article/leaders-across-party-lines-claim-facts-suppressed-as-up-police-forcefully-cremate-hathras-gangrape-victim/660129

pained at the death of the young woman'. On the face of it, it sounds sensitive and apt; it is true, after all, that Bharati died. And expression of pain at the loss of life seems fitting. But is it? Since it is incontrovertibly true that she was mercilessly pulverised and eventually killed, the term 'died' is entirely inappropriate. 'Death' fails to distinguish the demise of a person by natural causes, accident, suicide or murder.

To speak of the death of a person when she was murdered is grossly misleading. If used persistently and deliberately, it is nothing but unforgivable sophistry. It obfuscates truth. Likewise, pain alone is not an appropriate emotion in the face of a brutal murder. To not have feelings of anger, horror or outrage indicates an emotional and moral disability. Overall, then, expressing pain at Bharati's ghastly murder is an inadequate emotion accompanying a gross misdescription. Together, they hide the truth of the gruesome incident. In human situations, finding the right and the most appropriate description of what has occurred is often the difference between truth and falsehood.

Irrelevant Explanations

Such misdescriptions are not the only way in which powerful wrongdoers distort public discourse and evade responsibility. Very often, explanations that are otherwise factually correct or true are equally damaging. So, what is to be made of the explanations of the chilling assault on Bharati by reference to the male propensity for aggression, violence and control?

Consider the following example. An investigating officer enters a charred house and finds a can of kerosene and a used matchstick. As he exits, a reporter asks him how the house had caught fire. The officer answers that it's 'because of the presence of oxygen at the location'. Now, this account is not untrue, for nothing catches fire without the presence of oxygen. However, the response is entirely irrelevant and would send the news reporter into a tizzy. The answer is wrong because a good explanation needs to be not merely factually correct but relevant to the question at hand.

Surely, at the back of the reporter's mind is whether the house was burnt accidentally or intentionally, and if it's the latter, precisely who caused it and why. Finding the motive and attributing responsibility for the criminal act is vital. Likewise, it is probably true that males are prone to aggression. But, like oxygen, this is part of the standing conditions of specific acts of rape and murder. It is not explanatorily relevant in most cases of actual violence such as in Hathras. If our interest is in finding the precipitating causes for why Bharati was assaulted, we need to identify local social, economic, cultural and, perhaps, political factors. To provide irrelevant and general statements instead is a straightforward ploy to hide the truth and cover up a possible crime. Likewise, broadening the discussion in the immediate aftermath of the atrocity by speaking generally about rapes all over the country deflects from the specific atrocity in Hathras and lets its perpetrators get off the hook.

Identity of the Victim

This brings me to the third point, which is so obvious that I am surprised that I need to make it at all. To say that Bharati was assaulted and murdered and to stop there is being both economical with the truth and morally callous. The omission of a detail withholds the most crucial feature of the story, one without which what happened cannot be understood and explained. Horrendous as all rapes are, it was not just any woman who was brutalised by some men but a Dalit who was sexually assaulted and killed by 'upper-caste' men. This crime would likely not have occurred if it was not for Bharati's Dalit identity.[19] Indeed, she was reportedly gang raped and murderously beaten not only because she was a Dalit but precisely because in the past her family had resisted 'upper-caste' domination. Even Bharati did not remain mute as she lay battered; she named her perpetrators in her dying declaration.

So it is not false to say that a young woman was assaulted and murdered by brutal men, but to ignore Bharati's Dalit-ness and hide the caste-related nature of the crime is to fail to explain what happened; it is akin to providing a false account. For it is the criss-crossing co-presence of caste and gender that truly explains what happened to Bharati in Hathras. Ignoring or concealing this falsifies the account, even when no factually incorrect general statement or no outright lie is offered.

We cannot paper over the difference between the horrendous act of killing a woman out of personal hatred for what she did, killing her to assert brute male power and murdering her only because of her Dalit identity. In a caste-ridden society, some groups are imprisoned in their castes, facing horrendous consequences simply on account of

---

[19] Dipsita Dhar, 'Hathras Rape: A Caste Continuum,' *Outlook*, 1 October 2020, https://www.outlookindia.com/website/story/india-news-heres-why-caste-matters-when-a-dalit-woman-is-raped/361253

the families into which they are born and because of where precisely their families happen to be located in caste hierarchy.

The Inadequacies of Homilies

Usually, the same is true of our religious identity. This is why the targeting of Dalits or Muslims all over India or of Kashmiri Pandits only because of who they are brings in a dimension of violence that cannot be condemned by general homilies such as 'all killing is horrible' or that 'all rapes are terrible'. These truths and generalised statements tend then to obliterate the very reason for which some people are killed. To mistreat, discriminate and target individuals because of their colour, gender, religion or nationality is to commit a crime qualitatively different from other horrific acts. For it attacks and terrorises not just one person but her entire community. To omit any mention of these specific group identities, where relevant, is then to entirely misdescribe the crime and obscure its real cause.

In short, in cases such as the Hathras atrocity where caste and gender oppression are deeply intertwined, one cannot foreground gender in a way that prevents people from seeing the causal role of caste in the violent act. To de-emphasise this point is to falsify the narrative. To place emphasis on just one and not on the other is also to distort the account. This politically motivated sophistry is dangerous. By legitimising the crime, it helps perpetuate it.

90

Arrest the Virus of Arbitrary Power

In the early days of the lockdown when COVID-19 cases began to rise, we witnessed a second virus spreading equally rapidly in the country—the virus of communalism. But there is a third virus around, which is less spoken about: a virus eating into and severely corroding our democratic structure—the virus of arbitrary power. There is no better evidence of this than the denial of bail to a pregnant student-activist, arrested for creating disorder on an 'unprecedented scale' when all she appeared to have done was actively participate, like many others, in a protest against the Citizenship Amendment Act (CAA), 2019, proposed by the government.

Tyranny and Slavery

This arbitrary use of power, implied by the absence or selective use of law, is deeply troublesome—more so, when exercised by a democratically elected government. Frequent arbitrariness in the political domain leads to tyranny, quite like its persistent presence in the social sphere leads to slavery. Either way, it tramples upon basic human freedoms. But what, one might ask, is the connection between arbitrariness and the loss of freedom?

Individuals, communities or citizens cannot function freely without a stable set of expectations. By stabilising expectations, laws enable significant freedoms even as they restrict some others. To take just one example, once it is widely known that I am legally restricted to drive only on the left, I drive with greater freedom, knowing that headlong collision is unlikely. I regulate the speed of travel and calculate the time to get from home to office. This helps me schedule my work for the day and coordinate with others who likewise make their own schedules. By jointly accomplishing our goals, we enhance our freedom. Laws enable our actions and interactions to become broadly predictable. Many of our freedoms require that the arbitrary, by which is meant 'unpredictable, random or unexpected', does not throw us off balance. The arbitrary blocks freedom.

However, an even more basic feature of arbitrariness, one that produces much greater harm, is to be at the mercy of the whim or fancy of someone else, especially the powerful. Return to the traffic example. Suppose that two vehicles stop at the traffic light but just beyond the zebra crossing. The policeman, embodying the entire might of the state, issues a ticket, or a challan, to one but not the other. Worse, instead of fining the violators, he seizes the driving licence of a careful driver, who has stopped a good metre behind the crossing, merely because he dislikes the make of his car. Surely, this arbitrary implementation of the law is grossly unjust. This shows that the minutest aspect of daily life—travelling to work—can be dependent upon the arbitrary opinion of someone else. When power is exercised arbitrarily by the state, a person is made to act not in accordance with a legitimate, general rule but at the pleasure of state officials. The most extreme example of this is political enslavement, where an entire people is colonised and subjected to the will of the colonisers and laws, good or bad, flow from the like and dislike of the colonial masters.

This is equally true of the arbitrary exercise of social power, for instance, under social slavery. A slave must comply with any—just any—whimsical order of his master. Since the master owns the slave, he is legally permitted to do just about anything with him. The slave breathes, sits, stands, eats, works and sleeps at his master's pleasure. He can be awakened and asked to work in the field at an unearthly hour of the night if the master so desires. He is never sure of what to expect from his master. One moment, he is an object of affection or charity, at the very next, he is treated with utter disdain or sold away, even killed. After all, the master can dispose of his property at will. Such arbitrary power was routinely exercised by the patriarch of the family, which continues even today. Likewise, unbridled capitalism is marked by an absence of law to regulate labour; workers can be hired or fired at will by the employer and no fixed hours of work exist. Unregulated wage labour works pretty much like slavery. Aren't domestic workers still treated like slaves at many homes?

The Emergency and Now

These examples strengthen my point about an inverse relation between arbitrary political power and freedom. In dictatorships, entire populations are subject to the whim of the supreme leader or a tiny elite. Who did not fear the midnight knock in the regimes of Hitler and Stalin? While the devastation they caused is well chronicled, smaller tyrannies abound in our world too. Even democracies contain authoritarian spaces within them where the law can be used to continuously harass opponents. Anyone who has lived through the Emergency knows that Opposition leaders were thrown in jail on the false charge of conspiring against the state, and thereafter a small crack unit began to arbitrarily control the activity of anyone politically significant. Surely that experience should have sufficed to make all of us realise the supreme value of freedom from arbitrary rule.

However, with the number of first information reports being filed at the behest of random persons on unsubstantiated complaints and little explanation, largely uncontested by a tired, silent political Opposition, one begins to wonder if we are headed in that awful direction once again.

Upending Rights

Consider the arrest of activists. Article 21 of the Constitution gives every citizen the right to liberty and security. No one can be deprived of their liberty and held without properly following procedures prescribed by law. Article 22 requires that anyone arrested and detained must be informed of the ground for such an arrest and must be brought before a competent legal authority within a prescribed time frame. Legal scholars have rightly pointed out that the best interpretation of this article requires that the grounds of arrest and detention must be reasonable. The grounds of preventive detention, to be used in very rare cases, must likewise assume that the suspicion of offence is well-grounded and based on available evidence and relevant information that satisfies any objective observer and not on mischievous allegations. But reality seems to confirm what every other Indian movie has shown about police acting on the caprice of a ruling leader and the law being used to harass citizens. Is suspicion always supported by available facts? Is the 'offender' really a threat to internal security or merely present at the scene of the 'crime'? Whatever the facts of the case, was the offence committed by a pregnant student–activist so grave that bail could not be granted until her fourth attempt? If ordinary persons could smell arbitrariness here, why could not the sessions judge? Anyhow, why fill our coronavirus-infested jails with what are largely political prisoners when other countries are releasing even non-political inmates? Minimum lock-up during lockdown should have been the political slogan in these catastrophic times.

Arbitrary curtailment of liberty existed under the previous state and central governments as well. This is deplorable. Yet, what is worrisome today is its frequency and brazen partisanship. We should remind ourselves that the participants in the 2011–2012 anti-corruption movement were not thrown in jail. Nor was the media muzzled when it went after the central government of the day. Why are political activists and journalists charge sheeted today for simply doing their job?

The Emergency was meant to be a watershed in the life of Indian democracy; it was a brief, critical phase when the Indian political system could have either gone the authoritarian way or mature into a democracy. By restoring faith in democracy, India passed one of its crucial tests and firmly took the second route. But are we on the verge of giving up the gains from that chastening experience? Has the struggle against the suspension of democracy been in vain? Have a small section of its victims now become perpetrators?

91

Police Terror and the Theatre of Law

The murders of Jayaraj and Benicks at the hands of the local police in Sattankulam, Tamil Nadu, provoked national outrage. The bare bones of the incident are widely known. A small shopkeeper is picked up for a trivial offence and taken to the local police station. His son too is detained. Both are mercilessly thrashed. The hospital to which they are taken admits that they have blood clots all over their bodies but gives false certificates of fitness. The magistrate remands them to judicial custody without examining their abused bodies, merely waving consent from far away. Within a couple of days, the two succumb to their grievous injuries.

State and the Law

What does this reveal about the nature of our state and the link between law and violence? The modern state emerged by gathering power dispersed among rivalrous local strongmen and depositing it in a single set of interrelated institutions now endowed with a monopoly of force and violence. These institutions were meant to function independently of the ruler; they do not belong to him and are not part of his personal estate. Instead, they work for the entire public.

The Jayaraj–Benicks case makes us doubt if such a modern, impersonal state exists in India. It shows first that our political institutions, including the judicial machinery, are far from independent of the will of the rulers; rather, they work at their personal command. Second, local policemen think of themselves as sovereigns in their own little territory—the executors of 'laws' they invent on the go. At the very least, they believe that they partake in the sovereign power protected by lawmakers sitting higher up. Indian society continues to consist of rival power groups, each with a 'private' police force at their mercy, coercing local populations to behave according to rules crafted at will. It is as if the entire country is splintered into little fiefdoms, each believing to have a monopoly of violence. Third, police brutality is a routine, banal feature of everyday life of the poor. The wanton actions of the police are woven into the fabric of daily social interactions. The police uniform plays a symbolic role—anyone who dons it has power, prestige and the backing of the entire official apparatus. This social superiority sanctions extralegal behaviour that often has the stamp of rampaging criminality. After all, nothing done by the Sattankulam police was by the rule book; everything from the first to the last violent moment was extra-legal. Far from safeguarding the legal from the illegal, the police embraced criminality. Jayaraj and Benicks appeared to be living not in a post-Independent constitutional state but under a police state in the colonial or pre-colonial era.

Law as Performance

Our society is meant to be governed by the rule of law implemented by a state above it and impartially arbitrating social disputes. In reality, it is an arena where everyone fights with all their might over material resources, power, status, ideas and, crucially, the control of the legal machinery. To get the law on your side brings enormous advantage, for once under control, it functions at your pleasure largely to benefit you. But since democracy requires that the law work for everyone, a performance must be staged to sustain this myth, a make-believe world created for ordinary people that 'all is well'. The performance of law courts is like the theatre or a film that seduces spectators into a reality of its own making. On most occasions, the lower courts are seen to be doing something when in fact they get nothing legally substantive done. They operate but do not really function. The discourse of the rule of law too is often a handy rhetorical ploy. The action of remanding Jayaraj and Benicks to judicial custody exemplified an infirm and callous judicial system designed to keep up the facade of the rule of law.[20] The magistrate did not even care to properly perform the law.

---

[20] M.K. Ananth, 'Man, Son Die in Custody: Relatives, Traders Complain of Police Torture,' 24 June 2020, *The Times of India*, https://timesofindia.indiatimes.com/city/chennai/man-son-die-in-custody-relatives-traders-complain-of-police-torture/articleshow/76539691.cmshttps://www.newindianexpress.com/sport/cricket/2020/jun/27/indian-cricketers-ravichandran-ashwin-shikhar-dhawan-call-for-justice-in-tamil-nadu-custodial-death-2162203.html

It is, of course, true that some committed police officers, such as the woman head constable Revathy, work overtime to maintain the integrity of the force. And whenever people begin to seriously doubt its efficacy, it is thanks to them that the law is temporarily allowed to work impartially as it should for everyone. But, alas, this happens only until its image as a credible agency is restored. After that, it is once again business as usual.

The proper functioning of the legal system is therefore the exception whereas the absence of rule of law and the lawlessness of local powers, the norm. Winners at the ballot box appear to earn the right to rule by arbitrary power. They control and regulate the whole populations at their pleasure, exactly as the maharajas of yesteryears. Our democracy allows us to elect those to whom we haplessly submit for five years. Not true? Pure hyperbole? The jury on this is still out.

Excessive Force

Undeniably, any system of law depends on the deployment of force. But its use must be consistent with the dignity of a person. The rule of law requires the presence of constraints on excesses. Excessive violence, for instance, torturing in pursuit of information and confession, is illegal in most decent societies. Yet Jayaraj and Benicks were victims of a surfeit of unwarranted violence. How does one explain this excessive use of force? Sadly, when a body is broken to bits and the face disfigured, there is not much left to respect. To mutilate a body is to demean and humiliate it. Excessive violence is meant to convey that the life of the victim is truly worthless.

Such humiliation is complete when the dismembered body is made public. The European thinker Michel Foucault argues that torturous spectacles common in medieval ages have given way to punishment in disciplinary institutions isolated from society. Yet, as we know, public lynchings have not disappeared in our own times. Indeed, residual elements of the public display of violence are evident even in the Jayaraj–Benicks case. Flogged in an enclosed public space, their bloodied bodies must have been brought to the hospital in full public glare, then taken to be shown to the public magistrate and, when declared dead, publicly handed over to the family.

So, what began as an alleged minor offence turned into a grave crime as the body was slowly ripped apart. With each strike on the bodies by an iron rod, the enormity of their crime rose, the impunity of police action deepened and the warning to others grew louder. Most of all, these mutilated bodies demonstrated the heavy price of dissent.

The Purpose of Brutality

In Thoothukudi, Tamil Nadu, surplus violence was inflicted with a distinct social and political purpose. In a Saturday feature article entitled 'When Protectors Turn Perpetrators', *The Hindu* reported that the day before detention, Jayaraj sympathetically went up to unpaid workers of a shop nearby asking them to stand their ground, even as an abusive policeman had threatened to punish them if they did not disperse. Upon learning this, the police felt that the act openly challenged their authority; it was an act of aggression not just on the state but also on their very person. From then on, their wrath knew no bounds. The *Hindu* also reported that illegal sand mining and the sale of illicit liquor are common in the area. It appears that any form of challenge to a police force that plays a key role in maintaining this corrupt and criminal order had to be dealt with swiftly and harshly. A crack in the system must not be allowed to open further; so it was filled immediately. An authoritarian rule works by fear, brooking no deviation. Jayaraj and Benicks unwittingly made the mistake of questioning the command of the local tyrant. Coming from an ordinary person, how can such a challenge ever be brooked?

The Jayaraj–Benicks case shows that without a proper rule of law we are all condemned to live in local tyrannies. How many more lives must we lose before its corrosive impact on our collective life is acknowledged?

92

Love in the Time of Polarisation

A new front has opened in the culture wars in India. After silencing academics and print journalists, conquering television news channels and maligning the Mumbai film industry, the trolls have made advertising the new battlefield. The release of the Tata-owned

Tanishq advertisement was followed by a manic backlash with complaints about hurt Hindu sentiment, threats of violence and an abrupt withdrawal of the advertisement. These threats were not empty; Tanishq showrooms in Gujarat and Madhya Pradesh were visited by goons demanding a written apology.

Message and the Attack

What is the advertisement trying to communicate and what is hurtful about it? An affluent Muslim family is seen organising a baby shower for their Hindu daughter-in-law. Marriage brings unanticipated tensions for the families of the couple and a particularly profound disturbance in the life of the woman who often moves into the home of her husband. Without an entire network of support led by the husband and the mother-in-law, this transition is painful. In the advertisement, the Muslim mother-in-law arranges a Hindu ritual, affectionately puts her arm around her surprised daughter-in-law and says that the custom of loving a daughter far outweighs the demands of religious tradition.

Playing upon vile communal instincts, the trolls attacked it for its 'secular' message. One extremist reason they offer is 'love jihad', allegedly a design to marry Hindu women with the sole objective of multiplying Muslim numbers to change India's demography. This is why these marriages, they say, are not a personal or family matter but concern the community and offend its morality. This intolerance of Hindu–Muslim marriage is entirely politically constructed. Instances abound of such marriages being turned into hell, at least in the initial years, by politically encouraged intolerance. The trolling must be seen in the context of a long-standing practice of politically triggered harassment of inter-religious couples.

A less hysterical reason is embedded in the assumption that the compatibility of two individuals due to their class, education and temperament is trumped by the natural incompatibility between a Hindu and a Muslim. This explains the social wrath against interfaith marriages, particularly between Hindu women and Muslim men. There is something in this argument: if conversion and a change of the bride's name is made a condition of inter-religious marriages, an objection against it is understandable. But this is not always true. In any case, this advertisement emphasises that the young woman remains a Hindu. This should take the wind out of the sails of the objector. If it does not, it is because of a third reason: the impregnable belief that inter-religious marriages go against incontestable social norms. Thus, for one 'realist analyst', the advertisement proves the disconnect of secular elites from Indian social norms. How unrealistic to expect that Indians will tolerate inter-religious marriage when social norms do not permit even inter-caste marriages within Hindus, Muslims or Christians?

Moreover, interfaith marriages are never arranged. The advertisement also appears to celebrate not only communal harmony but also 'love marriage', individual choice and the new egalitarian family that respects the distinctive identity and wishes of women. This provides an additional ground for conservative anger. Covertly, the trolls prey upon social anxieties surrounding the young falling in love, rebelling against the rigid traditions of community and giving women equal respect. The backlash against interfaith marriages comes from communalism's juxtaposition with this asphyxiating conservatism.

At Odds with Reality

This deeply conservative general portrayal of Indians is a simplistic myth at odds with the ever-changing, equally Indian social reality. Large towns and cities generate conditions for a partial collapse of the old community-dominated order. Public transport, the workplace, restaurants, malls, educational institutions, etc., all facilitate and encourage inter-caste and inter-religious intermingling. This real and virtual proximity generates conflict as well as opportunity for friendship that can transform into love and even marriage no matter how much it enrages the socially orthodox and intolerant. No society has ever managed to completely control the emotional life of individuals. Love marriages have a long ancestry. Even the Dharmashastras acknowledge and endorse love marriage—Gandharva vivaha—at least for the Kshatriyas. The epics speak of Kshatriya women choosing their husbands. Indian films build upon such long-standing socio-mythical archetypes and frequently support individual choice and love as the only basis for marriage. Given this countercurrent against caste- and community-based arranged marriages, is it surprising that the young dream of falling in love and marrying the person of their choice?

Not a General Trait

Moreover, the older generation is not as stubborn as it is assumed. At least in metropolitan cities, the initial period of social boycott and disapproval gives way to acceptance, forgiveness, accommodation and reconciliation, particularly after the couples have children. Many understand that beyond a point they cannot impose their own will on consenting adults. To ignore this fact portrays Indians as unalterable, heartless bigots for whom traditional custom has insuperable priority over love, which is an inaccurate depiction. A fanatical commitment to religious dogma may be common among habitual haters of other communities, but this a hardly a general trait of all Indians.

In short, social intolerance of inter-religious marriages exists but is exaggerated by the trolls. What then is the springboard of this intolerance and hostility? This is driven by the ambition of new power elites out to displace older ones. A minority within the majority community is forcing itself on everyone by claiming to be the voice of the people. It uses the rhetoric of 'the people' because in democracy anyone who claims the backing of the larger number gains social and political power. If mass opinion matters, large political benefits can be had from passing off a sectarian view as mass opinion. If a choice is to be made between curbing the voice of corporates and the voice of 'the people', as one television commentator put it, one must curb corporate voice. In reality, this wrath and hate is manufactured by a predominantly male-dominated discourse of new elites with a surfeit of power and money. Love jihad a is part of this discourse.

There Are Two Stories

In this polarised climate, it takes courage by a commercial enterprise to convey a message of understanding, acceptance, love and communal harmony. Instead of supporting it, most electronic and social media have openly chastised this effort. The Indian state has stood by passively, at best as a silent witness and at worse as irresponsibly backing the disruptors.

Much is at stake in India today. Not just communal harmony but also individual freedom, gender equality and freedom of speech, besides economic freedom and equality. Capitalist markets have many drawbacks but they allow buying and selling irrespective of a person's religion, ideology, race, colour and sexual preferences. The withdrawal of the advertisement undermines the principles of freedom and equality associated with a safe business environment.

It is not true that all Indians are resistant to social change or that Hindus are inveterate Muslim haters. Ground reports on ordinary people tell two stories, not one as the trolls and their followers would have us believe.

PART X

Hope in a Time of Despair

93

Chance Encounter with South Asian Wisdom

Taxis are mobile spaces that enable strangers to be physically proximate for a short duration. In an enclosed metallic 6x6-feet box on wheels, two individuals or a small group are accidentally thrown together. But if the passenger and the driver are so inclined, a taxi provides an opportunity for ephemeral social intimacy too. The journey cries out for conversation particularly if you seat yourself next to the driver. And when that happens, the episode can turn into an amateur ethnographer's delight, for it provides fleeting, meaningful data about a person, his society and culture, which can be stored in memory for future use.

We All Die Empty-handed

In metropolitan cities such as New York or Sydney, Indian visitors can't escape a chance encounter with Pakistani taxi drivers. Conversations begin with where are you originally from, and soon enough, the P-word is fluttering in the newly found common space. A lament curdles: how sad that India was partitioned—so unnecessary, so painful! And then the blame game begins: 'It is all the doing of politicians—not only of yesteryears but also of today's—whose avarice ordinary people fall prey to. If only people took matters in their own hands, but no politician allows that. We must live with our fate as separated brothers for whom reunion is forever denied.' The journey ends with a slightly mournful, feel-good bye. The driver refuses to take any money. The passenger insists that he can't take a free ride. Money is finally exchanged and reciprocal pleasantries bring the encounter to a close. I must have gone through this ritual hundreds of times in the last two decades. Away from their respective homelands, diasporic South Asians feel a special, fleeting bond that they fail to replicate when they return.

When I hailed a taxi on my visit to Sydney, one Abdul Mallick from Karachi stopped by the curb and asked me to get in. He had the look of a proper, god-fearing Muslim—a beard that would be perfectly V-shaped if it was not inordinately long, facial hair shaven away from squeaky-clean, shining cheekbones. He had no moustache. This is the kind of religious appearance that ordinary Hindus associate with a kattar Mussalman, or dangerous Muslim. The conversation had a predictable beginning but took an unexpected turn. 'Sir, I don't understand our politicians,' he said. 'They all claim to be true Muslims. But a Muslim's foremost concern is with what happens in the afterlife. He gets Jannat only if he does good in the here and now, right? But a politician in our country openly plunders his homeland and does no good to his holy land; all a politician in our country is interested in is amassing power and wealth for himself and his family. Why can't he realise that this does no good for his afterlife? He is simply not being a good Muslim.'

I was stumped but listened intently. 'And you know, Sir, they believe they are leaving behind a fortune for their family. But what do they get in return? When Benazir's family came to power after her assassination, did they go after her killers? No, Sir, these politicians only amassed more power and wealth for themselves. These people are rotten. They are so caught up in this terrible game that they have no qualms about betraying their mother or wife. Or perhaps, what they pass on to their families is greed for power and wealth. That is their legacy and their children's inheritance,' he said despondently.

Perhaps simplistic and too harsh on the family, I thought, but he had a point. The stakes in big-time moneymaking and power wielding are so high that ordinary values of love, affection and respect are easily set aside. This philosophical lesson was rounded off with a soulful rendering of four lines from Shailendra–Mukesh's immortal song from *Teesri Kasam*: '*Sajan re jhoonth mat bolo, Khuda ke paas jana jai, na haathi hai, na ghoda hai, wahan paidal hi jana hai.*' He said: '*Sab yaheen dhare ka dhara reh jayega, Janaab! Phir kyoon yeh mara maari*' (You're not going to take anything with you after you die, so why hanker after power and wealth)? 'Yes, Sir,' I nodded in agreement.

Forgetting Life's Purpose

But are the really wealthy and the powerful listening, I wondered. Ruthless accumulation of wealth and power is at the expense of the nation, not for its sake as it is sometimes claimed. Nor is it in the true interest of the family, who has no special claim anyway. Largely induced by wilful self-assertion, it is aimed at momentary pleasure for pride and glory in the immediate here and now.

As I got off and walked towards my hotel, I chewed over Mallick's sagacious reflections. According to him, today's politicians seem to have forgotten the very point of human life—why we are here, what makes our life worth living and what gives it meaning. They give politics a bad name by overlooking its real point—to use collective power to realise the common good—he might have added. But why only blame politicians? Are we not all complicit? Have we all not forgotten the point of our vocations—law, medicine, education—and lost a sense of the overall purpose of human life?

It is hard for me to judge whether he interpreted Islam correctly. But indisputably, that was his interpretation of what true Islam required and what a true Muslim ought to do: abjure limitless pursuit of power and wealth for the sake of a better afterlife. But then, would a Hindu with an otherworldly inclination say anything different to contemporary politicians and builders of business empires who happen to be Hindus? It is hard not to conclude that despite all the manifest difference the lived religion of ordinary South Asians, in taxis or outside them, contains ancient folk wisdom. Alas, the excessively wealthy and the extremely powerful are impervious to it.

94

A Prayer for Our Times

As all of us ordinary citizens recovered from the Pulwama carnage and wondered how the government would respond to this latest instance of cross-border terrorism, one television channel showed us poignant images of grieving relatives of the fallen soldiers. While a few, driven by moral hatred for the perpetrators, were understandably crying for revenge, others, even at this moment of utmost suffering, spoke of the futility of retaliation. 'It would only bring similar suffering to fellow humans,' said one widow from the rural hinterland. Hers was a cry for peace, not for vengeful violence. 'War can only be the last resort, after everything else has failed,' she wisely counselled.

War and Patriotism

Alas, yes, war is sometimes necessary, especially in self-defence. But one doesn't have to be an unconditional pacifist to acknowledge the misfortunes it begets or to decry war mongering. Nor is the readiness to go to war the only indicator of patriotism. True, patriots must be prepared to die in defence of their patria—mother or fatherland. But is anyone any less a patriot if she strives for everyone in his country to flourish and to live peacefully and happily, leading life to its fullness? Fighting the daily challenges faced by her countrymen, seeking to improve their lot, always loving them and their habitat and expressing this love in word or deed as the occasion demands is the everyday vocation of a patriot.

A country at war is different. War is disruptive, and because it is lethal and involves human sacrifice, a patriot must eschew any bravado about it. This is particularly expected from contemporary leaders, patriots who never themselves go to war, unlike the past where the ruler who declared war was expected to always lead from the front on the battlefield. After all, it is our army officers and jawans who die, not the ones who call for and support war. Our rulers move about with elaborate security to protect their own lives. If they don't allow others to play with their lives, they must ensure that no one plays with the life of their countrymen, most of all our soldiers. Decisions on war must be taken responsibly without haste, not for spectacular effect or as tactical ploys in a game.

The inner workings of the human mind are mysterious, however. For it is not these thoughts that crossed my mind when I saw those moving images on television. This reasoning is retrospective—thoughts that occurred to me post facto. At that time, a strange melange of emotions—feelings of grief, despair, shame and nostalgia—curdled up and then suddenly, from nowhere, the lyrics of an immortal song by Sahir Ludhianvi, set to tune by Jaidev and sung melodiously by Lata Mangeshkar in the 1961 Dev Anand classic *Hum Dono*, came unbidden to mind: *Maangon ka sindoor na chhutey, maa behenon ki aas naa tootey* (may no one be widowed; may no mother or sister lose hope of their loved one returning).

Prayer for Peace and Wisdom

In the film, these lines are a part of a prayer for peace led by the wife and mother of a major of the Indian Army missing in action—a prayer not only for their own loved one to return home safe but for the wives, mothers and sisters whose loved ones are also involved in the war. Death in war is an interruption—an anomaly. It takes away from us young, active and lively persons who have not yet lived their full life. When a soldier dies in the prime of his life, he leaves many tasks unfinished, many relationships incomplete and millions of desires unfulfilled. And according to popular belief, when a person at the height of his powers meets a bloody, violent and untimely end, his prana or atman remains in limbo, trapped in no man's land, leaving the body without reaching wherever it is meant to go and hovering around us. May this never happen to anyone, says the poet: *Deh bina bhatke na praan* (may the spirit not abruptly detach from the body and wander restlessly).

But this mellifluous song is more than a comforting prayer for peace. It subtly points fingers at those who injudiciously push us into war and the economically strong and politically powerful who bring war upon us for their own benefit and nefarious purpose: *O saare jag ke rakhawaale, nirbal ko bal dene waale, balwaanon ko de de gyaan (jnana)* (you who watch over the entire universe, you who empower the weak, may you also grant wisdom to the mighty).

'Jnana' here refers not simply to knowledge but also wisdom, moral insight and indeed conscience. May the rulers rule with a conscience; may they be able to distinguish right conduct from wrong. Really, only such people should guide us when we are faced with the dilemma of whether or not to undertake morally retributive action.

And this is not all. The prayer then becomes a plea that we all be endowed with sanmati—to put our intelligence to good use, to have sound judgements and that we all have a conscience. Why? Because unsound judgements, faulty moral reasoning and suspension of good sense are not the lot of leaders alone but also of those who support them and legitimise their actions. It is after all we, ordinary folks, who are swayed by war hysteria. Those without good sense get the leaders they deserve. May the gift of sanmati be bestowed upon us, for only people with sanmati can rein in leaders who have lost all sense of good and bad, right and wrong.

A Civilisational Anchor

But who is this prayer addressed to? '*Allah tero naam, Ishwar tero naam*' (You whose name is both Allah and Ishwar). In this, his masterstroke, Sahir invokes not only Gandhi but an entire centuries-old religio-philosophical legacy of the subcontinent in which all traditions are believed to share the same semantic universe that enables the god of one religion to be translated into the god of another. This is inclusive monotheism at its best, where God is one but referred to in different traditions by different names. And so, the prayer is addressed to Allah, Ishwar and implicitly the god of every religion.

With men spewing venom, not satisfied with fighting a war with their own fellow countrymen and itching to go to war with others, nothing (empathy, reason, dialogue) seems to work. Helpless spectators, no longer in control of their collective life and in sight of a looming disaster on the horizon, often break into a prayer. What else can those stripped off agency do but hope that somehow good sense will prevail and all of us will be delivered from the collective insanity that shows no sign of loosening its grip? Thus, those who believe in one god, invoke him; those who believe in gods and goddesses, invoke them; and those who believe in neither, hope for some good fortune to fall in their lap. That is why this is a prayer for our times: we offer this prayer to You—Allah to some and Ishwar to others—that You miraculously bring an end to needless killings, give wisdom and conscience to the rich and powerful, and peace and good sense to everyone.

95

A Wishlist for New Governments

In every year of the general election, political analysts and psephologists forecast which party will get the largest number of parliamentary seats, and if it fails to secure a majority, which alliance partners would it seek to form a government with. Men, women and even children play this guessing game. Passionate discussion, intense arguments and mudslinging become a national pastime. I confess I too get irresistibly sucked into it.

But sometimes I desist. Instead, I share with friends my list of expectations from the new government, regardless of the party or coalition that forms it. Suspending personal preference and keeping in view our collective interest I ask what the country urgently needs in the immediate future.

I have deliberately pruned this list down to just five needs, not necessarily in order of importance.

Respect Law and Be Humane

First, the new government must enforce the rule of law. This means expelling arbitrariness from the exercise of power; political decisions must not be grounded on the caprice of a single individual or group. No matter how powerful or wealthy, no one must be above the law, which must be applied even-handedly. There must not be one set of criminal laws for one group and quite another for other groups. The rule of law must not be fractured by the diktat of a mob, as in recent cases of lynching. No criminal should be allowed to roam freely with impunity. Can the newly elected government for once side unambiguously with victims of collective violence rather than with perpetrators?

In a related point, it is shameful enough that a civilised society discriminates on grounds of religion, language, race, gender or caste, but to target a group because of any one of these and kill, maim, oppress or humiliate it is downright obnoxious. Will the elected government stop this abomination and do all it can to prevent any expression of hate or occurrence of violence and build a more inclusive society?

Second, a government is expected to provide relief to citizens who are in dire need of material help, for instance, victims of cyclones and floods, and farmers in calamitous distress. Every government is also meant to undertake major structural reforms to alleviate chronic poverty. Underlying such efforts is the assumption of the impoverished as mere biological organisms who require food, nutrition, clean water and air. But a caring government must also view its beneficiaries as people who value friendship, family and community, have the capacity to reflect and self-reflect, need to tell stories about themselves and imagine new worlds. Will the new government design policies that look at human life in all its richness and complexity and support organisations that attend to the social and psychological consequences of material deprivations?

Respect Institutions

Third, our government must respect the independence of institutions. A society is sustained and nourished by collective effort. Nothing of significance is achieved by one group alone but by apportioning tasks to different groups. As work is divided among groups with appropriate but different skill sets, each generates its own specific rules, norms and values. Institutions are practices governed by domain-specific rules and norms. If a nation is to realise its goals, it is crucial that public institutions such as the university, the press, the judiciary, the central back, the election commission, the police and investigative agencies remain in the hands of able, qualified personnel who possess a deep understanding of not only the point of these institutions but also how specifically each contributes to the overall functioning of society. Elected leaders must ensure that these institutions work in tandem to realise collective purpose; they must not capture and run them according to their whims. They must facilitate their respective functions rather than arbitrarily interfere, misuse or abuse institutions. How can a government appoint someone to head an academic institution who have no clue about norms of intellectual production and scholarship? How can the Sahitya Kala Parishad, Lalit Kala Akademi or the Film and Television Institute of India be administered by a person with little understanding of art, literature or cinema?

Listen to Criticism

Fourth, an elected government must listen to what ordinary people say about it—good or bad. It is even more duty-bound to pay heed to public-spirited intellectuals whose entire social role is to assess, evaluate and criticise those who wield power or have the potential to cause systematic harm to ordinary people. Those who can't stomach dissent or protest are unfit to rule.

Protect Cultural Heritage

Finally, every society selectively remembers a part of its past to pass it on to future generations. For, if we don't remember the past for the sake of the future, even our present is irrevocably destroyed. Indeed, no human society can grow unless future generations inherit the archives of the past. Our collective heritage is a usable past chosen to construct a collective future. Such cultural heritage can be found in tangible objects such as monuments and intangible objects such as ideas, values and symbols. Rather than exploit this heritage for narrow political gains, we need a government committed to rescuing it from destruction and to connect traces of the past with a living present. I am told there are hundreds of thousands of old Pali and Sanskrit manuscripts decaying in different parts of the country, pedagogies of traditional learning are on the verge of disappearance, oral traditions are becoming extinct and hundreds of languages are fading away. These are irrevocable losses. Will the new government focus on protecting this fast-decaying heritage rather than spend its time in cursorily renaming streets and cities to suit its political agenda?

96

A Moment for Indian Liberalism

Liberalism is probably more challenged in India today than in any other democracy in the world. Why? First, conservative communities appear to have gained untrammelled power in recent times. Self-proclaimed custodians of caste and religion are perpetually breathing down the necks of young men and women, dictating who they must meet, converse with, befriend and marry; what they should eat, wear, watch or read; whether or not they can use mobile phones; and, even, where they can go and when. By encroaching on the most intimate relationships of love and friendship and interfering in matters of pleasure or habit, they suffocate personal freedoms and violate the very basic norms of individual choice.

Second, people find it increasingly difficult to express themselves freely. A public culture of hurt sentiment, violated collective honour, offence and alleged humiliation, and the social and political license to react to it in whatever brutal manner possible have created such a climate of fear that creative artists, intellectuals and even ordinary persons in public conversations hesitate to speak up their mind and look over their shoulder to see if big daddy is watching. The threat of social intimidation and legal harassment makes public expression so expensive that people would rather stay silent or remain aloof from public life.

Third, large corporations and the government have access to virtually every detail about us, making us vulnerable and insecure.

Methods of surveillance become opaque even as they expose us against our will. The minutest details of one's private and intimate life are available today to large, powerful organisations at the press of a button. Is it not frightening that to call or visit friends and family we must undergo CCTV cameras, fingerprint scanner and face recognition?

Fourth, confidence in the rule of law is badly shaken. Is there any assurance that the law will be enforced even-handedly, indeed, that it will be enforced at all? On the contrary, we often fear excesses by official agents at every level of government, worry that power will be abused, that some person in charge of law and order will behave lawlessly, even brutally.

Freedom to Say No

What do power of the state, community and individual choice and expression have to do with liberalism? Everything. The term 'liberalism' has come to mean different things to different people and is associated with (a) demands for greater equality, (b) defence of individual reason and autonomy, (c) a tool against moral conservatism, (d) cosmopolitanism and humanism and (e) free markets. When overused, it suffers from what happens routinely to words with wide currency—it generates less light, more heat and even greater cacophony. Yet, a moment's reflection shows that one value has always lain at its heart: the freedom of an individual to say no—to say that enough is enough and that something ominously coming towards me up close, stalking me, is no longer bearable and must be stopped; that there is a little world of my own, my private universe, that no one may enter if I do not give permission and that a place exists in public for me too that must not be impeded as long as others are not harmed. In my largely private but also partly public world, I must live without fear or favour.

One such bulwark against habitual and pervasive acts of cruel interference is the dismantling of private armies commanded by powerful custodians of communities and the creation instead of an impartial public power (the state) governed minimally by the rule of law—a law that protects my mini-kingdom where I am sovereign and liberates me from fear itself. But then the same rule of law must also shield me from arbitrary, unexpected and unnecessary acts of state coercion. Whatever else liberalism might come to mean, it stands for personal freedom in the face of intrusion by every form of organised power. Indeed, classical liberalism in Western societies emerged precisely in response to persistent attempts to throttle the then bourgeoning assertions of individual freedom by oppressive communities, a meddlesome church and abusive state power.

In this minimal sense, the term 'liberal' no longer has a restricted spatial or temporal application. It has a much wider usage and has resonated in India with acts of renunciatory Brahmins, and with movements led by the Buddha, Mahavira, early Lingayats and those inspired by Nanak, Kabir, Akka Mahadevi and Mira as well as Phule and Ambedkar. This 'thin' liberalism has nothing uniquely Western about it. Indeed, there are modern liberalisms and ancient ones, and just as there have been liberalisms in the past, there will be liberalisms in future. The message in all these is common, clear and simple: don't force anything down anyone's throat and stop the deliberate infliction of physical or emotional pain on individuals, especially upon a weaker person, no matter how valuable you believe your cause to be.

An Inevitable Revolt

If the current climate of oppression or violent threats continues, a revolt against the current set-up will invariably arise. Young, self-reflective men and women, especially those facing continual restrictions, Dalits, Other Backward Classes, poor Muslims and people from smaller towns and rural areas will seize the moment and demand greater opportunity to exercise individual choice and freedom of expression. Is a new liberalism—different from the one articulated by traditional, metropolitan English-speaking elites and shaped profoundly by Indian cultural conditions—just round the corner?

97

The Politics of Everyday Life

Past societies have appeared to relentlessly deprecate everyday life. At least those elites who have written extensively about the good life have always made a distinction between a life lived in pursuit of the higher good by chasing whatever in their view was of ultimate worth and a life with little worth or significance. Everyday life was always listed under the latter category—ubiquitous but utterly insignificant—in complete contrast to a life of contemplation or an adventurous life of war, conquest or politics, or one in the service of a high art or religion in which humans are said to fulfil those transcendent values in which they encounter 'their essential being'.

It is true that not all traditions relegate everyday life to insignificance. The life of the householder (grahastha) in the Brahmanical tradition was worthy, self-fulfilling and endowed with religious, perhaps even philosophical, significance. Jain and Buddhist traders also endowed mercantile life with value, as did, arguably, the European bourgeois with the Protestant ethic. However, even these traditions deemed the daily life of the majority of labouring people as possessing no intrinsic value.

Now there is a grain of truth in the idea of the apparent insignificance of everyday life. The mere fact that something is repeated everyday makes it dull, mundane and boring. It is too familiar to generate a sense of surprise or excitement. Everyday life is routine, recedes unnoticed into the background rather than be in the foreground of our experience and appears to be trivial. What excitement can be generated in brushing one's teeth in the morning or in cleaning, cooking and washing? What enjoyment can be derived from the drudgery of these chores? Indeed, even activities that give one an initial kick become tedious overtime and are best avoided—something from which one needs a holiday.

With such images in mind, many philosophers have observed that the everyday symbolises some of the most alienating features of human life. The repetitive nature of labour and the fatigue that ensues—the burden of housework and raising children, among other activities—led thinkers such as Heidegger to designate the everyday as the domain of 'inauthenticity, triviality and error'. For the poor, the everyday is more than just boring and dull. It is relentlessly arduous: assembly line work, substandard conditions at home, obligatory use of jam-packed public transport, the struggle for daily bread, not to speak of the deep inhumanity embedded in, say, manual scavenging. Such an existence could deprive anyone of imagination and reason and permanently dull the senses and the mind, if it were not for the incomprehensible, mysterious quality of the human spirit.

In places such as Europe, the significance of the everyday life was properly acknowledged only after the spectacular horror of the war ended. When the French state was demilitarised and ordinary people began to receive adequate food and other supplies, everydayness emerged as an important enough category of thought. Interest in the everyday was subsequently revived after the realisation that the carnivalesque character of the student–workers revolt of May 68 in Paris, in which everyday life was suspended for a few weeks, was ephemeral and unsustainable. However, in India, the salience of the everyday jumps to the eye almost every second. The everyday, in whatever form, is all that the people have. It is its very inescapability, its ability to suck the majority of the people into a daily grind, to deny them virtually everything they need or want and to turn them into a bundle of frustrations that might compel them to rebel against conditions steeped in indignities. A war or revolt is not needed here to imagine the relief we might experience when released from the pain of everyday living or to dream of a better here and now.

I imagine everyday life is hellish for the destitute. But consider the life of an average middle-class person in most Indian cities—an endless wait at the bus stop for service that is late or for a three-wheeler that does not run by meter or for a train that never arrives on schedule; a tap that is perpetually dry, failing electricity that makes a hot day insufferable and the evenings without television, the only form of entertainment; queuing up every month to pay the bills; running from desk to desk to rectify a wrongly calculated tax but to no avail; getting interrupted by repair men just when reaching the climax of a thriller; being compelled to use filthy, foul-smelling public toilets or walking with supreme concentration on uneven sidewalks and garbage-filled streets for fear of stepping into potholes or cow dung; suffering an anxiety-filled night as a young daughter heads back home in dimly-lit streets; reconciling with children forced to play in accident-prone by-lanes; fearing dengue or malaria; facing unavailability of beds in hospitals; awaiting an ambulance that fails to arrive in the golden hour, and if it does, not reaching the emergency on time; and when it rains, streams sprouting everywhere as traffic snarls.

Add to this, contaminated water and unbearably polluted air and the misery is complete. Indeed, many of these travails afflict even the upper middle class no matter how hard it tries to buy good health, clean air or fast cars. Is not every one of the 800 million mobile users in India, rich or poor, a potential victim of state surveillance and a continuing target of the cannibalising instincts of big corporations? Everyday life is continuously disrupted by the inefficiency or machinations of the state and MNCs and by our own thoughtless complicity.

These disruptions will not disappear on their own or by the goodwill of benefactors, nor can individuals on their own prevent them. Even daily resistance by well-meaning but isolated individuals is insufficient to undo the damage. These largely privately enjoyed benefits can be had only with resolute collective action. How else can change in these abysmal conditions be effected except by a surge in collective protest? Only collective politics can sustain everyday life. A broad alliance cutting across all regional, religious and caste differences is required to restore the dignity of everyday life. We need a politics that seeks a transformation of life in its smallest everyday detail and helps all of us enjoy its rhythm and texture.

It seems to be inevitable that the politics of the next decades will be around people's need to have a smooth, uninterrupted and dignified everyday life—clean air and water, sanitation, better roads and public transport, uncontaminated food, a secure private life, to name just a few. Politics will be around the fulfilment of basic needs to secure a minimally decent life. We all desperately need the simple business of living a life and a government that delivers it. Rather than chase utopias, politics in the near future needs to set its eyes firmly on the everyday life and the woes that beset it.

After all, how long can the everyday be waylaid by sensational promises of a grandiose future, hollow but spectacular events and, indeed, the festivities of elections?

98

The Power of Ordinary People

When Mahatma Gandhi went to England in 1931 to attend the Second Round Table Conference, one of his close aides suggested that he retreat for the weekend to Oxford in order to reflect on the 'big questions of principle involved in negotiations'. It would also afford an opportunity to have informal, relaxed conversations with some British statesmen. The philosopher A.D. Lindsay, Master of Balliol College, extended an invitation, which Gandhi accepted. He reached on 26 October with his secretary Mahadev Desai, son Devdas, his English disciple Mira Behn and his friend C.F. Andrews. To ensure his safety, he was escorted by a large detective, who seemed even larger in contrast to the diminutive Gandhi. Whether or not he performed his other duties I do not know, but he sure brought a goat from the nearby hill when the master was unexpectedly asked if the college served goat's milk. The goat, tied to a tree in the college's main quad, came in very handy. Gandhi was spared from going out of the college and allowed to sit on the floor in his room to have his usual diet of milk and fruit.

Addressing Indians

The Mahatma found time to address all of Oxford's fifty Indian undergraduates, most of whom turned up in Indian clothes, including some women who sat spellbound in resplendent sarees. A few who came in Western attire made sure they wore an Indian turban. 'Among students, I always feel at home because I am a student,' Gandhi opened his address. 'If you begin by cross-examining me, we shall know each other better. Will you please make yourself thoroughly at home with me? I am not a geological specimen.'

The first question to him was on the future of women in India. 'The future of the women in India is that they will be equal in every respect to men, if not superior,' he said. He answered questions about separate electorates for Muslims and the 'Untouchables'. He was asked about his views on the creative power of socialism. Without batting an eyelid, Gandhi replied that 'it might be a creative power if it did not depend on force'. An Englishman asked if he believed in the good faith of England. Gandhi answered that he had good faith in England to the extent that he believed in the good faith of the human race. He went on: 'I have definitely come to the conclusion that the total sum of human energy must be directed for the good, otherwise the world would have been destroyed long since. As a consequence, I trust England, although I have been bitten so often, not once but many times. I expect that the English nature will be converted one day and will respond.'

Religiosity and Ethics

The *Oxford Mail* reported that Gandhi was struck by the beauty of the little town, and on his way to the poet Edward John Thompson's house, he got off the car several times to admire its towers, spires, bridges and college quadrangles. Later, Gandhi met visitors at the Master's Lodgings (Lindsay's home) at Balliol, including Madan Mohan Malaviya, Sarojini Naidu and several British parliamentarians. Also among the visitors was Lindsay's son, a tutor in Wales, who ventured to ask with some hesitation: 'People want to know how far are you a Christian?' This clearly meant how far Gandhi had travelled from Hinduism towards Christianity. Gandhi, always quick-witted and clever but also wise and truthful, adroitly sidestepped this question. He deliberately took it to mean something quite different. How far had he, Gandhi, followed the teachings of Christ? How deep had he dug and how much higher had he gone by following the example of Christ? Just then the senior Lindsay himself entered the room. 'Well, here is your father,' said Gandhi. 'Could he tell how far he is a Christian. He will not be able to tell you and neither am I.'

For Gandhi, each of us must truthfully answer how far we have achieved spiritual growth or self-perfection. In saying this, Gandhi communicated two central points of his ethical and religious thinking. First, the futility of conversion—an act that assumes that a person belongs exclusively to one or another religion, never to both, and that he should belong to a religion superior to all others. Gandhi rejected the idea of intrinsic superiority of one religion over another and the imperative of constricted, exclusive belonging. Second, the importance of multiple attachments. If, as he believed, the whole point is to dig deeper and go higher, then why can't a Hindu follow the teachings of Christ? Why would that be inconsistent with the true teachings of Rama, Krishna, Buddha, Nanak or Kabir? Why should anyone be restricted to a single source of inspiration?

To his Christian friends, he seemed to suggest that men and women can find the resources of self-realisation, work out salvation from within their own tradition and that no need exists to change mere labels. To people more generally, but particularly to fellow Hindus, he seemed to say that no religion can bind him absolutely. Indeed, on some issues, his own views were too closely interwoven with Christianity to be entirely Hindu and too deeply infused with Hindu and Jain ideas to be called Christian. Although Gandhi died a Hindu and remained unflinchingly so while alive, he probably exemplified the spirit of Christ more than any other man of his times. One might say, as the philosopher Margaret Chatterjee reminds us, that he responded to the teachings of Christ because he found confirmation in them of what he received from his own multiple traditions.

Collective Action

A friend of Lindsay told him that he should not think of Gandhi as a saint trying to be a politician but rather as a politician trying to be a saint. But both he and his wife were convinced that having Gandhi as their guest was like having a saint in their house. The one facet of Gandhi that utterly impressed Lindsay was his conviction that nothing could be God's will if it was not understood by ordinary, unlettered people. It is often thought that for Gandhi social transformation can be brought about only by a change in the moral character of every individual person. While Gandhi undoubtedly stressed the need for self-transformation, it is absurd to conclude that for him collective action was relatively unimportant. One of Gandhi's great contributions to social and political thought is that an enormous creative power is released when ordinary people of good will—without the trappings of power, wealth or fame—come together. Such solidarity can offer the most effective resistance to unjust exploitative social practices and political tyranny. The power to transform the world flows from the collective non-violent energies of ordinary men and women, a lesson that the high and mighty, steeped in social orthodoxy or propelled by authoritarian instincts, ignore at their peril.

99

The Return of the Secular

It was both touching and comforting to hear a reply by Nikhil, a young student from Jamia, to an unexpected question—What does Jamia mean to you?—put to him by a television anchor. After a long pause Nikhil said, 'It has given me tehzeeb, an understanding of the samvidhaan, and taught me to read, write and think. When I joined Jamia, I had no understanding of India. This university has made me understand my country. I will work to the end of my life to realise Gandhi's vision. I want my secular India back.'

Mentioning Gandhi was entirely appropriate. For Gandhi's contribution to an everyday understanding of secularism is massive, one that is different from at least three other understandings. First, the political secularism of Western Europe and North America in which some form of separation between the church and the state is required to defend equality and individual liberty but has no room for the idea of fraternity or community, which is crucial in deeply diverse societies. Second, the more legal and philosophical–constitutional secularism of India. Immensely complex, nuanced and comprehensive, and cognizant of the deep diversity as well as oppression within communities, here the state is required to maintain a principled distance from all religious communities in order to reduce institutionalised religious domination. This secularism is concerned to prevent inter-religious domination as much as to fight religiously grounded caste and gender hierarchies and fanaticism within religions. Finally, the secularism practiced in recent times by most political parties in India—what I have called 'party-political secularism'. This secularism does not really deserve to be called so because it is unprincipled and opportunistic, plays footsie with the most orthodox, bigoted and regressive elements of all religions, is concerned solely with seeking and maintaining power, and willing, for self-interest, to engineer riots or capitalise on inter-communal estrangement.

In contrast, Gandhi made secularism simple. All religious communities inhabiting a particular territory must live with continuing ease and comfort with one another. This is a people-dependent notion and was already, Gandhi believed, a part of the Indian consciousness, a rich resource within public discourse and a social norm but, alas, jeopardised in modern times by communal politics. To counter it, a support is needed from the state that is not partial to any one particular religion. Moreover, whenever any estrangement or hostility ensues, the state must help restore communal harmony. To perform its primary duty of maintaining fraternity and to prevent political alienation, the state must distance itself equally from all religions.

It was heartening to find so many young women and men all fired up about the Gandhian vision of secular India and be out on the streets to defend constitutional secularism as they understood it. Four things about what they conveyed are noteworthy. First, the fundamental injustice of policies with unambiguous discriminatory intent. This is unconstitutional and offends the dignity not only of those discriminated but also of every citizen in the polity. In major nation-wide protests in which countless people participated, it was made clear that any law or policy that discriminates on the basis of religion is not acceptable. Besides, the whole idea of proving one's citizenship by producing documents before government officials is abhorrent—any one born in India must be presumed to be an Indian citizen and should not be compelled to demonstrate this. To do so would cause severe and unnecessary harassment. Many protesting students are convinced that the CAA is discriminatory. Is it? Now, Article 14 provides for equal protection of the law within the territory of India. Suppose that a foreign national from Europe commits a grave crime in India. Should he be treated differently from other Indians? Would the law be differentially applied simply because he is, say, a European Christian? No.

Analogously, suppose that illegal immigrants fleeing persecution in their own country enter Indian territory and needed to be identified and investigated for possible deportation. A uniform criminal law should apply here too. Either all should be given refuge or all deported by due process of law. No one within the territory of India, Indian citizen or foreign national, must be treated differently. Students appeared to have imbibed this simple logic.

Second, the rejection of the politics of hate and revenge. Such divisive policies, the peaceful protestors seem to suggest, disrupt peace and stability by generating a vicious cycle of resentment and mutual hostility. To be sure, conflicts and skirmishes have not been uncommon between communities in the past but a deep division between them occurred only when a pernicious ethno-nationalist ideology was imported into India in the nineteenth century with tragic results in 1947. Young people in India appear to have realised that leaders of the current government have not learnt any lessons from those dark events and continue with policies aimed at consolidating a pan-Hindu identity defined by hostility to the other.

Third, the public acknowledgement by young Hindus of the contribution of Muslims to Indian culture and civilisation and to constructions of Indian notions of civility. Young women and men wearing skullcaps, hijabs or the bindis, fitting stereotypical ideas of what Hindus and Muslims look like, asserted that their own religious identity is not defined against other religions. One can be Hindu without being anti-Muslim and vice versa. Indian citizens cohabit a shared social and public space not through mutual toleration but by actively accepting one another and are committed to participating in each other's suffering and destiny. They conveyed that they shall not tolerate attempts to breach civic friendship.

Likewise, norms of public etiquette, civility and refinements in pubic culture have been shaped in India by multiple religious traditions in which Muslims have played a prominent role. For example, the qawwali and ghazal are as much a part of our culture as the bhajan. Aren't some of the greatest bhajans in Hindi films written by Sahir Ludhianvi and Javed Akhtar, sung by Mohammad Rafi, Lata Mangeshkar and others to compositions by Naushad and A.R. Rehman? It is not for nothing that even the actor Paresh Rawal, BJP MP, was compelled to remark that he was stunned by the demand to ban Firoz Khan from teaching Sanskrit at the Banaras Hindu University.[21] India's popular culture cannot be imagined without Rafi and Naushad, he reiterated, and demanded an 'end to this idiocy'. Firoz is no flash in the pan. There is a whole tradition of such scholarship that harks back to Dara Shikoh, Akbar, Tughlaq and Amir Khusro and continues in Modern India with renowned Sanskrit scholars such as Mohammed Hanif Khan Shastri and Pandit Ghulam Dastagir.

Finally, they made it amply clear that an obsession with religious identity takes focus away from pressing issues of everyday life of the vast majority of Indian people. No more divide and rule, as one of the posters averred; the business of government is to facilitate a better everyday life for all ordinary citizens, including Hindus and Muslims, and not destroy it. The reappearance of secularism in Indian public discourse, initiated by young Indian students, is surely a matter of relief and joy to those who aspire to protect India's diverse cultural heritage, defend its Constitution and wish every Indian to have a better standard of living.

100

What We Owe to the Mahatma

Where does multiple, forceful Hindu assertions of the past few years leave Indian secularism? Some say that secularism is in tatters. But can it also be claimed that it is needed more than ever before?

---

[21] PTI, 'BHU Protests: Paresh Rawal Supports Muslim Sanskrit Professor, Appeals to Students to Not Engage in "Idiocy",' *Hindustan Times*, 20 November 2019, https://www.hindustantimes.com/bollywood/bhu-protests-paresh-rawal-supports-muslim-sanskrit-professor-appeals-to-students-to-not-engage-in-idiocy/story-oZm7J9f5LHFWbKFzHh5xRJ.html

Two related but equally distinctive conceptions of secularism developed in India: one, constitutional and principled distance model; the other, communal harmony model attributed to the Mahatma. I believe this second Gandhian conception, equally distinctive, is in need of desperate revival. What makes it distinctive and why is it needed? To answer this, a comparison with European conceptions of secularism would help.

Secularism: Europe versus India

The background of the emergence of political secularism in Europe is profound religious homogenisation—dissenters and adherents of non-dominant religions were expelled or exterminated during and after the wars of religion. Rulers publicly confessed allegiance to one of the many churches in these predominantly single-religion societies, thereby consolidating a strong alliance between the state and the dominant church. Trouble began, however, when this church became increasingly politically meddlesome and socially oppressive. The key issue then was how to tame the power of the church. The state's disentanglement from the dominant church (church–state separation) was necessary to realise a number of goals, including the enhancement of individual liberty and equality. But for this secularism, tackling religious diversity was simply not an issue because it had already been liquidated in all kinds of ethically undesirable ways.

By contrast, in India, deep religious diversity was not an optional extra but a part of its social, cultural and historical landscape. Gandhi understood this and never tired of stating it: India is 'perhaps one nation in the ancient world which had recognised cultural democracy, whereby it is held that the roads to one and the same God are many, but the goal was one, because God was one and the same. In fact, the roads are as many as there are individuals in the world.... The various religions were as so many leaves of a tree; they might seem different but at the trunk they are one.' Gandhi dismissed the idea that there could ever be one religion in the world, a uniform religious code, as it were, for all human kind.

Deep Sociability

What is needed then is due recognition of different religious communities and to ensure comfort and trust among their members.

This was viable because for Gandhi all humans had a fundamental desire for what might be called deep sociability. They value human relations as an end in itself. They desire a constructive relationship with others. Why else would they be motivated to seek agreement even when it was not really necessary? Why, upon realising that they can't resolve disagreement on one issue, would they seek agreement on something else? Why are they motivated to renew conversation after it has been violently disrupted? Why, after a period of mutual recrimination, breakdown and silence, do people still begin talking to one another? Humans simply can't do without one another, and no matter how much they like to be with people of their own ilk, they invariably also need to live with those with whom they differ and reach out to people they disagree with.

The world's religious diversity—the impossibility of there ever being one religion for humankind—makes mutual respect, equal regard and communal harmony a necessity. Gandhi believed that this can become a reality by virtue of the human quality of deep sociability.

Humans occasionally wish to live independently of their communities, but as participants of historically embedded cultural and religious traditions, they also meet each other as members of religio-cultural communities. They must actively shape these encounters and ensure that they do not become bitter or turn sour but be good, decent, friendly and respectful. Humans can't really be good to each other unless they are respectful to each other's religious and philosophical traditions.

Gandhian Secularism

Gandhi felt that a large part of the responsibility for maintaining communal harmony lies with communities themselves. But there are times when this communally sustained harmony is disturbed. When this happens, the state has to step in. And for this to be possible, it cannot already be aligned to any one religion but must be distant from all. Secularism then marks a certain comportment of the state whereby it distances itself from all religio-philosophical perspectives in order to promote a certain quality of sociability and fraternity between communities. This makes Gandhian secularism distinctive. Unlike modern Western secularisms that separate the church and the state for the sake of individual freedom and equality and have place for neither community nor fraternity, the Gandhian conception demands that the state be secular for the sake of better relations between members of all religious communities, especially if they are mutually estranged. The Gandhian conception is indispensable in times of religious disharmony.

This Gandhian view did not stem from strategic considerations but was grounded in deep conviction. It is sometimes said that Gandhi's views were influenced by Jaina teachings. 'All religions are true and all have error,' he said, implying that all religions are inevitably partial, incomplete and fragmentary so that different traditions need to complement and enrich one another rather than behave as mutually exclusive rivals. Without denying this philosophical lineage, I would claim that Gandhi's views were shaped even more by the wisdom tradition of the ancient world, in which gods and goddesses of each cultural region are different yet a part of the same semantic universe and, therefore, mutually related and translatable. As a result, no culture denied the reality of the gods of another culture but always found ways to accommodate them. For instance, the god of one culture could become a member of the family of another culture (Ganesh is the son of Shiva and Parvati). A new god could be created by merging half of one God and half of another (Hari-Hara). Most of all, a relation of equivalence or identity could be established between them (Rudra is Shiva), making it possible to claim that the gods of different cultures are the same but called by different names. Gandhi was inspired by these traditions, particularly by the habit of establishing equivalence, and extended this insight into the new world religions. Thus, he claimed that Ram, Allah and satya (Truth) refer to the same entity. If this is so, every attack on someone else's god is a denial of one's own god; every claim that one's own god is better than the other's tantamount to the humiliation of one's own god.

Yet, the realisability of Gandhian secularism depends on faith in the popular wisdom tradition, which in turn is sustained by a certain idea of popular moral agency. When good, God-loving, ordinary men and women free from the trappings of power, wealth and fame—which is precisely what makes them ordinary and good—get together, they release non-violent creative energies that morally sustain and improve our world. Alas, it seems that such men and women have gone missing in our times. Gandhian secularism is badly needed, but who will ride it out?

Subject Index

Name Index

About the Author

Rajeev Bhargava was born in 1954 and educated in Delhi and Oxford. He is currently an honorary fellow at the Centre for the Study of Developing Societies (Delhi) and the director of its Parekh Institute of Indian Thought. He was also the centre's director from 2007 to 2014. He has taught at the University of Delhi and Jawaharlal Nehru University (Delhi).

Bhargava has lectured, taught and held visiting professorship at several universities. He has been a fellow at Harvard University (Massachusetts, US), University of Bristol (UK), Institute of Advanced Studies (Jerusalem), Wissenschaftskolleg (Berlin) and the Institute for Human Sciences (Vienna). He has also been a Distinguished Resident Scholar at the Institute for Religion, Culture and Public Life, Columbia University (New York), and the Asia Chair of Sciences Po (Paris), and between 2015 and 2017, a Berggruen fellow at Stanford (California), Tsinghua (Beijing) and New York Universities. Between 2014 and 2018, he was a professorial fellow at the Institute of Social Justice, ACU (Sydney). In 2022, he was a senior research fellow at the University of Leipzig (Germany). He is an honorary fellow at Balliol College, Oxford (UK).

Bhargava's work on individualism and secularism is internationally acclaimed. His publications include *Individualism in Social Science* (1992), *What Is Political Theory and Why Do We Need It?* (2010) and *The Promise of India's Secular Democracy* (2010). His edited works include *Secularism and Its Critics* (1998), *Politics and Ethics of the Indian Constitution* (2008) and *Politics, Ethics and the Self: Re-reading Hind Swaraj* (2022).

Bhargava comes into his own when he is in the classroom. Lately, by contributing regularly for *The Hindu*, he has also become more publicly engaged. He lives in Delhi with his wife, Tani, who will soon publish her first novel. They have two daughters: Aranyani, a Bharatanatyam dancer, and Vanya, an intellectual historian.

About the Author